The circle of Eros

Elizabeth Stevens Prioleau

The circle of Eros

Sexuality in the work of William Dean Howells

Duke University Press Durham, N.C. 1983

© 1983, Duke University Press

Printed in the United States of America on acid-free paper

Library of Congress Cataloging in Publication Data

Prioleau, Elizabeth Stevens, 1942–
  The circle of Eros.

  Based on the author's dissertation (Ph.D.—Duke)
  Bibliography: p.
  Includes index.
    1. Howells, William Dean, 1837–1920—Criticism and
interpretation.   2. Sex in literature.   I. Title.
PS2037.S48P74   1983   818'.409   82-14788
ISBN 0-8223-0492-9

207326

Contents

Preface

The present study has had a long evolution and involved the help of many friends in many places. *The Circle of Eros* first took solid form as a Ph.D. dissertation at Duke University and was written in Durham, North Carolina, Charlottesville, Virginia, and St. Louis, Missouri. At each place I had the good fortune to find superb facilities and friends.

The Barrett Collection at the University of Virginia laid the groundwork for my study and was supplemented by the faculty there, particularly Harold Kolb and Douglas Day. In St. Louis I found equally good resources at Washington University. It was Howard Nemerov who pointed me to the classical tradition of erotic thought. The St. Louis Psychoanalytic Institute was also instrumental. Without Dr. Stephen Post's instruction in psychoanalytic theory and his careful reading of my autobiography chapter, I would never have attempted a psychological interpretation of Howells. My thanks, too, to the Howells Center at Indiana University at Bloomington which gave me carte blanche to their library and letters. During the final preparation of my book I made liberal use of New York University Library and the New York Public Library, and appreciate their many hours of hospitality.

At every stage, from inception to dissertation to book, Professor Edwin H. Cady sustained and nourished my work. When it was still unfashionable to talk about sexuality in Howells, he encouraged me to explore it and steered me through every stage of the journey. He provided much more besides: inspiration, counsel, and the sharpest critical eye I have ever found. It is impossible to overestimate what he gave me, both as the preeminent Howellsian and as a guide and friend.

Not least is my husband, Dr. Philip Prioleau, who read and reread my manuscript in countless forms, and lent me—waking and sleeping—his ear, patience, and fine intelligence. He and all my family, Mr. and Mrs. Hugo Stevens and Dr. and Mrs. William H. Prioleau, made sacrifices too numerous to mention.

Finally, I would like to thank my editor, Reynolds Smith, whose scholarship, style, and taste were invaluable in the preparation of this manuscript. In addition, I am grateful to the University of Virginia Library, the University of Pennsylvania Library, Brown University Library, the University of Southern California Library, and Houghton Library at Harvard University for allowing me to quote from the Howells papers in their collections.

E.S.P.

New York City
1982

Abbreviations

Throughout this study, the following editions of the works of W. D. Howells have been used. All citations are noted in the text prefixed by the appropriate abbreviations.

AH *April Hopes*, ed. Kermit Vanderbilt et al. (1888; rpt. Bloomington: Indiana University Press, 1974)

BT *A Boy's Town* (New York: Harper & Brothers Publishers, 1890)

DTW *The Day of Their Wedding* (New York: Harper & Brothers Publishers, 1896)

FPB *The Flight of Pony Baker* (New York: Harper & Brothers Publishers, 1902)

FC *A Foregone Conclusion* (Boston: James R. Osgood and Company, 1875)

HNF *A Hazard of New Fortunes*, ed. Tony Tanner (1890; rpt. London: Oxford University Press, 1965)

K *The Kentons* (New York: Harper & Brothers Publishers, 1902)

LFA *Literary Friends and Acquaintance: A Personal Retrospect of American Authorship*, ed. David F. Hiatt and Edwin H. Cady (1900; rpt. Bloomington: Indiana University Press, 1968)

LG *The Leatherwood God*, ed. Eugene Pattison (1916; rpt. Bloomington: Indiana University Press, 1975)

LLH *The Landlord at Lion's Head* (New York: Harper & Brothers Publishers, 1897)

MF *Mrs. Farrell* (New York: Harper & Brothers Publishers, 1921)

MI *A Modern Instance*, ed. William Gibson (1882; rpt. Boston: Houghton Mifflin Company, 1957)

MLP *My Literary Passions* (New York: Harper & Brothers Publishers, 1921)

MYLC *My Year in a Log Cabin* (New York: Harper & Brothers Publishers, 1893)

NLM *New Leaf Mills* (New York: Harper & Brothers Publishers, 1913)

OEC *An Open-Eyed Conspiracy: An Idyl of Saratoga* (New York: Harper & Brothers Publishers, 1897)

QM *The Quality of Mercy* (New York: Harper & Brothers Publishers, 1892)

RL *Ragged Lady* (New York: Harper & Brothers Publishers, 1899)

RSL *The Rise of Silas Lapham*, ed. Walter J. Meserve et al. (1885; rpt. Bloomington: Indiana University Press, 1971)

SD *The Shadow of a Dream and An Imperative Duty*, ed. Martha Banta, Ronald Gottesman, and David Nordloh (1890; rpt. Bloomington: Indiana University Press, 1970)

SOP *The Story of a Play* (New York: Harper & Brothers Publishers, 1898)

SRL *The Son of Royal Langbrith*, ed. David Burrows (1904; rpt. Bloomington: Indiana University Press, 1969)

TFA *A Traveller from Altruria* in *The Altrurian Romances*, ed. Clara and Rudolf Kirk (1894; rpt. Bloomington: Indiana University Press, 1968)

TSWJ *Their Silver Wedding Journey*, 2 vols. (New York: Harper & Brothers Publishers, 1899)

WOC *The World of Chance* (New York: Harper & Brothers Publishers, 1893)

YOMY *Years of My Youth and Three Essays*, ed. David J. Nordloh (1916; rpt. Bloomington: Indiana University Press, 1975)

Prologue

It used to be said that people thought William Dean Howells "either a master or an ass." "There [was] no middle ground."[1] Over his long career (1852–1920) in which he edited *The Atlantic Monthly* for fifteen years, published almost a hundred books, and pioneered the critical battle for realism, he was always the subject of intense controversy. Now, despite a recent spate of Howells scholarship, the danger seems to be that he will slip from the middle ground of neutral respectability he has occupied for the last few decades and fall into total neglect. Somehow he has ceased to excite and engage the American reader. The man whom Henry James once called a "glossy antelope"[2] has become associated with stodginess, prudery, temperance, domesticity, and dullness. To the modern consciousness, Howells appears quaint, if not irrelevant.

What I have attempted is frankly iconoclastic. I have tried to dislodge the official image of Howells and suggest new possibilities. I have chosen the most controversial topic of all: sexual passion in his life and work.

At first glance, Howells and sexuality seem to be an unlikely—even ludicrous—combination. The love scenes in his best known fiction are undeniably prim by today's standards, and his early pronouncements on decency in literature, epitomize nineteenth-century fastidiousness. Then there is Howells's life itself. Externally he was the solid burgher who stares so mildly out of his photographs—monogamous, bourgeois, and moderate, a man who lived out no libidinous dreams.

Yet a closer look at his biography and writing reveals a powerful passional dimension. Henry James called his friend "much more passionate"[2] than he, and Howells's novels were considered risqué by his contemporaries. Beneath the bland Dean's facade, Howells spent a lifetime centrally engaged with the deepest, most explosive sexual issues. More remarkably, he himself changed. He began as a priggish young editor of the *Atlantic Monthly*, with an early neurotic terror of sexuality, and ended as one of the leading exponents of frankness in literature. He grew lenient to the point of advocating "scandalous" reforms like divorce and trial marriages, and his fiction moved from filigree indirection to bold erotic allegory. Not everyone will like this reconstructed version of Howells, but if my thesis provokes controversy, I will at least restore some of the original vitality to Howells criticism, when he was denounced as an ass or hailed as a genius, and his novels were devoured by young girls for the "love-parts."[3]

Although the old accusation that Howells never dealt with sexuality has been silenced, the effects of that attack still color Howells criticism. One reason is the size and clamor of the assault. During the nineteen twenties almost every major critic joined the hue and cry against "Aunt Prudence Heckleberry"[4] Howells. He became a whipping boy in the revolt against Victorian repression, and was denounced in unforgettably scurrilous and colorful terms as a "pious old maid,"[5] who wrote watered prose for "fibrous virgins, fat matrons, and oleaginous clergymen."[6] It was not until the fifties that revisionists cautiously suggested that Howells was unprudish about sexual matters, and even pre-Freudian in some of his insights. Edwin H. Cady and others pointed to his reputation in his own day as a "fleshly" novelist, and showed how he surpassed his contemporaries in confronting passion and writing about it.

Nonetheless, the impression persists that Howells was sex-shy. Although Lionel Trilling, for example, admits Howells's bias toward pleasure, he denies his acquaintance with "the dark gods of sexuality."[7] Edward Wagenknecht's biography, for all its advances, still maintains that "the grosser temptations of men made no appeal" to him.[8] With a more existential slant, George Carrington and Kenneth Lynn portray Howells as a man whose knowledge of sexuality was not too scant, but too searing. Through his neurotic hypersensitivity, they claim, Howells glimpsed the "black heart's truth,"[9] then withdrew in horror to his domestic interiors. In either case, the twenties legacy lingers on—albeit muted and modernized.

Recently, there have been signs of another trend. A number of articles have examined the theme of marriage in his fiction for hidden sociosexual currents, and still others, applied psychoanalytic techniques to his work. The best of the latter include studies of the homosexual implications in *The Shadow of a Dream*, and the sexual tensions in *Their Wedding Journey*.[10] On a broader scale, John W. Crowly has explored Howells's "psychic" stories and discovered a persistent incestuous motif. But no one thus far has attempted a systematic investigation of the sexual text and patterns in Howells, particularly as they relate to his prose and "neurotic" biography.

In trying to accomplish all this—to simultaneously expose the hidden sexual threads in the novels, and weave them with the rest of Howells's history—I have drawn greedily on every critical tool. In order to "see" the eroticism that Howells's readers saw, and place it in context, I have plundered Victorian American social and literary history, from medical manuals to dress codes to etiquette to popular fiction and culture. I have also taken a close look at the texts themselves, fine-combing published versions, word changes, and penumbras of meaning.

But by far the most rewarding approach, both for understanding the novels and life, has been psychoanalysis. Howells provides an unusually fertile subject for this method. First there is his writing. Not only was he the undisputed "psychologist of the age,"[11] whose special interest was sexuality, but he acknowledged a latent text beneath the apparent one. "You can convey an idea by suggestion," he once admitted, and through it, write "a novel of intense passion . . . without the help of one embrace from beginning to end."[12] His creative habits are also psychologically intriguing. Although he gestated novels for several months, he wrote by a kind of free association, using memory for inspiration and changing plots or characters spontaneously. "Most of my observations," he said, "have been unconscious," and again, "writing . . . is only remembering the history of your own life."[13]

His life makes a psychoanalytic application still more fruitful. A strangely fearful child who suffered phobias and nightmares, Howells endured three psychological collapses during his adolescence and early youth. Thereafter and to progressively lesser degrees, he was plagued by various neurotic ailments. All of this he recorded in detail at the turn of the century in five autobiographies and dozens of essays. Such richness of material presents an alluring opportunity: the chance to get beneath the ostensible text in the love stories, to watch the imaginative rendering of his biography there, and match that with the conscious accounts later.

To say that I have relied heavily on psychoanalysis, however, does not mean that I have followed it cravenly or programmatically. I have avoided "schools" and handpicked theories and insights according to need. One of my first concerns was never to impose patterns or philosophies on Howells's work, but to let the material dictate treatment. If I have invested some unlikely objects with sexual significance— such as dogs, Indians, and coffee—it is because they were erotically charged for Howells. Finally, it should be emphasized that psycho- analysis is only a theoretical model for psychic life, a useful construct rather than ordained truth, and therefore has to be used in the spirit of caution and humility. This is especially true when the subject is no longer alive and is as complex, as various, as Howells was.

Although my major sources are postmodern, Freud, of course, un- derpins my study. From him, I have taken the whole concept of neu- rosis, childhood sexuality, the unconscious, repression, and far too much to name. For clarity it may be well to define certain terms I use frequently. By sexual I mean not only genital sexuality but the whole sensuous/affective life of man, including the polymorphous impulses of childhood. According to Freud, the primitive infantile feelings never vanish, but remain beneath the threshold of consciousness, sur- reptitiously steering our lives. If these early wishes—particularly the Oedipal ones—cannot be reconciled with the ego, a neurosis is said to develop. Neurosis, properly defined, involves a conflict between ego and id, flight into illness, and consequent bondage to the past. Cure requires confrontation with the repressed desires, followed by cathar- sis and compromise with the ego.

Where I have expanded on Freud has been on issues of art, myth, and human happiness. Due to an innate atavism, resistance to change, and antagonism between civilization (the reality principle) and grati- fication (the pleasure principle), Freud believed the chances of either cure or a fulfilled life were slim. Here, I have sided with the more sanguine moderns who give the ego influence in therapy and accord the cultural environment key importance. I have relied particularly on Erik Erikson's work with the mature ego, and his schema of stages through which the psyche passes toward health. The neo-Marxists, Herbert Marcuse and Norman O. Brown, have been influential too, with their conviction that the hostility between civilization and plea- sure is not inevitable and that work and play, discipline and freedom, can merge in a nonrepressive instinctual order.

Marcuse and Brown have been further useful since their ideas par- allel Howells's native Swedenborgianism and since they stress a thera- peutic view of art. Art, they contend, is a central weapon against repression and liberates the instinctual joys of childhood. Simon O. Lesser's hypothesis in *Fiction and the Unconscious* refines the neo-

Marxists further. Fiction, he says, does more than simply restore pleasure: it ventilates and resolves psychic conflict. Ernst Kris's psychoanalytic theory, which he developed around art, argues that imaginative work permits controlled regression to the repressed unconscious, and therefore, furthers catharsis and cure. "Regression in the case of aesthetic creation," he explains, ". . . is purposive and controlled . . . the process involves a continual interplay between creation and criticism, manifested in a painter's alternation of working on the canvas and stepping back to observe the effect . . . aesthetic creation may be looked on as a type of problem-solving behavior."[14]

If Freud, then, gave me a vocabulary with which to discuss Howells's emotional difficulties, his successors gave me a theoretical framework with which to explain the psychosexual progressions in his life and work. Through his fiction, Howells was able to gain access to the buried conflict in his past, and gradually (with the help of his prose) achieve the self-knowledge and erotic integration which marks his later years. Karen Horney's emphasis on the union of neurosis and culture also points up how neurotic Howells's age was, how he had to heal a cultural schism while he mended his own. Since his task pushed him beyond his times, I have often used Jung's mythic terminology in order to place Howells in a larger historical context. As he neared psychic wholeness, his language grew overtly archetypal, with special emphasis on circle imagery.

In dealing with his sexual texts as a whole, I have again tried not to stress or manipulate the facts. Of course, the obvious question is why Howells's eroticism hasn't been noticed before if it is so visible. The answer, I think, lies in the "sexual revolution" of the past decades, whose blaze of explicitness may have blinded us to the nuanced, sepia sexuality of Victorian fiction. Although nineteenth-century writers could not use D. H. Lawrence's "phallic language,"[16] they could still say a great deal about sex, more than we perhaps realize.

To truly render the sexual experience—the full body-mind impact—is to move beyond description into the realm of poetry. As John Atkins points out in *Sex and Literature*, metaphor and suggestion have always been the preferred means of evoking sexuality, while graphic accounts have inevitably reduced it to a gymnastic routine. By these standards, Howells was a powerful and effective erotic writer. With a preternaturally sharp eye for sensual details, he used every conceivable literary device to portray the sexual drama: dialogue, allusion, symbolism, choreography, euphemism, and the entire "novel of manners" repertoire. He focused so tightly and lingeringly on phallic and coital images, infused his love scenes with such palpable tension, and built his erotic climaxes with such finesse, that no sexual overreading is ever really necessary.

More interesting than Howells's erotic artistry, though, is what he had to say about Eros. As he worked toward his own self-integration, he also evolved a sexual ethic, a solution to the problem of passion. Despite the acknowledged failure of the sixties' revolution to better the lot of the sexes, there has been little recent discussion about a sexual morality—perhaps because of its noxious nineteenth-century associations. Yet every era has formulated an ethic for the instincts and agreed on the fundamentals with surprising consistency.

Since antiquity, sexuality has been acknowledged as a tremendous double-edged power. It was a constructive, creative force of the highest magnitude, but it was also dangerously destructive, capable of violence, depersonalization, and inhuman extremes of egomania, greed, and promiscuity. The common goal of love philosophers from Plato to Havelock Ellis has been to master the negative capacities without dampening desire, to blend soul and sense, law and lust in an associated erotic order. The order that best harnesses the creative energies of Eros has always been the same: a temperate, relaxed rule midway between license and repression.

Howells's age was tense and repressed to an extreme. The negative effects of sex were so exaggerated, as Howells exaggerated them during his adolescence, that suppression became the norm, and resulted in an unprecedented division of flesh and spirit. Over the course of Howells's fiction, he explored those inflated destructive capacities, found their true essence, then built a pleasurable ethic that harnessed the creative powers of sex and bound the dichotomies. By incorporating his opulent "free" childhood into an adult morality, Howells was able to fashion something unusual in American thought: an affirmation of sexuality that harmonizes the sexes and echoes the great erotic solutions of history.

On the other hand, it would be a mistake to claim too much for Howells. He was bound in real ways by his time and personality. To portray sex in its total complexity and strength, freedom of expression is, of course, preferable. A better grasp of Marcia's frigid ardor for Bartley in *A Modern Instance* might be possible if Howells had been able to tell us what happened when the lights went out on Canary Place. Because of Howells's own happy marriage and the domestic,

Victorian sympathies of the day, he could not imagine rotating relationships, homosexual liaisons, or single parenthood.

Yet, far from being an "Aunt Prudence Heckleberry," Howells was quite advanced for his time. Certainly his final erotic synthesis is uniquely committed to gratification, joy, and equality. As he worked toward this affirmation, his passage is never dull. The advances, deadlocks, compromises, lulls, and sudden, miraculous breakthroughs in his journey through Eros make an exciting, rare adventure.

To better chart his progress, I have not always dwelt on Howells's best-known work, but have concentrated on novels which highlight his erotic themes. I have even skimmed over fourteen years when Howells was most prolific since none of the fiction of that period advanced his sexual quest; he imaginatively wearied of "the everlasting question of the young man and young woman."[17]

During this impasse, however, Howells approached sexuality on another creative plane and began the autobiographies which took him to the core of his neurosis, to self-harmony and recovery of his lenient, sensuous past. By 1909 when he wrote his grandson a valentine that he had "rounded his ways,"[18] his fiction had also made a radical circuit, through the dark truths of negative sexuality, curving back to the gratifications of childhood, recovered in maturity.

I have, then, limited myself to one dimension of Howells, but been otherwise unlimited. I have used every critical resource at hand, and freely crosscut from nonfiction to fiction, showing how they intermesh and finally cooperate in the creation of Howells's erotic harmony. At last, what is awesome is how dynamic that harmony seems to have been, how the circle Howells traced continued dilating. Like the artist, Westover, who painted Lion's Head Mountain over and over because he found something new each time, Howells continued his exploration of Eros, stretching his limits and finding new wisdom until his death. The possibilities for study of this erotic dimension in Howells's life and work are equally endless. I have drawn only the first ring of a potential spiral of other scholarship, of expanding and limitless possibilities for Howellsians of the future.

The circle of Eros

The circle of Eros | *One*

Howells scholars have long agreed that "no more damaging accusation has been made than that of his prudery."[1] Yet his reputation as a reticent realist who avoided the truths of passion persists. His novels are thought to be tame and thin-blooded—ladies' books that ignore the fury and mire of the flesh, the darker impulses. Howells himself has an equally sexless image. The quiet family man Lionel Trilling depicted in 1951 is still the prevailing view of him; he is the "Mr. Papa" for whom "the grosser temptations made no appeal."[2] Moderation, prudence, fastidiousness, and nervous respectability have become almost synonymous with his name.

The nineteen twenties' critics and their successors who saw him as the personification of the Victorian moral establishment are responsible for this legacy. Howells's public persona has also contributed to his prudish renown. He remained married to the same woman, worked and lived successfully within polite society, defended "decency" in fiction, and when he spoke of himself, was often slyly ironic and self-deprecating. He frequently misled interviewers with his criticisms of love, and answered an imaginary niece's objection to the lack of "virility" in his novels with typical archness: "Good heavens, my dear! . . . I hope I'm a gentleman."[3] In the same spirit, he demurred in one of his autobiographies: "I, for my part, should not have liked to sail with Columbus" (*LFA* 150), thus confirming his repute for squeamishness and libidinal apathy.

Yet beneath these public selves was another Howells who contrasts sharply with his staid, prudish stereotype. As Edwin Cady has pointed out in his biography, Howells's inner life was anything but bland: it was filled with risk, pain, radical doubt, and tremendous upheavals. Most of all, it was profoundly passionate. Summing up the difference between them, Henry James wrote Howells: "[P]rimitive passions *lose* themselves for me . . . you are much more passionate."[4] On closer examination, the novels, too, are far from passionless. Read in the context of the age, they show a daring engagement with the theme of sexuality which extends over his entire lifetime. Within this theme, a portrait of the inner man emerges that reveals an ardent, courageous personality capable of enormous changes. The life and the erotic fiction, then, looked at in depth and side by side, provide a glimpse of Howells—the man and artist—that is unsuspected by the general reader.

The most common complaint made of him and his imaginative treatment of sex is that he consistently drew away from passion. If the novels are seen in the light of nineteenth-century norms, however, they display a progressive exploration of sexuality, carried further and further into the heart of Eros. Moving past the exaggerated fears of the times, they steadily uncover sexuality's true dangers and come at last to the demonic itself. Out of such knowledge, an erotic ethic takes hold in the turn of the century books that masters evil and reconciles sense and sensuousness in a triumphant, poised equilibrium. The novels in this way resemble a drama of sexual maturation, with a descent into tragic darkness followed by mastery and synthesis. At the same time they also chart Howells's maturation. Contained in the sexual theme is a symbolic record of his own integration. As the fiction investigated truths of the libido at progressively deeper levels, Howells increasingly penetrated the unconscious recesses of his psyche. He worked through his adolescent fear of sex—neurotic in its intensity—to the roots of that fear in infancy, and thus purged and conquered it through a process akin to psychotherapy, binding body and soul in a new psychic whole. The erotic victory in his final novels, therefore, is a double one and testifies to a confrontation with passion that was of the highest bravery. In the course of his encounter, as well, he said some things about sex which were decidedly un"gentlemanly." Sado-masochism, homoeroticism, and perversity all flourish in his studies of love, and he draws conclusions about these tabooed expressions of Eros that were bold and original.

Any examination of Howells and sex necessarily begins with the subject of his neurosis. His emotionally troubled youth and attendant sexual fears are the standard starting points in discussions of his prudery. For the boy who suffered such torments over the flesh and the "lower" impulses, his home environment was surprisingly unprudish and pleasure loving. His father was an early follower of Robert Dale Owen, the utopian advocate of divorce and birth control,[5] and a later disciple of Emanuel Swedenborg, the sexual mystic. It was in this lenient, sexually celebratory faith that Howells was raised as a child. Swedenborg, unlike other Christian prophets, believed in a union of body and soul and envisioned a heaven where enhanced sensuous and sensual delights rewarded virtue on earth. His *Conjugial Love* was an extended paean to human passion, with an ethical system which was tolerant, shrewd, pragmatic, and "advanced." While he enshrined monogamy and damned promiscuous, selfish love, he defended feminism, divorce, and permitted occasional indiscretions. William Cooper's receptivity to Swedenborg's erotic liberality is evident in his memoir which recounts casual kissing and a free love liaison with easy-going impartiality. Howells's mother seems to have been equally relaxed about sex. Howells remembers her as a gay, high-pulsed woman, who once rolled in the grass for ecstasy and who bravely took a "compromised" village girl into her home.

The preindustrial Ohio of his boyhood, as well, was remarkable for its freedom of sexual expression and comparatively lax moral standards. In his autobiographies, Howells recalls the "traits of primitive civilization" (*BT* 130) that prevailed there: the bacchanalian election days, the casual courtships, the simple manners, the royal liberties permitted young boys. For Howells it was a time when "life was rich unspeakably" (*MYLC* 43). With a nearly hyperaesthetic sensitivity to the sensed world, he reveled in the backwoods intimacy with nature, the joys of his informal home, and the unsupervised pleasures of the still rustic Midwest. Acutely impressed by physical beauty, he never forgot a childish vision of flowering peach trees and responded to the Ohio spring with "rapture": "It [was] all like some foretaste of the heavenly time" (*BT* 83), he reminisced. Swimming naked in the canal, roaming the woods with packs of pet dogs, he and his friends lived out a dream of "savage freedom" and longed to be the Indians who inhabited the outskirts of town. The nucleus of his boyhood was a home that was the "light of heaven" to him. His love for his mother, her sumptuous meals and delicious coffee made his home life a uniquely gratifying one. Swedenborg was his "lightning rod" against danger, and in such a family he early acquired the ambition to be Apollo, the god of "sunshine" (*BT* 53, 229, 21, 81).

Yet, paradoxically, Howells's youth contained disproportionate amounts of darkness and terror. His habitual gloomy-mindedness earned him the nickname "Old Man," and "more fears than hopes" filled his childhood (*BT* 238, 16). An ambivalence about the sensuous

pleasures he enjoyed so much seems to have been at the root of his
anxieties. His was the classic neurotic conflict as Freud defined it: ego
and sexuality were in deep, chronic tension. From the first dark vision
which accompanied the memory of the peach trees—a man drowning
in the Ohio—negative associations continued to intermesh with his
happiest experiences. The woods he prowled with delight were also
full of ghastly dangers. Ghosts and filthy savages lurked on all sides,
making life as much a "prison" as an endless frontier of pleasure (*BT* 1).
The celebrants he watched blithely on election day became a symbol
of menace in a drunken miller at Xenia and, despite Swedenborg's liberalities, he developed a horror of hellfire and the devil. The light of
home was not strong enough, either, to obliterate the terrors of the
night. Nightmares, haunted by "loathesome reptiles," [6] and fantasies
of disease and death, plagued his youth. At an early age, he imagined
he would die prematurely and throughout the long Ohio summers,
suffered hypochondriacal delusions. Tellingly, the disease was linked
to the instinctual joys he loved most. From a dog, the mascot of his
boy's world expeditions, he believed he had caught rabies and he fan-
cied he had the symptoms of hydrophobia. The same "delicious water" in which he "rioted" (*BT* 48) with abandon brought on sensations
of smothering and panic.

His home was the scene of tensions as well. Paradise that it was, it
was often a painful place for the young Howells. The mother he adored
had a "quick temper" (*YOMY* 20), which sometimes exploded capriciously, and the rivalry for her affections was stiff. There were six
other brothers and sisters, and the Oedipal friction was severe enough
for Howells to have once told his mother that he wished his father
were dead. Until his teens, the fear of her loss was so keen, he could
not leave home without crippling attacks of homesickness. In Freudian terms, this overattachment to her was the dynamic center of his
neurosis. In the free expression of his instincts were desires that were
either forbidden by his mother or incestuously tied to her in fatally
punishable ways. Hence the dangers in sensuous release. Freud would
say, too, that his symptoms—the hypochondria, ghosts, and nightmares—were fantasized retaliations for those tabooed wishes.

When he reached adolescence, the ambivalence grew patently sexual. With the "radiant revelation of girlhood," and "unlimited social
freedom" came a parallel fear of the "lower" impulses (*YOMY* 90, 92).
He adopted the strategy of repression. The boy who swam naked now
bridled at a nude painting of Adam and Eve, refused to speak to a

fallen seamstress in his home, and developed a "devilish ideal of propriety" (*YOMY* 37). Three times his nerves cracked under the strain. In his nineteenth summer, his hypochondria returned with a vengeance and, exhausted from overwork, he listened to the death watch in the wall each night. The next year, working as an editor on the *Cincinnati Gazette*, he found the spectacle of girls in restaurants and a sordid station house so upsetting he collapsed with homesickness and left his job. Again, on a reporting assignment in Columbus, he came down with vertigo and went home to recuperate. Afterwards, he was able to control his symptoms and launch a successful literary career, but the price was a lingering prudery. He achieved sanity through suppression.

During his editorial stint in Columbus, he dedicated himself to the cult of pure womanhood and clean literature, denouncing the "shameless" Walt Whitman. "You must shrink from his contact,"[7] he advised, and chastised a friend who investigated a prostitute's suicide. He even foreswore the blandishments of the theater. When he married lively, warmblooded Elinor Noyes Mead, however, his puritanical zeal relaxed. He moved to Venice, expanded his moral vision, and enthusiastically embraced its rich, complex, and hedonistic culture. Yet beneath his new content and broadened perspectives, the unresolved sexual conflict remained. A defensive squeamishness surfaced repeatedly throughout his years on the *Atlantic Monthly* and well into middle age. He found it a "horror"[8] to watch a girl in a leotard in Boston, argued for literary reticence, and wrote Charles Eliot Norton in 1878: "What I can't abide is the matter between Helen and Casanova . . . it's odious."[9]

On the basis of these and similar positions, he earned the stigma of prude and "old maid." Even if his views had not changed, the social-historical milieu considerably extenuates his maladjustment. As Karen Horney points out, every neurosis expresses a cultural difficulty in some accentuated form.[10] Howells's "puritanism," then, was only a heightened reflection of his age's official norm. From the beginning, the cultural climate reinforced and aggravated his instinctual conflict. The death and disease he dreaded during his youth were the penalties promised by Victorian physicians for unrestrained sexuality. "Indulgence is fatal . . . it leads to a 'house of death,'"[11] one warned; and another threatened boys who masturbated with attacks of hypochondria.[12] At almost no other time in Western history was the fear of passion so extreme. For reasons hard to determine, sex became a metaphor for chaos and old night and was said to cause every possible malady, from the nightmares Howells endured to his morbidity and 1858 "giddiness."[13] The special sigla of this dangerous impulse were primitive races and drink, a key perhaps to Howells's terror of Indians and the drunken miller.

His adolescent apprehensions seem to have been colored by his environment as well. Fallen women, like the seamstress in his home, were "horror[s]";[14] nudity, an abomination; and cities were breeding grounds for lust and corruption. When he moved to Columbus, his repressive strategy received enthusiastic support and ratification from the community. Polite Ohioans in the fifties banned theatergoing and his editor there admonished him: "Never, *never* write anything you would be ashamed to read to a woman" (*YOMY* 126). In Boston he came under the sway of the genteel leaders at the fount of the purity cult. As editor of the *Atlantic*, his mentors were the chief apologists for Victorian respectability—literarily, scientifically, and philosophically. For Lowell and the literati who befriended him, "any grossness of speech was inconceivable," and their muses, "not merely very nice young persons but really ladies" (*LFA* 193, 111). John Fiske, a Darwinian advocate of the lower instincts theory, dedicated *Myths and Mythmakers* to him, while Henry James, Sr., taught him a bloodless version of his native Swedenborgianism. Put into perspective, then, Howells's fastidiousness appears less extreme and his neurosis more comprehensible. The popular assumptions about sex exploited and fostered his inner ambivalence and endorsed the suppressive techniques he used to quell it.

What his erotic novels show, though, is first a progressive revolt against this spirit of denial and then a gradual resolution of his neurotic split. Beneath the conscious positions he took, beneath his public facades, his imagination worked steadily toward cure and the lost pleasures of childhood. To use Ernst Kris's terminology,[15] his creativity permitted a form of controlled regression, in which he would "remember" his early difficulties, purge them, and unite his divided psyche. With each novel, he probed deeper into his instinctual fear until he came to the primal core of his anxiety (his Oedipal desires included) and recovered the sensuous joy of his past. Herbert Marcuse and the neo-Marxists would say that his imagination was more than therapeutic; it was by definition committed to "freedom from repression . . . uninhibited desire and gratification" from the start. Over the course of his fiction, both functions can be seen in operation together, striving toward the fulfillment of his love theme at the turn of the century. When he achieved the erotic "marriage" in the novels, he achieved his own totality through the same circular route to maturity. He "returned from alienation"[16] to his bodily self, by facing and mastering the demonic, and ethically integrating blood and spirit. Just before he died, he celebrated his combined psychic and eroto-literary accomplishment with the image of a circle—the archetypal emblem of completeness. Speaking of love in general and his marriage in particular, he said, "the marriage ring is . . . a circle rounded in eternity."[17] He had freed himself from his past, finally, from his first sexual ethic, from the confines of his era.

To reach that goal required the labor of a lifetime. In five slow stages, Howells inched toward full tragic knowledge and the affirmation beyond it. The first phase brought him to the adolescent level of his conflict. Progressively these three novels focused in on exaggerated sexual fear. At the same time they more and more repudiated a repressive solution and invoked the old images of pleasure—in all their ambivalence. The result was a stalemate at the end of each book, with a savage sexuality on the one hand, invalidated controls on the other, and an unassimilated, contradictory subcurrent of pleasure. By *A Modern Instance* (1882), the ambivalence had grown extreme and the oppositions critical: death cancelled out every erotic option.

Howells's sexual theme achieved escape from this stranglehold in *April Hopes* (1888). Through a dramatic shift of perspective, he was able to strike a compromise with pleasure and tentatively endorse a reasoned, temperate, relaxed ethic. But, in a third development, *The Shadow of a Dream* (1890), Howells rejected compromise for a deeper investigation of sexuality. Before the primitive, infantile truths that he found, his newly enlightened ethic disintegrated. A crisis ensued like that of *A Modern Instance*, only worse. Erotic value retreated further from reach, the sensuous evocations were sharper and as ambivalent as they had been in childhood. Thanatos triumphed again.

The fourth developmental period was one of quiescence and incubation. While the sexual quest lay relatively fallow, he launched an autobiographical exploration in which he intellectually retraced his imaginative footsteps. After the anagnorisis of *The Flight of Pony Baker* (1902), he returned to sexuality in his fiction and entered the final, golden stage of his inquiry. With *The Son of Royal Langbrith* (1904) he produced the first of the sexual affirmations which filled the decade. He reintroduced demonic sexuality (clarified by his personal history) and surmounted it with an ethic that restored the gratifications of childhood. Purged of negative associations, pleasure became absorbed in a morality of the finest maturity. Antinomies fused, and his last novel raised the erotic victory into a fertility myth.

Throughout his erotic theme, as it evolved from fear and division to affirmation and synthesis, the language of Howells's childhood experience is the dominant idiom. Sexual evil breeds death, darkness, nightmare, and suffocation and its special harbingers are dogs, snakes, savages, and alcohol. Swedenborg's rhetoric permeates every evocation of negative sex. The devil, hellfire, filth and deformity—all the properties of damnation in *Conjugial Love* (so disproportionately perceived by the young Howells)—emanate from sexual sin. By the same token, the early pleasures provide the vocabulary of positive Eros. The early, informal Midwest serves as a reference point of "good" sexuality, like the sensuosity he experienced there. The "rapture" of the woods, natural beauty, and unfettered bodily enjoyments form the fabric of his erotic affirmations. Inextricably woven into them, as well, is the pivotal image of home: its light, warmth, and cornerstone, his passional mother. And if Swedenborg's infernal prophecies pervade the portrayals of evil, so his celestial ones inform the celebrations of sexual blessedness. Throughout his sexual theme, this private language supplies a continuous key to the meaning—tracing the path from dissociation to integration and unlocking the deeper reaches of his erotic drama.

There are other, more standard keys to his erotic fiction which supplement his personal code. Although, like the traditional amorist writers, Howells could not be explicit, he loaded his novels with a wealth of sexual implication. Drawing on established conventions, the innovations of contemporary Europeans, and his own intuitive methods, he became a consummate erotic artist. He skillfully deployed euphemisms—either shared by his generation (such as "undisciplined") or of his own invention (such as "fascinate")—that were most calculated to arouse the semiconscious sensitivities of his readers. Allusions, from art and literature to etymological love, enrich his sexual theme and his symbolism ranges far and deep. He culled the natural, mechanical, and social worlds for imagery, concentrating on phallically and coitally suggestive words. In the proliferation of canes, cigars, flower and fruit motifs, he was abundantly pre-Freudian.

Perhaps due to his playwriting experience, his dialogue is also a superb instrument of erotic communication. Packed with double-entendres, breathless tensions, and racy comic byplay, it registers sexual sensations from the most nebulous to the most tremendous. With theatrical instinct, he artfully staged and costumed romantic episodes. He made material settings refract lovers' passions and choreographed their movements exactly. When he combined these techniques for maximum effects—in climactic scenes, for instance, like seductions and declarations—he was able to elicit the very pulse and urgency of desire. His eye for sensuous detail grew preternaturally sharp; his pacing became symphonic and his euphemisms explicit.

As Howells's sexual theme expanded, his style matured with it. The further he carried his investigation toward intrapsychic depths, the more he left his famous "cabinet-picture manner,"[18] his subtleties and detailed documentation, for psychological realism. His methods gained economy and force, gathering a poetic brilliance. By his last novel, he had entered the realms of myth and folklore. The euphemisms turn literal (his protagonist actually fascinates his victims); the symbolism becomes archetypal and the allusions elemental. With allegorical compression, settings contract into psychic landscapes, and the characters (costumed like masquers) seem to dance their parts and speak in recitative. At the end, each of Howells's erotic techniques came into high relief; the artistry he developed and honed over a lifetime attained a clarity as limpid as the one he reached in his love theme.

As Howells began to study sexuality in his fiction, there were intimations of the direction it would take. His imagination inclined toward pleasure and away from repression and sought out the darker manifestations of the libido. His first three serious explorations of sexuality open onto his adolescent apprehension of that darkness, while they increasingly endorse sensuality and repudiate the remedy of denial. The conflict builds with each novel, until *A Modern Instance*, where the contradictions mount to a deadly climax.

In *A Foregone Conclusion* (1875), the first of the group, he adumbrated the main issues of his erotic books and established the problem he would have to solve. The three protagonists represent the two character types he used to study passion and illustrate the opposite ends of his immaturity spectrum. Florida Vervain and her priestly lover are the oversexed, under-controlled prototypes through whom he explored "natural" sexuality in his work, and Henry Ferris, the model of overcontrol, through whom he probed the mysteries of repression. Both embody imbalances Howells would seek to redress; juvenilities, he would refine. With their immature lack of discipline,

Florida and Don Ippolito generate extraordinary pain and discord. Florida's mismanaged and flammable passions create one mishap after another and finally lead to the priest's death. He, meanwhile, is the incarnation of everything to be feared in unchecked sexual regression. He is the mythic "fool," who harbors the chaotic impulses (especially the perversions) and inflicts confusion on himself and others.

What is significant, though, is that the respectable consul, Henry Ferris, causes even more damage through his repressive ethic. In this, he forecasts the future direction of the novels, at the same time that he enunciates their central quest. When, torn by fear and envy of the priest, he stands at his window and tries to untangle the "truth of the secret" (*FC* 241), he voices the mission of the sexual theme. Latent in *A Foregone Conclusion* are two other incipient trends. Excessive repression, it is suggested, exacerbates Don Ippolito's and Florida's intemperance and promotes their final sterility. So, too, the ambivalence encroaches. There is a genuine equivocation about the sensuous setting and characters: Venice is both celestial and wicked; Florida's garden, voluptuous and bug-infested; Don Ippolito, a knight and a dog.

Howells's second study of passion brings the problem home to America and heightens all of its terms. The uninhibited, sultry Mrs. Farrell of *Private Theatricals* (1875) demonstrates a sexuality more disruptive and brutal than anything in *A Foregone Conclusion*. As living proof of Darwin's theories, she reduces a New England colony to pandemonium with her natural savagery. Egotism, jealousy, sadism, and violence vie openly during her seduction of the community. On the other hand, the orthodox culture which Ferris represented has grown in destructiveness. Not only does it actively encourage Mrs. Farrell's excesses and frigidity, it condemns the society to the rule of the death instinct. Whether genteel outsiders or the simple natives, the prohibitive ethos has leeched the landscape of life and value, leaving the barren legacy of sentimentality and neopuritanism. With the absence of a viable morality, the ambivalence increases. If Mrs. Farrell is a wild animal (Swedenborg's term for the damned), she is also an image of supreme pleasure.

In *A Modern Instance* (1882) these oppositions reach a total crisis. Free sexuality, as the wanton Marcia and Bartley Hubbard attest, leads to nothing less than death. The wickedness they perpetuate and their fatal ends dramatize the sexual terror of the age and thus, of the adolescent Howells. Yet with this extreme, deathbound vision of passion is a parallel one of the orthodox morality. The "official" purity creed generates a lifelessness and venality which extend out of a New England colony to Boston and the Western frontier. And like that of *Private Theatricals*, it fosters the Hubbards' prodigalities. Death and negation finally weigh both sides of the erotic equation, unrelieved by value or meaning. Simultaneously the impulse toward pleasure gains ground. Moving closer to the early gratifications, the sensuous subtext converges around Middlewestern themes: the inhabitants, beauty, and relaxed mores. But the conflict has also grown critical. Lenient, vernal Indiana is corrupt and sinister and Bartley, who escapes there, a petty criminal. In him the ambivalence comes to a head. When he lights out for the West, the plot collapses and winds down to the bleak anticlimax. It was also when Howells, drawn to the quick of his adolescent feelings, himself broke down. His Columbus neurosis had resurfaced and the repressive controls failed.

By *April Hopes* (1888), after the tentative breakthrough in *The Rise of Silas Lapham* (1885), he was able to loosen the deadlock and establish a temporary detente with passion. The great transformations of the late eighties—his defense of realism, rebellion against convention, and discovery of Tolstoy—permitted a realignment in his erotic theme. The undiscriminated fear recedes and is replaced by a more complex, tolerant attitude to sex. What had been implied in the novels gains new emphasis: orthodox repression is now the handmaiden of negative Eros. With the blame transferred to the genteel establishment, a positive sexuality becomes possible in the unconventional world, the locus of Howells's pleasure principle. Under the aegis of four "outsiders," a rudimentary erotic ethic, based on reason, moderation, selflessness, and relaxation, emerges. Among these characters is a free-spirited, embryonic heroine; but she, like the other three, cannot implement her beliefs. Although it has been envisioned, sexual maturity is still on the horizon.

In *The Shadow of a Dream* (1890), this realistic compromise dissolves before deeper, more tragic libidinous truths. Moving beyond the alliance of respectability and sexual evil, Howells descended to the pith of the "secret," the unconscious springs of passion. He went past his adolescent fear into the infantile recesses of his terror. He penetrated Don Ippolito's regressive impulses and tapped the demonic—the classic dark side of Eros. Through Douglas Faulkner and his dream, the perversions, as well as the savagery, rise up in their primal anarchy. The temperate narrator (reflecting the *April Hopes* solution) cannot defeat these realities logically and finally succumbs to them himself. His only recourse when the plot lies in the shadow of chthonic sexuality is to fall back on the invalidated, lethal tactic of denial. Death, then, closes in on the novel in the same way that it did in *A Modern Instance*, except with graver consequences. Suppression carries the double threat of sterility and salacity while the sexual truths go beyond exaggeration to the source of fear. Yet the infantile fear could not be touched without unleashing the pleasure too, and the portrayals of beauty and luxury are stronger, more defined than ever before. With it, the ambivalence climbs proportionally, creating a tension so paralyzing that the only escape is the death of the two lovers. Never had Thanatos enjoyed such an unqualified, crushing victory.

Rather than escape through illness, Howells temporarily withdrew from his sexual theme this time. Having cut to the bone of his neurosis, having exhumed the ultimate fear and the accompanying gratifications without discovering a way to contain or resolve them, he put aside the erotic quest for fourteen years. The novels either restate the problem in a lower key like *The Landlord at Lion's Head* (1897) and *The Kentons* (1902), either move out to socio-economic concerns, or show the sex weariness of *The Day of Their Wedding* (1896). Howells's letter to Charles Eliot Norton in 1892 typifies his fatigued, almost ascetic mood: "I doubt if I shall ever write another story in which mating and marrying plays an important part. I am too old for it, and it does not interest me."[19] The lull in his fiction, though, was a tremendously fruitful period. After *The Shadow of a Dream*, he began a succession of autobiographies in which he consciously examined the ground his imagination had charted. He looked squarely at his neurotic conflict and fear and searched for the "secret" behind them. With each memoir, as in successful psychotherapy, he came nearer the crux of the difficulty, until he found the tabooed, infantile emotions he had intuited in Faulkner's dream. From the sadistic, vagrant impulses, he progressed to the incestuous foundations of the libido, all the while recalling the sensuous joys with increased vividness. Like the novels, the same fear-pleasure dichotomy prevails throughout the first books. After *The Flight of Pony Baker* (1902), however—where Howells exposed the Oedipal nerve of his neurosis—the opposed sides start to knit. Psychoanalytically, the purgation made this synthesis and renewed ego control possible. More and finer clarifications occurred in the later autobiographies, but 1902 marks a watershed in his development—best visible in the erotic novel which succeeded it.

The Son of Royal Langbrith (1904) is a radiant testimony to his achieved self-integration. With the accumulated wisdom of his decade-long inner scrutiny, he returned to the chthonic truths of *The Shadow of a Dream*, personalized, intensified them, and gave them an affirmative ethic. The dark drives Faulkner shadowed forth, Royal Langbrith and his son act out in reality. Sadism, promiscuity, megalomania have their blackest, most terrifying figuration and the infantile perversions, the first lucid treatment. In James Langbrith's narcissism and Oedipal attachment, Howells reified what Ferris had feared in Don Ippolito; he dramatized the inner logic of neurosis. The definition of "fool" becomes complete. By the same token, the pleasurable undercurrent in the novels solidifies. Tragically informed and ethically strengthened, it manages to master demonic sexuality (as in a maturity myth) and establish erotic harmony. The joyous modalities of childhood—the West, equality, freedom, beauty, passionate womanhood—return, incorporated into the adult consciousness. Howells's nineties' apatheia literally dies out of the plot, and a positive Eros floods the book. In one of his happiest finales, James and Hope Langbrith celebrate a love which brings together every antinomy and radiates life, concord, and the light of common day.

His novels afterwards enlarge and perfect this synthesis. *Through the Eye of the Needle* (1907) portrays a utopia of sexual freedom and equality and *Miss Bellard's Inspiration* (1905) chillingly retells the marriage of Marcia and Bartley, ripened into a middle-aged *mano a mano*, with a comic ending. But his last work of fiction, *The Leatherwood God* (1916), provides the ultimate consummation of his sexual theme. With mythic condensation, the tale recapitulates and elucidates his entire erotic drama. The controlling images are the childhood ones; the setting, his past; and the characters, densely autobiographical. Personifying both his childish fears and his own "bad" boy-self, the Leatherwood "god" also distills everything Howells had learned in his fiction about negative Eros. A snorting stallion, Joseph Dylks is an apotheosis of the lawless id and his religious pretensions, the highest expression of the connection between repression and lust. When he dies, demonic sexuality suffers its worst, most unqualified defeat. Moreover, the forgiveness which follows his rout represents a positive integration of these powers—the ideal goal of therapy and erotic morality.

The affirmative side of the "secret" achieves just as luminous a clarification. The quest for pleasure crystallizes in an ethic that restores the childhood gratifications, transfigured by adult wisdom. The two halves of value, the passionate Nancy Billings and shrewd Squire

Braile, move through maturity tests toward a tough, resilient erotic poise. Men and women, flesh and spirit, public and private realms coalesce in a harmony no less perfect because it is "realistic." Death and evil remain absolute and implacable. But Eros is strong enough in this ritual comedy to acclaim life over death, to sensualize the whole environment with its fertilizing power. Howells's infantile ambition to be Apollo, god of light, has been fulfilled without sacrificing any of the pleasure. The novel is a hymn to the liberties, primal satisfactions, and loveliness of the preindustrial West, structured on an ethic which stems from Swedenborg. The use of his father's religion, sexual idealism, and story for his inspiration is a final testimony to his accomplished maturity. In the classic proof of Oedipal transcendence, he became reunited with his father. He had completed an epithalamion for his sexual theme.

Although elements of his ethic seem Victorian—the monogamy, fidelity, "decency," and domesticity—he surpassed his temporal limitations. While he healed his neurosis, with its heightened expression of the cultural norm, he also mended the division of his generation, aligning himself with universal erotic values. He broke through the excessive, wholesale nineteenth-century fears to the demonic constants in sexuality. From Socrates to Freud, the great amorists have all located a destructive, animal core within Eros and agreed on its properties: greed, egotism, promiscuity, perversion, and violence. Their remedies for passion have resembled Howells's as well. In the search for a mean between the extremes of restraint and license (each of which ends in impotence) they have unanimously espoused a balanced, associated ethic. Ultimately, this is the ideal enshrined in the literary convention of marriage. It is the union of opposites, the wedding of the sexes, soma and psyche, freedom and security, self and society that Donne's poems extoll. It is the concord of Spenser's garden of Adonis, with the "wilde Bore" mastered and caged.[20] Without Howells's achieved inner harmony, his supreme solution would have been impossible. For as Socrates realized at the end of the "Phaedrus" that is where every sexual value finally starts and ends: "Give me beauty in the inward soul," he prayed after the long erotic argument, "and may the outward and inward man be at one."[21]

With the successful integration of sexuality in his fiction and psyche, there was a change in Howells's public persona which has been largely ignored. As in the novels, he gradually departed from the orthodox morality of his time, and came to advocate "the grossest material honestly treated."[22] Reversing his reticent realism decrees, he openly attacked censorship, the hypocrisies of civilization, and defended the "indecent" modernists against popular abuse. His "Editor's Easy Chair" at *Harper's* was a forum for sexual discussion, in which he proposed a series of *avant-garde* ideas: easier divorce laws, subsidized lovers' bowers in parks, feminism, and an art of love for married couples. For his era, he was daringly advanced—an iconoclast—and the positions he took, courageous.

If his youth was a time of fear and queasiness, his adult life was a long record of risks taken and won. Richard Chase accuses Howells of "real laziness."[23] On the contrary, he tackled what psychiatrists call "the equivalent of the labors of Hercules"[24] and pressed his love theme to new frontiers. Neither Henry James, who psychologized sex into pure spirit, nor Mark Twain, who remained torn between his St. Joan and Queen Elizabeth, were able to extend Eros as far. Few American writers, for that matter, have been able to resolve the perennial dichotomies of the sexes, head and heart, liberty and containment. Almost as interesting as this last achievement, though, is the way Howells arrived at it. Through a process he admitted was a "psychic puzzle"[25] to himself, his creative mind strove surreptitiously and stubbornly for forty years toward wholeness. His imagination forced a confrontation with the unconscious essence of his neurosis and insisted on the recovery of pleasure. After 1902, it joined his conscious insights for a powerfully built, elaborated erotic synthesis.

Such a view of the interior, creative Howells in relation to sexuality requires a reassessment of his reputation. He was a richer natured, deeper, more audacious personality than has been believed and an amorist writer of the greatest sophistication. Stylistically, his treatment of passion ranks with Shakespeare's, Flaubert's, and Colette's and his affirmation, with the best erotic thought.

The sculptor, Augustus St. Gaudens, who modelled Howells's bas-relief, had a dream about him that encapsulates his engagement with Eros. He saw him withdraw a gun on a ship at sea, take aim, and shoot the planet Venus out of the sky. As it fell in a bright arc to the horizon, the astonished St. Gaudens realized the stars were nearer than he thought. Venus *was* the target of Howells's attention the better part of his career and he did hit its meaning dead center, bringing passion down to the human horizon. Another modern myth presents a more popular version of the same parable. The young hero at the end of *The Centaur* by John Updike watches the planet Venus with his father and asks the question which becomes his life's quest: "Can you steer by it?"[26] The classic question, on the other hand, has always been how can man steer Venus, how can he harness the chthonic powers and convert them to life and pleasure. That, essentially, was what Howells asked at the beginning of his sexual theme and what his imagination, with pain, patience, and the support of his active will, answered brilliantly for him at last.

A Foregone Conclusion: The beginnings of a sexual theme | *Two*

Howells called *A Foregone Conclusion* (1875) his "first novel."[1] It was also his first major treatment of passion, a distinct breakthrough. Confronting sexuality directly, he set his love story in voluptuous Venice and cast it with three highly sexed protagonists. The resulting triangle tragedy covers only a few short months, involves four people and never leaves Venice, except for the epilogue. So confined is its compass, so minute its scale, Henry James likened the book to a miniature painting. But within this brief novel, the principal motifs of the sexual theme are all adumbrated and the central quest defined. As James observed in the same essay: "He has outlined his field; [he only has to] fill it up."[2]

The three major actors in the drama become prototypes of the individuals who would dominate Howells's erotic writing. The steamy heiress, Florida Vervain, and her priestly admirer, Don Ippolito, are the first of the over-sexed, undisciplined characters in his work, and Henry Ferris, the consul, the first of the puritans. Each represents an opposite maladjustment Howells would investigate and eventually repair over his career. Through his passionate personalities like Florida and Don Ippolito he was able to explore the nature of sexuality and examine its innate dangers. Ferris's prudery, on the other hand, gave him access to the mysteries and dangers of repression. Ostensibly, the instincts contain all the peril in *A Foregone Conclusion*. Florida's fevered behavior stirs up a tempest of misunderstanding, jealousy, and pain, and the priest's intemperance explains the original title, *The Tragedy of Don Ippolito*.

But at a deeper level, the respectable consul causes the greater misery through his squeamishness. Because of his exaggerated fear of sex, the tragic issue of the tale is assured. Indirectly he foments a triangular conflict, blights Florida, and speeds the priest to his death. For that reason, perhaps, Howells changed the title to the line from *Othello* in which Othello falsely accuses Desdemona: Ferris's misconceptions cause the same tragedy. And like Othello, too, he does not escape unscathed. His distorted fears lead him to a psychological breakdown which he survives only by psychic and creative self-mutilation. He suffers a traditional maturity test, the passage through the dark underworld of the subconscious. Amidst his ordeal, he asks what the rest of the novels will try to answer, the "truth of the secret" (*FC* 241) to the sexual riddle. The "secret" would gradually unfold, but Ferris's failure would be a motif repeated for the next three decades.

For all its "delicacy"[3] and "cabinet-picture"[4] subtlety, *A Foregone Conclusion* created "something like a scandal"[5] in genteel America. It is intensely sexual. From allusion to dialogue, Howells loaded his small canvas with a vibrant, palpitant eroticism. Turgenev, the unrivaled "master of the love story,"[6] showed the way to this new sexual dimension. Howells discovered him two years before he began the novel and the effect was overwhelming: "It was like a happiness I had been waiting for all my life" (*MLP* 171), he recalled. Through Turgenev he found a safe way of talking about sex in Comstockian America and important devices for conveying it. Using Turgenev's dramatic method, he learned to avoid censorship through the feigned absence of the author from the story and to pack in a maximum amount of sexual meaning—inconspicuously. Adapting Turgenev's atmospheric effects and compressed details to his own ends, Howells reworked the materials from *Venetian Life* (1867) to highlight his sexual theme. The San Lazzaro of his travel book, for instance, metamorphoses, through his careful emphases of sensuous particulars, into an objective correlative for Florida's passion. Scenic descriptions duplicate erotic moods, and Venice's sexual history contributes throughout to the love theme.

In his range and richness of figurative language though, he surpassed Turgenev. PreFreudianly, canes, candles, and phallic flowers proliferate, reflecting the libidinal wishes of the characters. Don Ippolito's fountain, which jets up in Florida's garden, is a prime example and grows, with the advance of the romance, into a major central symbol. Certain distinctive patterns of Howells's sexual imagery also begin to appear: the polarities of light and dark, life and death, heat and cold, freedom and entrapment. Other characteristic methods Howells introduced in *A Foregone Conclusion* are the euphemisms, such as "fascinate" and "kiss," which so shrewdly exploited the sensitivities of his readers,[7] and the erotic allusions from literature, painting, and history. His finest artistry, however, went into the portrayal of his characters' sexual temperaments and encounters. Every detail—their names, physiques, gestures, and dress—is libidinally telling, and their surroundings radiate their sensuality. Their scenes together are intensely passionate. Dialogue scintillates with double-entendres, innuendo, and desire, and their movements resemble a *pas de deux*. In certain peak episodes, like Don Ippolito's moonlight tryst with Florida in the garden, all of these techniques combine for powerfully sexual crescendos.

So dramatic is Don Ippolito's part in the story that he has often been seen as the leading character.[8] Beyond question, he is one of Howells's most memorable creations, setting up resonances (as Gregor Samsa and Nana do) in the unconscious, subrational regions of the mind. Not until the end of his life was Howells again to portray such a complete example of uncurbed, infantile sexuality. Don Ippolito's puerility becomes clear at his first appearance in the book. Reinforcing the clues provided by his name, which signifies "Spanish cavalier" (*FC* 58) and horse (the archetypal id animal), he introduces himself to the consul by offering him an emblem of his immature libido—a model cannon that explodes prematurely. Ippolito's romantic good looks and frequent blushes further establish his passionate temperament, and the "sensitive nose" (*FC* 2) he rubs continually hints at autoerotic expressions of it. During his initial interviews with Ferris, he presents a classic Victorian image of incontinence. He is puerile, "soft," "womanish," "dreamy," "ineffectual," and the town "crackbrain" (*FC* 4, 5, 16)—everything the nineteenth century feared from sexual undiscipline.[9] Don Ippolito's apartment and hobby mirror his instinctual abandon. The rooms he lives in are covered with his own "quaint and childish" frescos. Vines "flourish up the trellised walls, with many a wanton tendril and flaunting leaf" and blossom in "lavish clusters of white and purple all over the ceiling" (*FC* 47). An aura of degeneracy surrounds the disordered studio. The inventions he concocts there are thinly disguised fantasies of sexual intercourse and, significantly, each contains a fatal, childish defect. In an insinuation of narcissistic propensities, one is a camera designed to take a self-portrait.

Through his uncontrolled surrender to his instincts and the infantile perversions, Don Ippolito creates havoc in himself and for others in the tale. The passion he rashly develops for Florida excites her maternally, and misleads and alienates the true object of her affections, Henry Ferris. At the same time, the consul takes such fright at the priest's regressive sexuality that he draws away from erotic involvement with Florida. Indirectly, then, Don Ippolito frustrates and destroys their romance. Far worse, though, is the way he bedevils himself with his intemperance. He abandons himself to a tragic course that ends at last in his death. From the shadow, cold, and privation of his monastic life he rushes toward the warmth and light of heterosexual love, only to be plunged back into deeper darkness.

When he meets the Vervains he emerges from his "stinted" (*FC* 142) circumstances and stygian alleyway into a sun-drenched patio brimming with sensuous abundance. Mrs. Vervain gives him a "breakfast of hot beefsteak, eggs and toast, fried potatoes and coffee" (*FC* 66) and her daughter greets him in all her *volupté*. Precipitously, Don Ippolito's life begins to change. Giving rein to his sensuality, he discards his clerical robes for a waistcoat and a phallic shaped hat "with a very worldly, curling brim" (*FC* 76). He repairs the fountain in Florida's garden so that it spirals up over the naiad statue at the center: the first of the tumescent images which accompany his erotic awakening. As his infatuation builds, he plays a piano and church organ simultaneously until the "notes swell" (*FC* 86), and he heroically lifts the gondola from the mud on the Brenta Canal.

By contrast, he physically wilts in his clerical role, collapsing and dropping his candle during the Corpus Christi procession. His confession to Florida afterwards of his discontent as a priest and her encouragement prompt the series of steps that lead to his downfall. Overcome by passion, he stands in the sun, watches the trains (one of Freud's favorite phallic symbols), and then decides to leave the priesthood. He flies to Florida and in a rash moment blurts his love for her. It is his moment of ecstasy. His fountain leaps up "like a tangled skein of silver" (*FC* 208) in the moonlight, and, transported by a sense of "release and triumph" (*FC* 209), he unburdens his heart. When Florida reacts with horror, the images of light, elevation, and power turn to darkness and collapse. The fountain suddenly expires; he covers his face with his hands, and the night deepens. "The whole edifice of his dreams, his wild imaginations, had fallen into dust" (*FC* 213). Florida tries to console him, but he retreats into the "dense shadows" (*FC* 223) of the canals where he slowly pines away under the weight of redoubled deprivation. To a lunatic's curse of "dog of a priest" (*FC* 227),[10] he totters off to his final sickbed, dropping Mrs. Vervain's rouleau of money behind him. On the surface, he undergoes a conversion, during which his "darkness" (*FC* 236) vanishes before a religious illumination, but his condition undercuts the validity of his salvation. His sensibilities are dulled, his hands "weak, chill, and nerveless" (*FC* 235), and he dies hopelessly. In essence, he had no choice: his identity was too dominated by his sexuality to survive its defeat. Without finding a way to vitally integrate and control the force of Eros, he succumbs to Thanatos.

Florida Vervain resembles Don Ippolito in that her sexuality takes an immature—if more complex—expression. In her case, however, rather than fixating at the infantile level, her sexual orientation is adolescent, the desires still unfocused and either too tightly reined or too extravagantly released.[11] Because she cannot responsibly manage them, she seduces the priest, repels the consul, and orchestrates both her and Don Ippolito's doom, all uncomprehendingly.

As in the priest's case, Florida's initial scenes in the novel graphically illustrate her erotic disposition. She sweeps on stage like the classic hot-blooded heroine in literature: tall and buxom, with "masses of fair gold hair" (*FC* 19), deep voice, and ivory skin, she blushes violently and seems to impersonate her name. She demonstrates a temperament as tropical as Florida, and a beauty as lush as the fragrant, profuse Vervain (verbena) flower. Her garden symbolizes her rich, untutored sensuality. The flowers, designed to make the "greatest show of blossom" (*FC* 62) with the least tendance, bloom amidst "wanton" statues of nymphs and surround a "careless naiad" in a fountain at the center. As Florida's passion mounts, the naiad "increase[s] its fervors day by day" (*FC* 74).

She does not simply hurl herself to her impulses as the priest had done, however, but describes a more circuitous downward path. Somewhere between "a woman [and a] . . . child" (*FC* 92), she cannot resist lavishing her sexuality on the priest and, when her real romance sours, actually displacing her frustrated desire onto him. This is the meaning of the novel's allusion to Potiphar's wife. Like Joseph in the biblical story, Don Ippolito becomes a victim of feminine provocation. From the moment of their introduction, Florida behaves in a sexual manner toward him. She blushes, devours him with her eyes, and invites him to instruct her. When he responds with his new "worldly" clothes, she signals her approval and enthusiastically accepts his gifts, including the fountain. It is on the Brenta Canal trip, though, that her serious overtures begin and Don Ippolito becomes the unwitting dupe of her disappointments with the consul. Smarting under Ferris's sarcasms, she overreacts to the priest's intimacy, and worsens the damage with an extravagant, handholding apology. The setbacks with her lover which follow heighten her interest in Don Ippolito. Impelled by "the fascination of [a] pathos she could not fully analyse" (*FC* 138), she pries a confession from the priest, then endorses his vocational misgivings and encourages him to be a "man" (*FC* 146). He, in turn, collapses under the stress of his conflict during the Corpus Christi parade.

Her next intervention tips the balance in his struggle. Arresting him at the garden gate, she assails him with all the symptoms of an infatuated woman. Breathlessly, amid tears, blushes, and long gazes, she entreats him to leave the priesthood and assures him that his failure to act would make her unhappy. They celebrate his decision in her garden, where she insidiously provokes his fatal declaration. Again, with sexual carelessness, she barrages him with seductive cues. She warmly pledges her faith and friendship, puts her hand on his shoulder and, in a symbolic sanction of his erotic release, lets him play the fountain. The result is his climactic announcement and defeat. Afterwards he warns her of her sexual irresponsibility and cautions her that she should not love a man's soul alone. But she ends their relationship with the most voluptuous display of displaced passion in the book. She seizes his head in her hands and buries it in her breast; thence dispatching him to the "dense shadows" (*FC* 223) of his alley and his untimely death.

Ferris's reaction to this incident, his desertion of Venice and Florida, dramatizes the harm she brings on herself through her thoughtless seduction of Don Ippolito. By her erratic sexual behavior and intemperate dalliance with the priest, she succeeds in thwarting her life almost as fatally as he. As her hopes sink one by one, she falls into the priest's postures and encounters the same, engulfing darkness. Her first meeting with the consul provides a model of how she alienates him with awkward vacillations between hauteur and provocation. Instead of receiving his gift of flowers with composure, she blushes, murmurs "delicious!" (*FC* 19), and buries her face in the phallus-shaped hyacinths. Alarmed, Ferris begins to satirize her mother, which arouses Florida's arrogance for the rest of the San Lazzaro tour. On the way back, Ferris retaliates with further mockery until she suddenly issues an overture comparable to a raised skirt today. Directing "her eyes full upon him," she pushes "her sleeve from her wrist" so that he can see its "delicious whiteness" (*FC* 31) and lets her fingers trail through the water. The impact is immediate: he beats a burlesque retreat and leaves her inflamed. She throws his hyacinths into the canal and clasps "her hands to her face" (*FC* 38).

In later meetings, her hot-cold oscillations increase, driving Ferris further afield. During a promising tête-à-tête in her garden, she defeats herself again by first censuring the consul's levity, and then drawing up so close to him with "bold innocence" (*FC* 92) that he bolts for the gate. The Villa Pisani episode both demonstrates the dynamics of her self-destructive course and marks a turning point in her love life. She begins the trip with a flagrant display of her two most alluring instruments of seduction: her hands and eyes. She flaunts her hand at Ferris so that "he could not help worshipping its lovely forms" (*FC* 96) and blatantly ogles him. But because of the attentions she displaces upon Don Ippolito, the consul becomes angry. He peppers her with barbs, rouses her hauteur, and finally provokes her explosion at the priest. Her love affair enters a skid. Recoiling in "cold disgust" (*FC* 108), Ferris takes refuge in his studio and strengthens his defenses. Florida's conciliatory visit ends in a brusque dismissal. It is here that another, more regressive sexual manifestation enters her romance. Perhaps the consul's abrasiveness had attracted her in the first place, but his rudeness makes his appeal openly masochistic. Despite his insolence during the Corpus Christi procession, she truckles to him with "distraut humility" (*FC* 151) and decides that a woman's life should be "a constant giving up" (*FC* 155). Nonetheless, he abandons her, and the images of darkness and flaccidity that surround Don Ippolito enfold her. She, too, drops a candle in despair and covers her face with her hands until she leaves Venice behind a black veil.

By the epilogue two years later, she is still no older, wiser, or better coordinated sexually. Pursuing the incompatible consul to an art gallery, she proffers herself with "her old directness" (*FC* 250) and immediately flares up in angry arrogance—a seesaw that continues unchecked through his declaration. It is only when he is walking out for the second time that she stops him with an impulsive marriage proposal.

Marriage, however, does not change her. Besides the same fluctuation between too much and too little instinctual control, there is an additional hint of sexual frustration in her union with Ferris. Still without proper management of her will, still masochistically inclined, she tries to lose her "outwearied will" (*FC* 260) in a total submission to her husband. Yet the result is a mysterious "vacancy" (*FC* 261). As in Venice, she turns to another object to relieve her frustrations with Ferris: this time, her children. Her maternal displacement upon Don Ippolito, then, becomes permanent and ironically infected with her unresolved sexual maladjustments. Caught in the whipsaw of her

"haughty humility" and "tigerish tenderness" (*FC* 261), her children
shy off (like their father) and prefer him. Ultimately, Florida's fate is
as unhappy as the priest's. Rejected as a mother, unfulfilled as a wife,
she carries her sexual imbalance with her into middle age at the end
of the book—there increasingly to imperil her own and her family's
happiness.

When *A Foregone Conclusion* first appeared, Ferris's part in the drama
was all but ignored. Henry James referred to him as a "likeable," "good
fellow," a "makeweight in the action,"[12] and *The Nation* dismissed him
as "the American gentleman"[13] of the piece. Though perhaps too close
to the norm of the times to be appreciated, he may nevertheless be the
novel's most interesting character. Prudish, stiff-necked, and repressed, he is no more mature than the other two and creates the
greater discord in the story. In an ironic twist on *Othello*, he errs not
through excessive passion but through his excessive sexual fears. The
expressions Don Ippolito's and Florida's passion take are those most
calculated to arouse his deepest terrors, and he scapegoats them accordingly. At the same time, his exaggerated reserves lead him to a
nervous collapse from which he learns and gains nothing.

As with Florida and Don Ippolito, his name, bearing, and environment reflect his sexuality. Ferris means "like iron," and his gestures
are retentive and offish. He habitually brushes dust from his clothes,
steps away from others, and retreats to his balcony (the equivalent of
the Vervain garden and the priest's apartment) when threatened. These
indices of his prudishness, though, accompany pointed references to
his lust. In the opening passages, he is seen crossing two "gilt lance-
headed staves" (*FC* 3) above his bookcase and striking his "stick on the
smooth paving stones" (*FC* 17) as he watches girls go by. His all-
important obliviousness to his impulses appears from the beginning.
On his way down the calle, he buys aphrodisiacal hyacinths for Florida "in ignorance" (*FC* 20).

Externally, Ferris is a man superior to the instincts, a sophisticate
beyond the appetites of "lower" men. Every sexual innuendo in the
book elicits his caustic barb, every off-color reference, his contempt.
But as the plot unfolds, it becomes clear that he is overrepressed to an
almost neurotic degree. Before he meets Florida, he had long "denied
himself [the] pleasures" (*FC* 69) of feminine companionship, and, with
her, the reasons soon emerge. The conflict between his desires and
fear of them has incapacitated him to the extent that he cannot con-
duct a courtship without destroying both the object of his affections

and himself. Behind his injuries to Florida lurk two anxieties that compete with his desires: the fear of sexual evil and the fear of being "fooled"—precisely what her volatile sexuality is most designed to arouse. His abuse of Florida and her mother on the San Lazzaro trip stems directly from these terrors. Frightened by Florida's passion when he gives her the hyacinths, he vents his apprehensions on her mother, whose racy chatter about Byron and her too early marriage fulfill his worst suspicions of the daughter. A volley of wisecracks ensues, aimed at deflating improper feminine ardors. His next attack reveals another anxiety. Beside the arrogant Florida in the flower garden, he suddenly balks and retreats behind her: "'What a fool!' he said to himself" (*FC* 27).

As his fears mount with his attraction, his injuries to Florida increase. Out of anxiety at his own defenselessness, he ridicules the priest to her, which only fans her maternal zeal and speeds their estrangement. His visit to confide his "undefined . . . formless" (*FC* 91) apprehensions about Don Ippolito brings his two fears into sharper focus and predicts their consequences. While he suffers a "pang" (*FC* 88) of passion for Florida and plays autoerotically with a twig in his hand, he abruptly criticizes her "quick temper" (*FC* 89)—a standard nineteenth-century index of lasciviousness.[14] Mindless of her embarrassment, he blunders forward with his attack of the priest, forcing her to his defense. Friction grows until Florida is reduced to her old San Lazzaro ploy. She draws closer to him, looks at him with "bold innocence," and so entices him that he gasps with a "delicious thrill." But, as before, he draws back and leaves her with a parting, "Good heavens . . . I'm a fool to have spoken to you" (*FC* 92).

On the Villa Pisani tour, these opposing impulses reach a climax and his persecution of Florida becomes overt. With the advance of his passion, which now makes him "worship" (*FC* 96) Florida's hand when he sees it, is a parallel advance in his terrors—exacerbated by the presence of Don Ippolito. The theme, then, of his satire on the boat trip out is sexual sin. He needles the priest with hints of clerical corruption and goads Florida about Venetian debaucheries while he sketches her. The resulting portrait reveals both his second fear and the harm his suspicions cause her. Afraid of her *érotisme*, he has (as Don Ippolito tells him) drawn her without "color" (*FC* 106), and afraid of seeming foolish, with too haughty a look. When Mrs. Vervain asks him for a happier expression, he responds tellingly, "And give her the appearance of laughing at me? Never!" (*FC* 106). Florida's scene with Don

Ippolito both forecasts the sort of laughingstock she might make of him and confirms his sense of her bestiality. He recoils in "cold disgust" (*FC* 108), lambastes her "savagery" (*FC* 109), and rids himself of her as fast as possible.

Afterwards, his defenses become adamantine. He takes refuge in his studio and repels Florida when she pursues him. Although she has never seemed "lovelier" (*FC* 125) to him and "his soul tremble[s]" (*FC* 128) in her presence, he rebuffs her advances and dispatches her alone to find a doctor for her mother. Symbolizing his new defensiveness, he turns his painting to the wall as she enters, then refuses to help her because "he did not care to invoke a snub" (*FC* 126). Amidst bitter reflections on her "ugly temper" and his possible humiliation, he disposes of her with misogynistic grandeur. From his perch on the balcony he watches her fumble toward the doctor and feels "superior to the whole fitful sex" (*FC* 129).

Yet he perpetuates a worse crime against her. After one more meeting, in which he confirms her "vulgarity" (*FC* 131), he gives her the advice that triggers her traumatic confrontation with Don Ippolito. In a pompous lecture on the priesthood (which includes an ominous remark about women accepting celibacy better), he tells her a priest should leave his profession if he loses his faith. Thus she comes to sanction Don Ippolito's wild dream. Nor does Ferris help prevent the crisis once the misunderstanding sets in. Fearing Florida's sexual impropriety and his own dupery, he fails to warn either Don Ippolito or the Vervains of the disaster ahead. When his intervention comes, it is too late: he sees the tableau of Don Ippolito and Florida in the moonlit garden and assumes the worst. Assured of her venery, he stalks off for the last time, allowing Florida to pilot her mother through Europe alone and unfriended. Not only does he heighten Florida's labile and immature sexuality with his fears; he sins against her humanity and possibly precipitates her mother's death.

As his last transgression demonstrates, Don Ippolito also falls victim to Ferris's conflict. An embodiment of Ferris's deepest fears and desires, Don Ippolito plays the part of a "shadow self" in the drama, externalizing Ferris's inner warfare and becoming his scapegoat. If Florida is Potiphar's wife, Ferris is the Potiphar who unjustly punishes Don Ippolito. Because of his fear of being tricked, he makes sure that the priest becomes "fooled"; because of his terrors of sexual evil, he makes sure that the priest meets the fate of the sexually damned. Yet, for all of his persecution of Don Ippolito, he suffers more in their relationship. Like an underworld guide, the priest leads him into an encounter with his submerged, subconscious self that turns into a nightmare ordeal. At the end, Ferris says truly: "We might well curse the day we met" (*FC* 239), for Don Ippolito drives him to a psychic breakdown from which he never fully recovers.

In an apt symbol of the priest's significance, Ferris trips and falls in his dark entranceway the first time he visits him. Throughout the triangle love story, Don Ippolito provides a projection of the dark forces that rend and finally defeat him. Ferris is the fool and sexual sinner of his anxieties as well as the rival who stands in the way of his desires. The worse his conflict becomes, the stronger his hostilities grow until he lashes out at the priest with mindless hatred.

The most obvious component of his "complex resentments" (*FC* 234) against the priest is jealousy. From the moment Florida and Mrs. Vervain mention him, his competitive instincts flare. He warns them to "spare [their] romance" (*FC* 36) and snipes sarcastically: "I didn't arrange for him not to fall in love with her [Florida]" (*FC* 55). Later his aggressions turn malicious as Florida diverts her libido more and more onto the priest. Targeting Don Ippolito's courtesy and gallantry (exactly what he lacks himself), he abuses him at every opportunity. He mocks his courtly efforts to speak English during the Vervains' breakfast, criticizes his stylish dress, and burlesques his civilities without stint on the Villa Pisani trip. Besides the pain he causes, he also kindles Don Ippolito's passion by increasing Florida's sympathy. His spontaneous visit after the fountain is repaired illustrates how his jealousy promotes her displaced affections. He listens to her praises of the fountain with a "pang" of envy, then defames Don Ippolito in such a way that Florida goes overboard in his defense: "[I]n any case . . . I can't believe any wrong of him" (*FC* 91), she exclaims. Later he wakes up and sees a symbol of his jealous malice before him. A "spear of light" (*FC* 95) lies across his painting of the priest pointing to his heart.

Fear, however, accounts for the deepest level of Ferris's hatred. The priest comes to personify the evil Ferris dreads in sexuality. With his exaggerated anxieties, he envisions Don Ippolito as one of the Venetian clergy Howells mentioned in *Venetian Life*[15]—the famous libertines of the decadence. This is the meaning of his dark hints of "various scandals" (*FC* 82) associated with Don Ippolito's profession. What begins in a haze of suspicion ends in blazing hatred, as Ferris more and more experiences the very underground impulses he attributes to the priest. Just after his high-tension exchange with Florida at San

Lazzaro, he visits Don Ippolito's apartment and immediately finds it suffused with hints of salacity. The grape trellis mural reminds him of the "doors of degenerate places" (*FC* 47–48) and the studio seems to have a "sinister effect . . . as if some hapless mortal [were] in contact with the evil powers" (*FC* 49). Unnerved by these imagined signs of prurience, he abuses Don Ippolito's inventions, beginning a critical offensive that ends in the priest's dependence on the Vervains for his success in America. As with his jealousy, his sexual anxieties only fuel Don Ippolito's calamitous hopes for Florida's love. After Ferris's thoughts stray to Florida's "full lips" (*FC* 72) in church, he upbraids the priest for imaginary perversions; after Ferris's eyes "worship" her soft, white hand he accuses Ippolito of the desires of the old *villegiatura* clergy: both times drawing his rival and lover closer together. His portrait of Don Ippolito encapsulates the lechery he projects on him. Determined to paint the "lingering pagan" (*FC* 75) in him, he gradually succumbs to a "sinister" (*FC* 82) look he perceives, making the picture hard and "conventional" (*FC* 183). Aptly, he entitles it "A Venetian Priest" and, aptly, Florida loathes it.

Don Ippolito is also the "fool" of Ferris's apprehensions. He represents an incarnation, as the fool archetypically does in mythology and folklore,[16] of the anarchic unconscious, the buried regressive urges. All of the primal helplessness, puerility, and effeminacy he fears in sexual surrender he sees writ large in the priest, especially the nearer his own surrender comes. With the same effect of his other sources of aggression, he makes Don Ippolito seem foolish, thereby increasing Florida's misdirected ardors. The initial "disgust" Ferris feels toward Don Ippolito centers on a dim sense of "pity" (*FC* 17) that gains definition as soon as he visits him. There the childishness, the disorder of his surroundings strike him with revulsion, and he flinches at the priest's naive faith in the Vervains: "Could he really have been so stupid . . . ?" (*FC* 54) he wonders as he flies away. The fate he dreads in such trustfulness materializes on the Brenta Canal. When Don Ippolito is reprimanded, he turns away in "cold disgust" from the "helpless thing" (*FC* 108). His rising passion clarifies his hostility further. There is a womanliness about the priest's helplessness, he tells Florida, that inspires repugnance, that makes him seem "dreadful" (*FC* 154). To this she responds predictably: "Shouldn't you be very sorry for him?" (*FC* 154)—thus squeezing the fatal triangle tighter.

Though Ferris violates and hurts Don Ippolito and fosters his downfall, he injures himself even more through his prudish complexes.

During his obsession with the priest, he descends further and further into the heart of his conflict until he breaks down. He enters the chaotic, infantile realm of the subconscious; but, unlike the hero of a maturity myth, does not finally prevail.

The climactic scene in which he scapegoats the priest for his ambivalence touches off his inner ordeal. The three strands of his hatred converge and he denies Don Ippolito the advice that would save him. He hears the priest's love confession with a "pang" of envy, gasps prudishly, "You? You! A priest?" (*FC* 189), and winces at the regressive, vulnerable image he presents. Repelled by his "terrible position" (*FC* 193), he watches him glide before him "like a tall, gaunt, unhappy girl" (*FC* 192) and steels himself against his pleas for help. He turns to his balcony and dispatches him coldly to his ill-omened interview with Florida: "I cannot advise or warn you" (*FC* 195), he snaps.

While Ferris stands facing his balcony, the world suddenly turns upside down "like sights in a mirror" (*FC* 194), and his introspective voyage begins. When Don Ippolito (his mirror image) leaves, he sinks into a dark engagement with his subconscious, nether self. An "anguish" he cannot master envelops him and as night advances, he sits paralyzed in his chair: "It was all a shapeless torment; it held him like the memory of some hideous nightmare prolonging its horror beyond sleep" (*FC* 196). At last he goes to the Vervains, where he watches the embrace which leads him into deeper darkness. He stumbles down the black calle behind the guiding figure of the priest toward a complete nervous collapse. Unable to "give his trouble certain shape" (*FC* 229) (as neurotics typically cannot), he prowls the streets by night and travels across a sea of "molten fire" (*FC* 228) to Malamocco—the degenerate colony of *Venetian Life*.

During a later interview with Don Ippolito, Ferris drops to a still lower level of his conflict. As Ferris remarks when he sees him on his sickbed, they meet on "strange ground," and it is on this ground of the irrational that his "complex resentments" (*FC* 234) take full possession of him. The "coil of suspicions, misgivings, and fears" (*FC* 235) flames out in a burst of hatred against the dying man. With the condensation of a dream, he conflates all the sources of his aversion—the jealousy and two fears—into one culminating accusation: "He felt merely that this *hapless* creature had profaned . . . what was *sacredest in the world to him*" (italics mine) (*FC* 234). The priest's attempt to befriend and illuminate him meets with icy disdain. Ferris turns his face away convinced of his unchaste involvement with Florida. At the height of Don

Ippolito's denials, the fear beneath his hostility spews up: "I'm afraid," he exclaims, "the same deceit has tricked us both" (*FC* 239). As an answer, the priest kisses him on either cheek, but Ferris goes away unpersuaded and unmoved.

That night he reaches the nadir of his chthonic ordeal. Wherever he walks through the dark streets he ends up, as though pulled toward his own center of gravity, at the priest's door. In an agony of confusion, he stares at his window trying to "spell from the senseless stones the truth of the secret" (*FC* 241). Yet the "secret" eludes him, his hatred returns, and after a sleepless night, he plans a climactic denunciation. When he arrives, he finds Don Ippolito has died and the housekeeper, seeing his wild visage, delivers the final judgment: "[M]adman" (*FC* 241), she cries at Ferris.

In contrast to the lunatic's jeer, which heralded the priest's conversion, the housekeeper's cry brings no awakening to the consul. Although he thinks himself cured of his "long debauch of hate and jealousy and despair" (*FC* 242), he appears in the epilogue as sexually apprehensive and immature as ever. If he bungles his romance with Florida through his fears in Venice, he botches it in the same way two years later in New York. Despite his newly "clear[ed] mind" (*FC* 249), he is still too paralyzed by anxieties to contact Florida and quails at a casual reference to her temper. Their eventual meeting at a museum activates the old conflict with renewed force. He mocks her defensively and delivers a declaration hedged with terrors. "Remember that I was such a *fool* as to be in love with you," he retorts when Florida tasks him for his neglect, "are you trying to make a *fool* of me?" (italics mine) (*FC* 252). His next assault demonstrates both his fear of sexual sin and his own equivalent salacity. When he confesses his "black" (*FC* 251) suspicions to Florida, she shudders at his revealed prurience and shrinks away. His reaction, as on the Brenta Canal, is to retreat: this time into sulkiness, egotism, and self-pity. Even after they are wed, his conflict shadows his life and marriage. Because of the "hot temper which he had dreaded from the first," he only loves Florida "after his fashion" (*FC* 260) and leaves her with an inner "vacancy." Armored thicker in defenses, he laughs at her "excesses," and patronizingly distorts her character into extremes of "unfathomable" (*FC* 261) innocence and arrogance.

He retains an equally warped view of Don Ippolito. Over time, his enmity diffuses into a baffled prejudice that provides revealing insights into his own development. Rather than his former accusation of carnality, he now charges the priest with passionlessness—a reflection of his burned-out marriage with Florida. Yet, mirroring his increased defensiveness, he harps on the priest's foolishness. Don Ippolito was the quintessence of "helplessness, dreamery, and unpracticality," he complains, a naif whose "inadequacy" (*FC* 262) would have doomed him in America. The envy that gauged his desire has attenuated and the conflict receded further into unconsciousness and confusion. "He's a puzzle, he's a puzzle" is Ferris's last assessment of the priest.

There is a mordant irony in these concluding judgments that conveys the full measure of the consul's self-ruin through his repressions. The foolishness he condemns has descended on *him*, despite his strenuous avoidance of passion. Supine on gondola pillows, dependent on Florida financially, and failed as an artist, he has become the helpless, emasculate, and doomed figure he imagined the priest to be. His injured arm, like Rochester's blindness in *Jane Eyre*, provides a visible image of this castration. His "civilized" suppression of his neurosis, ironically, has brought him the exact fate he dreaded in sexual release. By burying his conflict, by hardening his defenses against it, he has starved off the live center of his identity, his creativity. As his friend comments when he sees his painting: "It's hard and it's feeble" (*FC* 247). Another kind of Thanatos, besides Don Ippolito's, has befallen him: death to his own potentialities and selfhood. The last line is resonant with his fate. Ferris's attitude toward the priest—and by extension toward himself and life in general—"is not the least tragic phase," the book concludes, "of the tragedy of Don Ippolito" (*FC* 265).

Repression, then, proves the greater villain. The excessive controls perpetrated by Ferris's conflict cause the true, permanent injury in the tale. Don Ippolito's and Florida's lawless libidos create misery and confusion, too, but they are the more vital, sinned upon characters. There is also a suggestion, developed in the later novels, that the creed of denial conspires in their sexual uncontrol. Paired with their extravagances are repeated references to the renunciations forced upon them from without: social in Florida's case, religious in Don Ippolito's. No viable, satisfying means of taming their passions exist, while the suprarepressions work steadily to force their impulses underground into perverse, overheated expressions.

Joined to this implied critique of repression is a covert sympathy for pleasure. Descriptions of Don Ippolito's rapture, Florida's full-blooded beauty, and the Venetian spring which embodies them are richly, lyrically sensuous. All of the affective language in the book centers on passional enjoyment and bounty. Yet an ambivalence cuts through every sexual celebration. Florida's garden is hemmed with bugs, the Brenta Canal of the *villegiaturas*, with "weeds and mosses" (*FC* 99), and Don Ippolito's inventions, like the lovely fountain, issue from a "sinister," littered studio. The imagery, already at this stage, is Swedenborg's, the mystic whose erotic thought would dominate the sexual theme. Filth, infusoria, and vermin, in the vocabulary of Howells's childhood prophet, were sigla of sexual damnation; fountains, gardens, and feasts, of blessedness. The epithets "dog" and "madman" that are hurled at the consul indiscriminately are both *Conjugial Love* terms for the sexually damned. Although Swedenborg advocated a nonpunitive, sensual ethic, Howells had not yet differentiated between good and bad sexuality or grasped his "body mysticism."[17] As he wrote his father two years before he began *A Foregone Conclusion*: "I understand Swedenborg very dimly."[18]

Ultimately Ferris's conflict reflected Howells's own. His early prudery in Ohio masked a neurotic split which carried over into his adult career—his strong sexuality warring with his fears. The unintegrated core of pleasure in the book and the ambivalent ethico-sexual emphases reflect this unresolved tension. The irony at the ending is unstable: the conflict lingers on, unplumbed and unsolved. Yet, as opposed to Ferris, Howells's difficulty was not "neurotic" in the psychiatric sense,[19] since he consciously came to terms with it through his fiction. Seen together, his novels about sex can be read as an extended self-therapy, in which he probed deeper and deeper into the infantile strata of his conflict until he purged and resolved it. As his lovers grew toward maturity and sexual concord, so did his imagination, with the affirmations of his later life providing a brilliant testimony of his cure.

Books after *A Foregone Conclusion* would take up Ferris's quest of the "truth of the secret" and pursue it past his adolescent fears to the subliminal root of the problem. The sexual landscape darkened. Ferris's terrors clarified and materialized in the love stories through 1882, while the drift toward pleasure and against repression continued. If what Ferris adolescently fears in sexual sin and undiscipline is death, then his civilized suppressions also prove deathbound. A negative crisis will occur in *A Modern Instance*, after which the erotic theme breaks through to the unconscious, infantile recesses of sexuality. Throughout, Howells's intemperate protagonists would struggle toward vital control and his puritans learn to retrace Ferris's steps down Don Ippolito's dark alley, decipher the "secret," and meet the dying priest's demand for friendship. By the turn of the century, his two character types would attain a mature sexuality, fear vanish, and a pleasurable, associated Swedenborgian ethic enter in.

Here, though, in *A Foregone Conclusion*, all the major chords of the erotic theme have been struck and the mission enunciated. Perhaps with unconscious sexual intent, Henry James said of the book: Howells "has sunk his shaft deep."[20] Condensed into his small Venetian tale is the passionate womanhood he would school and glorify, the "fool" he would integrate, and the prude he would sensually heal. He would sink deeper still into the sexual mystery, extending his explorations further outward into the social environment and inward into the psyche. His erotic artistry would mature and advance. But with this first, dense-packed sexual tragedy, in which three lovers torment and foil themselves and each other, he had found a theme. He had only to work it into newer and richer erotic possibilities.

Private Theatricals: W. D. Howells and the *femme fatale* | *Three*

It was Howells's theory that in "the presence of mystery"[1] the typical American response was comedy. His own, after the baffling enigmas of *A Foregone Conclusion*, was also comedy—a sprightly spoof, *Private Theatricals* (1875). Serialized in the *Atlantic* and not published again until after his death as *Mrs. Farrell*, the book seemed to have disappointed Howells: "The present story . . . is a much slighter affair and lacks a strong motive such as that [*A Foregone Conclusion*] had,"[2] he told John Hay. The way the tale evolved while he wrote it may have disappointed him as much as anything. Just as his first "erotic" novel changed from the priest's tragedy into a complex, triangular drama, so his second metamorphosed from light to black comedy in the telling. Once again, his imagination led him against his conscious intent[3] toward the darker reaches of sexuality and the recovery (despite the contradictions) of pleasure.

On the surface, the novel could not seem further from *A Foregone Conclusion*. A seedy summer colony replaces opulent Venice. A cast of frivolous women replaces the three doomed protagonists; and the plot resembles not so much a downward, tangling spiral as an ascending chain of ironic climaxes. The leading character is a lusty widow, Belle Farrell, a vamp with none of Florida's innocence, Don Ippolito's pathos, or Ferris's depth. Nevertheless, *Private Theatricals* directly continues the Venetian tragedy. It presses forward the exploration of Ferris's fears and takes the argument against repression to new ground. Mrs. Farrell, essentially, is the consul's nightmare vision of Florida. She is the unregenerate "savage" of his worst apprehensions, who "fools" an entire community with her erotic allure. She reveals, in her personality and in the violence, confusion, and suffering she creates, the inner rationale behind Ferris's terrors. She is Darwin's sexual predator, the Victorian femme fatale. At the same time, the kinds of foolishness she inflicts on her victims broaden the definition of "fool" and show more precisely the kinds of irrationalities Ferris dreaded.

The psychic mayhem she generates with her undisciplined sexuality, however, is matched by the malignancy of the culture. By tracing Ferris's prudery back to its bases in 1870 America, Howells portrays a society that has grown moribund through overrepression. Tumbledown West Pekin furnishes an objective correlative for the country's sexual malaise, and the forces that created it are all on exhibit there: the decline of religious faith, the rise of social Darwinism, and the death of puritanism. The assembled natives and visitors have not only been leeched of life by this ethos; they have embraced sick substitutes for passion. Sensationalism, idealism, and sentimentality replace their denied sexuality and at last prove (as *A Foregone Conclusion* began to discover) to be in league with intemperance.

While Howells's imagination unearthed these findings, showing Mrs. Farrell's exploits in an ever darker light and invalidating the cultural values, his sympathies inclined more toward pleasure. The richest language, the brightest colors attend the vivacious, bohemian Mrs. Farrell, who midway through the novel dwarfs the other characters with their moral pieties into insignificance. There is a "sneaking fondness" (*MF* 184) for her within the text, similar to that the protagonists share. But, as before, ambivalence muddies the sensuous undercurrents. With a sharpening of both sides of the conflict, the rejection of sexuality and gratification increases in proportion to their attractiveness. Images of beauty and cruelty, sensuality and deadliness, coexist uneasily together, and the book ends irresolutely, overpowered by negations.

No wonder, then, that Howells wrote Edmund Clarence Stedman, amidst *Private Theatricals*: "No man ever felt his way more anxiously, doubtfully, self-distrustfully than I to the work I'm doing now."[4] What began as a breezy farce about the mass seduction of a summer colony, led him back, with stubborn insistence, to the tragic themes he had grappled with in *A Foregone Conclusion*. Once more the problem was universal sexual immaturity; and instead of blithely evading "the secret" (*FC* 241), he had instinctively drawn nearer to it. Mrs. Farrell lured him, with the development of the plot, deeper into Ferris's terrors, deeper into sexual ambivalence, and toward a more profound indictment of the ethic of denial.

Early in his career, Howells observed that comedy had the ability to circumvent social controls, to "escape a censor the most vigilant of public tranquility."[5] In *Private Theatricals*, he learned to implement this insight to the inestimable advantage of his sexual theme. Through laughter and nonsense he was able both to elude the nineteenth-century purity-watchers and convey passion more fully. Mrs. Farrell's routine about Gilbert's catch, for example, with its phallic play on "fish" and comic excitement heightens the erotic meaning two ways. It carries a risqué thrust (innocuously) and utilizes the aphrodisiacal power of laughter to evoke their sexuality.

Besides humor, Howells discovered other ways in *Private Theatricals* to make the sexual text bolder and stronger. Reflecting his intense interest in plays, he costumes Mrs. Farrell dramatically (in clothes that cling to her like plumage), transforms her settings into impressionistic backdrops, and showcases her *volupté* through her movements. Scenes gain an edge over "pictures,"[6] and dialogue, with an almost electric eroticism, assumes new prominence. Figurative language grows more elaborate and explicit. The whole village of West Pekin becomes a metaphor of sexual obsolescence and the phallic imagery expands to include cigars, rods, and knives. Beneath his "unconscious"[7] method, Howells's erotic art was thriving, gathering frankness, pith, and texture.

The story, ostensibly, follows a simpler plan than that of *A Foregone Conclusion*. Belle Farrell, a ravishing, sprightly femme fatale, invades a somnolent summer colony and one by one conquers its sex-starved natives and visitors. But as her seductions proceed, and even the sensible *raisonneurs* succumb to her blandishments, ugly truths about Eros increasingly loom up. Not only do the sadistic components prove to be more virulent than before and the regressions that occur in the act of sexual surrender become deeper, the repressive norms appear less effective and more pathological. Amidst her conquests, Mrs. Farrell explains the secret of her success, "[Y]ou did wrong to let me surprise [your] weak place" (*MF* 135). In each case, she exploits and exposes the deadliness of the official value system, leaving in its place her lethal sexuality and terrible, ambivalent appeal.

The scene of her sexual escapades, the summer colony of West Pekin, is an erotic wasteland. Howells once said that whenever he thought of the theme of "forbidden fruit" he always envisioned a "summer hotel as a probable scene,"[8] though the Woodward boarding house seems as improbable a place as might be imagined for a love story. The countryside is parched of life, the local residents are almost catatonic, the guests, in the throes of ennui. The surrounding farms lie barren and exhausted; and their houses, like the stone walls which enclose them, sink in ruins beside "gnarled and misshapen trees" (*MF* 1). Only the husk of religious faith remains. The "blank and bare" (*MF* 45) church in the middle of town rings a "terrible" (*MF* 46) bell every Sunday and the sexton annually slaughters the nesting swallows (an icon of Aphrodite) on the tower. The congregation, reduced to a handful of old people, sings in "cracked basses and trebles" (*MF* 48), nods mechanically through a "sandy desert of . . . discourse" (*MF* 50), and drives away down an avenue of grey-powdered trees. Grotesque and ungainly in outdated clothes, the natives trudge silently through a sterile landscape and meet like zombies: "When they had hornily rattled their callous palms together, they stood staring at each other, their dry, serrated lips falling apart, their jaws mutely working up and down, their pale-blue eyes vacantly winking . . ." (*MF* 3). The Woodwards, who own the farm-hotel, epitomize (as their name suggests), this wooden, lifeless asexuality. Mrs. Woodward married her "dreadfully dull" scarecrow of a husband from "duty" (*MF* 5) and produced two anemic children.

Nor do the boarders, genteel Boston women, supply much more vitality. In exile from their husbands, for whom they provide "scanty children" (*MF* 11), they languish in a weary swoon in a house full of bored and ailing women. They complain, sleep, and greet their weekending husbands like "the fishballs at the Sunday breakfast" (*MF* 10). Their pleasures consist of trivial artwork (like Ferris's) and a sensational "faith in romance" (*MF* 175) and "ideality" (*MF* 172). The exception among their ranks is the invalid Mrs. Gilbert, who presides over them with eighteenth-century majesty. With her whitened hair and regal air, she resembles a marquise of the enlightenment, "a powdered old-regime beauty" (*MF* 14), and repeatedly dashes cold baths of common sense on their romanticistic excesses. Yet even she will be critically tested by the impact of Mrs. Farrell on West Pekin.

Unlikely as it seems, then, the blasted community provides the perfect setting for Mrs. Farrell's assault; its dessication, offsetting and enhancing her "forbidden fruits." "As if by violence" (*MF* 14) she bursts in on the torpid farmhouse. Everything about her pulsates with sexual energy. Undisciplined and supersexed, she blazes *érotisme*. Confirming the suggestions in her name ("feral" and "La Belle Dame"), she impersonates the traditional minx in literature. Brunette, graceful, and curvaceous, she is a dazzling beauty who seems to be "a French painter's fancy of a Roman girl of the decadence" (*MF* 16–17). When she moves it is with the "freedom . . . [and] self-disposition" (*MF* 18) of a streetwalker. Like the original love goddess, she comes from the seacoast and, like the archetypal seductress, is a bohemian with an experienced, mysterious past. A Darwinian underlay also reinforces her lawless, high-voltage sexuality. She is a "child of unregenerate nature" (*MF* 149), whose kinship with the savage, tooth-and-claw "lower" world becomes a recurrent motif. Surrounding West Pekin are dense, untamed woods with which she becomes increasingly identified (as Florida did with her garden and Ferris with his balcony) as her siege advances.

Rightly, her first scene takes place there. Upholstered in a "stuff that cl[ings] to her shape" (*MF* 16), she springs upon a depleted berry pasture like a "well-millinered wood nymph not the least afraid of satyrs" (*MF* 17). The episode that follows establishes the source of her appeal and the role she will play in the story. Flaunting her sensuality before the meek Rachel Woodward, she leaps into woods that "joyously . . . accept [her] as part of nature," and falls upon the scant berries with a "frank, natural, charming greed" (*MF* 17). When she has eaten her fill, she lies back suggestively on a rock and launches a comic monologue that predicts how she will be able to play with fire in her flirtations and not get burned. She announces (ten years before Thomas Eakins was to lose his job at the Pennsylvania Academy for daring a life class) that she would like to draw from the nude, laughs it off, and then answers Rachel's retort about her preference for animal models with an even racier quip. "Well, and aren't *men* animals?" she gibes. She speaks only half-facetiously. For when two men actually come into the clearing, she puts this insight to work with brilliant results. She makes a blatantly animal appeal to them. Using a dropped handkerchief ploy, she approaches them in quest of her book with the "sweeping, undulant grace" of a deer and "floods" (*MF* 24) them with a come-hither look.

It is not her elemental attraction alone, however, which instantly infatuates one man and later the other. The oscillations that Florida practiced in "innocence" between hauteur and provocation, Mrs. Farrell uses consciously and artfully, with sophisticated refinements of her own. Exemplifying the Darwinian theory of the importance of "variety"[9] in sexual selection, she shuttles back and forth from saint to siren in each of her seductions. Thus the book, Keble's *Christian Year*, which she retrieves so voluptuously. Moreover, her vacillations are exquisitely aimed to hit the specific weakness of each victim. Her roles impersonate the various extremes of the culture's sexual schism, play upon them, and so baffle her captives into submission. That is the real secret, over and above her obvious sexual allure, of her West Pekin victory. That is ultimately how she is able to make "fools" of everyone and open a Pandora's box of sexual evil upon the sleepy New England village.

Before the story opens, she has already captivated the Woodwards. She has managed to fall ill upon them, a la Little Eva, while simultaneously playing on their secret attraction to sinuosity and pleasure: "She fascinates their straight-up-and-downness" a character observes, "by the graceful convolutions of her circuitous character" (*MF* 40). Their lovelorn son, Ben, is the one who summarizes her usurpation of West Pekin at the end when he says what a "fool" (*MF* 232) she has made of him.

Her first and biggest "fool," however, is the New York idealist, Wayne Easton. The author of a book on heroism, the disciple of the "highest dreams of self-devotion and courage and patience" (*MF* 29), he epitomizes the neochivalric faith that accompanied the cult of purity. His exalted madonna worship and "cut and dried" (*MF* 28) principles, however, bring him to his knees like another high-minded "knight"—the "wretched wight" of "La Belle Dame Sans Merci." For beneath his noble sublimations are sexual urges that contradict his ideals, frighten him, and make him easy game for Belle Farrell. Like Don Ippolito's nose-rubbing tic, Easton also has a telltale habit. He smokes cigars "self-reproach[fully]" (*MF* 42) and stealthily at night and confesses his fear of his inward impulses through his phobic reaction to horses—an ancient emblem of the id.[10] By directing her assault at this fissure in Easton's psyche, Belle breaks him down by degrees until she brings him so far into the irrational underworld that he suffers a mental collapse. His immature libido (no better than a shy "country boy['s]" [*MF* 30]) meets and fails the initiation ordeal, while Belle's continuing seduction of him yields ever harsher sexual truths.

His initial response to Mrs. Farrell is a "bewildered" (*MF* 25), spiritualized infatuation. Unconscious of his conflict, he eulogizes her as he draws "shameful solace from his cigar" (*MF* 42). "It's a face to die for!" he says chivalrously. But his next meeting with her reveals the other, "lower" side of his attraction and shows how she manipulates his division to her advantage. She appears before him in church in all her "grace and style and beauty" (*MF* 50) and lures him away from the sermon to reveries of her as a "Babylonian priestess" (*MF* 51). On the way back, she unnerves him further with an appeal to his chivalry that contains a darker appeal to his baser nature. She also gives him a preview of the fate he will meet in her clutches. Allowing him to "rescue" her from an unruly horse, she deluges him with sensual overtures and then capitalizes on his combined desire and sexual anxiety. She sees him wince at the horse, finger his cane while he inhales her "intoxicating mysterious odors" (MF 54), and she begins to whip the horse with the same sadism she will inflict on him. Easton, though, is too bowled over to grasp his danger, and can only blush and "thrust his cane into the turf" (MF 61) afterwards.

Later that afternoon, Mrs. Farrell completes her capture with an intensified assault on his sexual conflict. She leads him deep into a fern dell (the life force plant) where she plays his lust against his idealities so masterfully Easton loses his head. She drapes herself seductively across a rock, plies him with provocations, intimacies, and jokes, and makes him retrieve a snagged hat cord from her "warm, fragrant, silken" (MF 70) hair. When he retreats trembling, she abruptly changes tack and impersonates the "nun" (MF 71) of his purest dreams. To complete his confusion, she redoubles her advances. She plays with ferns like a fan dancer, whistles a "low, delicious note" (MF 73), and arranges to make an apology for her overly serious questions. At the voluptuous extension of her hand, Easton completely forgets himself and kisses it. In Howells's lexicon, this is tantamount to a direct sexual approach, and his response reflects it. "It was base, tyrannical, brutal!" he raves, "it was worthy of a savage!" (MF 95). With his sex-terror exposed, she consolidates her win by delivering a crowning blow to his dissociated sexuality. She gives him an "electrical" (MF 97) touch, along with an exalted plea for respect. Unable to withstand any more, Easton's mind whirls: "He seemed to be losing his fast hold upon things, upon truth and right and wrong" (MF 98). A breach of honesty with his old friend, Gilbert, follows and his ethical deterioration begins.

As his psychic and moral disintegration proceeds under Mrs. Farrell's seduction, her sadism grows. During their second excursion into the woods, he reaches a breaking point. Her arts and cruelties snap his strained mind-body conflict and he literally falls ill. The setting, appropriately, is the fiercest part of the woods where Mrs. Farrell's untamed id is at home. Her bosom heaves and her eyes glow in the primeval wild, and the aggressive-perverse components of her sexuality have full vent. Narcissistically congratulating herself on her faults, she induces Easton's love confession and treats it with mounting contempt. She allows him to fall at her feet, dispenses another "electric touch" (MF 128), and then toys with his anguish. She rebuffs him and reels him back in until she makes a final brutal demand to hear his worst sins. So besotted is he by this time that he complies and betrays his best friend. And she does not let him go without a promise to blame her (in a classic double bind) for everything.

His psychic collapse comes quickly. Morally trapped and rent by the irreconcilable claims of spirit and flesh, he passes out in the heat. In a dream he experiences a nightmare encounter with his repressed unconscious. Just as Ferris saw everything upside down when his subterranean ordeal began, so Easton's coma shows him the reverse side of his consciously held gyneolatry. Mrs. Farrell appears to him not as the lily maid he thinks he adores but as an exotic she-devil who arrives at his side in poisonous berries and laughs at him with Gilbert on her arm. He awakens no wiser from this underworld insight, though, and tries to fight his friend defending her virtue. Before he passes out again, he explains the moral anarchy to which he has been reduced: "But for once in my life," he tells Gilbert, "I didn't seem to be able to do the thing I ought. I couldn't understand my own action" (*MF* 156).

His long illness represents, with his fevered lapses in and out of consciousness, a classic maturity passage through the irrational, but he emerges unawakened and unregenerated. He rises up pale, weak, and tremulous, with his idealism elevated to new impossible heights. His further suffering is not only inevitable, it is masochistic. After listening to a litany of cruel confessions from Mrs. Farrell, he tenders a marriage proposal and grovels before her sadistic gambits. To her admission of unfaithfulness during his illness, he responds with a more exalted gyneolatry, hymning woman's love as "the divinest thing in the world" (*MF* 242). Then, "hurt beyond all solace" (*MF* 249) by her indifference, he agrees to absolve her of wrong and masochistically accepts her parting kiss, like Keats's "wretched wight."

His friend, Gilbert, presents Mrs. Farrell with a more formidable challenge. Sophisticated, pragmatic, reasonable, and perceptive, he sees through her immediately and warns Easton of his fate. But the lawyer, ironically, succumbs to her, too, and ends up "trembl[ing] from head to foot" (*MF* 222) in her presence. Again, excessive repression foils him. His cultivated sentiments—though better grounded than Easton's—are also overspiritualized; they discount his sexual needs and render him just as helpless before Mrs. Farrell.

Instead of neochivalry, Gilbert espouses a more common sublimation of the seventies—the cult of home and hearth. Pure, selfless feminity in the service of domestic well-being was the fulcrum of this faith. Accordingly, he pays homage to the prim Rachel Woodward throughout his visit. He hails her "vestal soul" and praises her "quality of homelike comfort" (*MF* 185). Beneath his lofty tributes, however, lies a covert attraction to ornament, sensuality, and a "spice of coquetry" (*MF* 60) that shows all too evidently in his appearance. Tall and handsome with a "very dark mustache branching across a full beard" (*MF* 23), he rises up out of the woods with his stylish costume and trouting rod like a cosmopolitan satyr. His ever-present fish basket— his fertility icon—further enhances his sexual image, as does his flirtatious relationship with his sister-in-law in which he bandies compliments and endearments like an erotic gourmet. He defends himself against these inclinations, though, with a firm "rational" exterior and a steady stream of reductive irony.

When he first meets Mrs. Farrell, for instance, he sagely assesses her as a restless flirt and humorously quotes Tennyson's lines about the calamitous Helen of Troy from "A Dream of Fair Women." But just as Tennyson's maiden metamorphoses from siren to innocent victim and enchants the dreaming youth, so Mrs. Farrell destroys Gilbert's defenses by alternately impersonating a *fille de joie* and a domestic goddess. She trades on his "angel in the house" pieties, exposes their inherent weaknesses, and thereby gathers him into her meshes.

The welcome she gives him after one of his fishing trips perfectly illustrates her strategy. She greets him in the role of a simple farm girl shelling peas and instantly assails him with "star-like" (*MF* 85) gazes and sexual invitations. When he retorts ironically she beats him at his game with an even shrewder use of humor. Under the protection of comedy, she plays up to his "lower" nature with lascivious abandon. She flatters, coaxes, and teases him, skillfully deploying a risqué pun from her Shakespearean repertoire. She sees Gilbert's catch and makes an elaborate play on the Elizabethan "fish,"[11] for his benefit: "What beauties," she jokes provocatively, "like flowers! . . . But not exactly the same perfume!" (*MF* 87). Still with comic immunity, she veers into the same sadism she used on Easton. "Twisting her slim shape round to take a handful of peas" (*MF* 89), she goads him until she hits the buried resentment in his idealistically overstrained friendship with Easton. Only after she has infuriated him does the comic assault cease, and then she manipulates his anger so that his inner schism is widened. Nobly apologetic, she bows over her peas and makes eyes at him through her eyelashes. The baffled Gilbert turns on his heel and leaves with a "short, sardonic laugh" (*MF* 94).

Easton's illness gives Mrs. Farrell the ideal opportunity to secure her hold on Gilbert. While she acts the part of a ministering angel, she extends her liberties with him, sidling up to him in a darkened hallway and delivering tremolo speeches. This time she meets his protective sarcasm with the meekness of a maidservant and asks for books on philosophy. Although Gilbert mocks these ruses to his sister-in-law, although he hails Rachel's "purity" (*MF* 185) and domestic graces, he falls straight into Mrs. Farrell's net.

She corners him in a setting as symbolically suggestive as the wild fern dell: a dark, swampy meadow with a consumptive tree in the center. Her seduction will drag him, too, into deadly, unwholesome regions of the subconscious. So weakened has he been by her machinations that he capitulates easily. He attempts a joke when he hands her a bough for one of her household projects, but she checkmates him with a vengeance. She flings the bough back at him and exploits his *hausfrau* ideality: itemizing her domestic virtues one by one—her devotion, selflessness, and longsuffering—she accuses him of cruelty and extracts an apology which she accepts with a series of eye-batting overtures. He all but falls at her feet. He tells her how "worthy" (*MF* 190) she is, and watches her leave as if "all sense [had] fled after her out of his face" (*MF* 191).

Like Easton's, Gilbert's passion involves moral and psychic decline. It also brings forward another theme in negative Eros—entrapment. While his friend lies bedridden, he progressively betrays him with Mrs. Farrell, reasoning "languidly" (*MF* 99) to his sister-in-law about the ties of friendship. At the depth of his infatuation, Mrs. Farrell stages a little farce for him to dramatize the state to which she has reduced him. Posing once more as a household goddess, she enlists Gilbert in yarn winding. As she holds him captive (literally) with his arms suspended in the air, she bombards him with her most enticing arts. She works him over with flattery, coquetry, and comedy and renders him completely spellbound. "Here I am," she exults, "as if I were weaving a spell around you!" (*MF* 194).

A threatening lecture from his sister-in-law finally awakens him from his swoon. But just as Easton emerged from his encounter with the irrational no better informed or integrated, so Gilbert leaves West Pekin in the same vulnerable, segmented state. Mrs. Farrell has the triumphant last word. She tracks him down on his way out of town and interrupts his flight with the grand finale of her conquest. With all the airs of the *mater dolorosa*, she implores him, as she postures seductively in the moonlight, not to think her a "heartless woman." He collapses, confesses his love, and bemoans his disordered, hapless condition: "What a fool I am!" (*MF* 223), he raves. When she seizes his arm, he breaks away with an accusation that is only an inversion of his domestic gyneolatry. He identifies her with the wife most feared by the religion of the hearth—the spendthrift who bankrupts her husband.[12] She has "beggared [him] in everything" (*MF* 224), he cries, as he rushes down a road that will eventually take him to South America.

With Gilbert's defeat, the ebullient mood begins to flag; the comedy grows strained and manufactured. The sexual truths revealed by Mrs. Farrell's West Pekin prank have turned sinister, her injuries, serious. Two friends have quarrelled and parted, both lost control of their reason, and both regressed into helpless dependence. Against her blandishments, which have become megalomanic and sadistic, their ideals are useless. Jealousy, strife, bondage, and fragmentation have taken over, held back only by an anxious humor. Further deepening the tints of the story are Mrs. Farrell's victories over the two level-headed women in the drama. Again, their surrenders are due to intrinsic flaws in the orthodox value system.

Mrs. Gilbert, the sybilline grande dame, is the voice of reason and temperance in the book. To the stream of romance-drugged petitioners at her door, she dispenses sane drafts of wisdom. She counsels common-sense courtships, restraint, fair play and, like her brother-in-law, has a canny grasp of character. Yet she, too, bears the strain of a suprarepressive seventies' morality. Her childlessness, invalidism, and nunlike seclusion at Woodward Farm (where her husband is always too busy to visit) all signify her sensual deprivation. A surreptitious inclination toward romance and excitement, therefore, coexists with her rationality and makes her fair game for Mrs. Farrell.

Her welcome of her brother-in-law makes the countercurrents in her personality plain. The object of her "romantic" (*MF* 31) devotion, he receives a reception that brims with sentiment and sensationalistic flourishes. She dramatizes Mrs. Farrell for him in florid colors, interspersing her critique of her "shabby-genteel" (*MF* 35) affectations with flamboyant tributes to her "streaks of genius" (*MF* 36) and "Beauty" (*MF* 38). When Easton arrives with his story of how he met her, she milks it for all its theater, and ushers the two into dinner with comic fanfare. By aiming at this discrepancy in Mrs. Gilbert's personality, Mrs. Farrell "throws" her so thoroughly that she ends up encouraging her brother-in-law in his passion and moral lapse.

Mrs. Farrell's first stab at Gilbert plays right into Mrs. Gilbert's romanticism. She buys the widow's "routine" over the fish her brother-in-law caught and announces histrionically the next time she sees him: "She had them for supper, and ate a great many—for your sake. . . . It's you she wants, William!" (*MF* 104–105). Mrs. Farrell's dual role as a "capable" (*MF* 176) nurse and sentimental fiancée during Easton's illness, with its appeal to both sides of her conflict, secures Mrs. Gilbert's "fall." She not only discourages Gilbert's interest in Rachel when he turns to her for help, she praises the woman who besieges him: "I always did have a sort of sneaking fondness for her, and now I'm determined to indulge it," she rhapsodizes, "I'm an ardent Farrellite!" (*MF* 184). Gilbert thus is betrayed by his own ally.

Even after Mrs. Farrell confides her treacheries, Mrs. Gilbert cannot break her "fascinat[ion]" (*MF* 33). Although she lectures Mrs. Farrell on duty, responsibilty, and realism in affairs of the heart, she answers Mrs. Farrell's question about whether she likes her "absently," admitting that she, too, would be a "fool" (*MF* 210) for her. By the time she gives Gilbert his melodramatic warning, she has been so far fooled as to become Mrs. Farrell's accomplice. She works her brother-in-law up to just the right pitch for the moonlight *coup de théatre*. With tears and fifth-act supplications, she barrages him with heroic commands and ends breathlessly: "I don't blame you for loving her— how could you help it? She is charming—yes, she charms me, too" (*MF* 219). At last she manages to part coolly with her, permitting herself just one "impetuous embrace" (*MF* 230). But when she sees her several years later she is swept into her orbit all over again. While condemning her narcissism, she "can't help," in the final analysis, both "admiring" (*MF* 259) her and defending her cruelties.

Even Rachel Woodward, the paragon of virtue, bows down before Mrs. Farrell. Despite the high morality she exhibits through the book—her industry, modesty, honesty, and plaindealing—she has also cut herself off from the life of the body and rendered herself vulnerable. Beside Mrs. Farrell in church she sings the "truer and wiser" (*MF* 50) note; but, like the other natives, she is the product of an exhausted and sclerotic puritanism. She "creep[s]" (*MF* 17) and crouches as Mrs. Farrell leaps across the meadow, fades into the wings when men approach, and espouses such stern principles that Mrs. Gilbert calls her "granite" (*MF* 14). She is too feeble to withstand a conversation about nudity, and she is identified with Rosa Bonheur, the transvestite painter. That is the *real* reason why neither man ever strikes up with her (despite their lip-service) and why Mrs. Farrell can enchant her so readily. The denied part of herself draws her to the widow with an implacable, unconscious logic. As Mrs. Gilbert says, Mrs. Farrell seems to mysteriously "thaw" (*MF* 40) her out. But the more Rachel falls in with her, the more she begins to dissolve emotionally and morally. At the same time, she becomes the victim of Mrs. Farrell's cruelest sadism. Already forced to relinquish the man she loves to her, she must also bear her continual mockery, insults, and unfinished dirty work.

When Mrs. Farrell parodies Easton's love-making to her, she reaches a breaking point. Torn between delight in Mrs. Farrell's spoof and pain and moral outrage, she loses control of herself. She laughs "helplessly" (*MF* 145) and then unleashes all her buried hatred in a wild harangue. Afterwards, Mrs. Farrell uses her apology (as she did with her other captives) to secure her grip. She softens her with endearments and laughter, and leaves her so unhinged that even through her tears Rachel blurts out at the end: "She did more than she meant . . . yes I like her. . . . Nobody could help that" (*MF* 253).

Yet if Mrs. Farrell has been able to foment all of this discord and misery through her attack on the official morality, she also falls victim to it herself. Not only do the refined sublimations—idealism, sensational sentimentality, and neopuritanism—encourage her sexual lawlessness, but suprarepression burdens her, too, with disease. Because there is no way to ethically mediate her sexuality, she suffers the reverse schizophrenia of the Victorian age. She is a body without a soul, physicality without spirituality, *bios* without personhood. Hers is the libido of childhood, with all its attendant narcissism and sadism. Incapable of real feeling, she uses comedy (in antithesis to Ferris) to defend herself from emotional, rather than sexual, intimacy.

Midway through her assault on West Pekin, her comic defenses, just like the book's, begin to erode, and she suffers her own maturity ordeal. Amidst the "long trial" of Easton's illness and the demands made on her humanity, she sinks into a deep melancholy (*MF* 179). She withdraws behind closed doors and eschews society except for the chthonic, skeletal figure of Mr. Woodward, whom she follows on his somnambulistic rounds through the potato patch. In the throes of her ordeal, she confides in Rachel: "It seems to me that I know how to feel," she exclaims, "but that I never feel" (*MF* 180). From her underworld immersion she perceives her exploitative and sterile sexuality. As though in a "dream" she sees Easton trapped in a prison while she waits paralyzed outside. She cannot stir herself from her "torpor" she tells Rachel; her heart "lies like a stone in [her] breast" (*MF* 181). If Rachel is "granite," Mrs. Farrell is equally rocklike, equally nonvital. At the end, after she emerges unhealed and untransformed from her *rite de passage*, she bewails her spiritual death to Easton and begs him to marry her and save her from herself. She turns out to be an even more lethal femme fatale than she seemed at first. Besides the outer destruction she causes, she is inwardly dead. With the impotency historically associated with intemperance,[13] she may also—as her fear of a penknife hints—be physically frigid as well. Rather than the promised Venus from the sea, then, she is an avatar of Thanatos.

A disturbing mood has settled over Howells's farce by the last chapter. The orthodox morality has proved ineffectual and moribund, and sex shows a ferocity and virulence unequaled before. Without a value to stay it, its negative powers have run roughshod over the book, reducing everyone to the very "fools" Ferris feared. No character, not even the deadly Mrs. Farrell, has been able to survive a journey toward sexual maturity.

What makes the ending more unsettling still, and makes it so unsatisfactory, is the final ambivalence. The sympathy for pleasure, which was inchoate and muted in *A Foregone Conclusion*, becomes overt in *Private Theatricals*. Threaded through the novel is a secret affection for Mrs. Farrell much like the one the characters feel. The narrative commentary surrounding her strains with contradiction: her greed is "charming"; her daring, "delicious" (*MF* 123); her woodland retreat both wild and "richer than anywhere else" (*MF* 125). So too, the langauge that accompanies her betrays fundamental tensions. Paired with scenes of her fiercest cruelties are lyric descriptions of her, especially during the forest interview where the landscape Howells paints resembles his tributes to the sensuous woods of his youth. Such is the force of her dialogue, as well, with its rich ornament, comedy, and vitality, that the esthetic sympathy falls all on her side. By contrast, the heroine of the piece, Rachel Woodward, cannot demonstrate her appeal textually but limps feebly through her paces, mouthing cliched, wooden pieties. The Swedenborgianism that Howells would later incorporate into his erotic books is in abeyance here. Evil sexuality (now registered more fully in Mrs. Farrell's egotism and mental imbalance:) remains confused with sensuality, goodness with pallor, while an unintegrated, covert movement toward joy, beauty, and the flesh pulls steadily against the direction of the plot.

The result is an epilogue that hangs suspended amidst dark, unstable ironies. The news of Gilbert's incipient romance with Rachel is undermined by Mrs. Farrell's final appearance in a production of *Romeo and Juliet*. Despite Mrs. Gilbert's caustic assessment of her beforehand, despite Mrs. Farrell's overbosomed, sensual portrayal of Juliet, she carries the day one last devastating time. Mr. Gilbert assures his wife that his "sense of right and wrong has not been shaken, like some people's by this enchantress" (*MF* 260), but he, too, falls under her spell as completely as the West Pekiners. In the wake of the drama critic's decision that she belongs in a "private theatrical" (*MF* 264), the infatuated Mr. Gilbert consigns her back to the arena where she wreaked such disaster before, there to work her deadly arts permanently. Why shouldn't she marry Easton and enjoy herself?, Mr. Gilbert asks as he leaves the play; he, Gilbert, would marry her, he insists. By the end, the defenses against her have crumbled further and the lethal truths she embodies have been loosened again with redoubled power. Worse still, the ambivalence festers on: Mrs. Farrell continues to "divinely fascinate" (*MF* 262) while the virtuous Rachel, praised throughout the book, languishes off-stage.

Amidst Mrs. Farrell's siege, Gilbert says fliply at one point; "You can't expect me to be very earnest about genteel comedy" (*MF* 200). The comedy, though, had metamorphosed all too earnestly. Whether he intended it or not, Howells had, by implication, indicted the entire mid-seventies' sexual ethos. Every expression of the official purity cult shows itself infirm and death-centered, and in thrall to a second form of death, the barbarous Mrs. Farrell. There is no live center of value, no positive sexuality; only a "sneaking," fragmenting "fondness" for her. West Pekin becomes a model of destructive Protestantism, "a pure culture of the death instinct."[14]

Howells's "slight" story, then, had apparently backfired. He had only pushed deeper into the tragic sexual realities he had broached in *A Foregone Conclusion*. The "strong motive" had been there all along, concealed and embedded like a time bomb in the novel. The secret pull of his imagination toward a gratifying Eros had heightened his critique of the orthodox morality and increased his creative ambivalence. His exploration of Ferris's fear, by the same token, had brought him nearer the exaggerated terrors (which were also his culture's) of his adolescence. Mrs. Farrell's overscale ferocities and the degrees of foolishness she inflicts—casting her victims into aggression, irrationality, helplessness, and confusion—precisely fulfill the mid-nineteenth-century cautionary literature.

Howells, though, called *Private Theatricals* his "prematurity."[15] A larger, more ambitious book was destined to flesh out the insights of his West Pekin drama. In *A Modern Instance* (1882) he would cover a wider canvas and not only find official repression sicker and deadlier but discover more murderous truths within his adolescent terror. The contradictory attraction to pleasure would build to a crisis point. The trap which was implicit and circumvented (albeit barely) in *Private Theatricals* would become explicit and impossible to avoid. That was seven years away. It would be still further before Howells could probe to the heart of the "truth of the secret" and provide a serious solution to Mrs. Farrell's playful question, "Oh! Why is it that there isn't some common ground for men and women to meet on, and be helpful to each other?" (*MF* 96). His protagonists would continue to make "fools" of each other, to persist in their maladjustments and cruelties. But with each advance toward the "secret," Howells moved further away from a wild pasture to a "common ground" and closer to a heroine who could harness Mrs. Farrell's passion, beauty, and élan for civilized, helpful ends.

A *Modern Instance*: Howells
and sexual tragedy | *Four*

Once, when a reporter accused Howells of avoiding tragedy in his fiction, he rejoined: "Don't you think there was something tragic in Bartley Hubbard before the divorce court?"[1] Of his novels, *A Modern
Instance* (1882) was to be his "great" tragedy, his direct confrontation
with the underlying truths in *Private Theatricals*. As the 1875 comedy
was being serialized, he saw Grillparzer's *Medea* and decided to write a
"New Medea," a novel that dealt "seriously"[2] and explicitly with the
sexual evils submerged in Mrs. Farrell's West Pekin farce. His Jason
and Medea were to be two libertines, like her, whose careers dramatize and extend her iniquities. Their "divorce"—the implied end of
her affairs—was to be the "motive," and the treatment "tragic . . .
[but] not wholly tragic." His prospectus to Scribner's explained: "I
think [you] can trust me . . . not to let the moral slip through my fingers . . . I should be ashamed to write a novel that did not distinctly
mean something."[3]

It was six years before Howells was ready—intellectually, emotionally, and artistically—to begin his ambitious novel. But when he
did, his imagination once more altered his plans. Working toward the
"secret" (*FC* 241) and reintegration of joy, his creative impulses led
him toward a crisis in his life and sexual theme. In what became the
most personal of his books, he struck the heart of his adolescent sex
terror and, at the same time, found no ethic to contain it. The orthodox culture, on an even wider scale than *Private Theatricals*, proved
corrupt and death-infested. The voices of moral order that saved
Grillparzer's *Medea* from being "wholly tragic" never materialized,
while Howells's protagonists sank into a puritan's nightmare of sexual
damnation. At the very climax of the novel, Howells's "moral" threatened to slip through his fingers, and he fell ill for seven weeks.

A deeper explanation of his illness might be not only that he exhumed phobic fears from his early adulthood without a value to re-

strain them but that he encountered his primal conflict as well. The same imaginative instinct that drove him to invalidate the suprarepressive sexual norms also lured him further toward the redemption of pleasure. And with the desire to redeem pleasure, his self-division rose proportionally. More, the ambivalence touched the raw nerve of his own autobiography, since he modelled his Jason, Bartley Hubbard, "from [him]self."[4] When Bartley escaped, Howells's contradictory reactions to him (and to his own sexuality) may have escaped too. The "stress of self,"[5] as Edwin Cady suggests—a divided self—became intolerable. A worse dilemma than the loss of a moral, then, threatened Howells when he collapsed; his "distinct" meaning was in danger of eluding him.

The rest of the book is a record of Howells's attempt to recover a "moral" and meaning for his "New Medea." Again, though, his imagination baffled his conscious efforts, insisting on return to his adolescent fear, on denial of repression, and on the restoration of pleasure. Rather than easing ambivalence, the tensions increase and the novel ends in a negative stalemate. Free sexuality culminates in violence and death, orthodox morality in more death; and the contradictions build to a bitter climax. In keeping with this new mood, Howells changed the title to Jacques's sardonic speech from *As You Like It*. His remark to the reporter gathers a deeper meaning: his novel had become existentially tragic. He had been forced to a crisis point in his psychic and creative development; he had either to find another approach or submit to sexual immaturity, confusion, and death.

In 1876, on the heels of the Grillparzer performance, he began his "New Medea," but discarded it after two chapters. Before he could implement his vision, he needed the catalyzing events of the next five years. His private life, the national mood, and artistic influences from abroad, all provided him with the necessary materials and vision for his daring project. The late seventies were a time when the public temper coincided with his adolescent sex phobia, while his faith in official answers began to erode under the pressure of personal distress. During his final years as editor of the *Atlantic*, his "good great time"[6] was on the wane. As early as 1876, after a summer of his wife's "wretched"[7] health, he complained to his father about conventional Boston and expressed a desire for "repose and retirement"[8] in the country. By 1880, he spoke of "melancholy" and the "loss of fresh passion."[9] His daughter Winifred had suffered the first of what seemed to be nervous breakdowns (perhaps evoking his own adolescent ones) and had not responded to any of the orthodox cures. Accompanying his despair was an increased pessimism about sexuality. His fiction continued to draw closer and more seriously to the dark side of the "secret," [10] and one of his letters complained that he could no longer bear to be pained by the problem of "Helen and Casanova." [11] Yet, as though consciously exploring his own dark side, he visited a police station house like the one which horrified him as a young man in Cincinnati, wrote an essay about his nightmares, and revisited Xenia, the site of some his worst, earliest teenage anxieties.

If the changes in his personal life drove him nearer the fears of his youth and further toward distrust of prescribed solutions, the sexual climate of the age continued to foster these developments. There was a tone of crisis about sexuality during the late seventies and early eighties that was almost without parallel in America. Advice books warned of the doom and corruption in indulgence, [12] and the *Atlantic* ran an article advancing the Schopenhaueresque thesis that the sexual will led to "final and total destruction." [13] An ultrarestrictive puritanism accompanied this cataclysmic fear. Howells's editor was threatened with obscenity charges for *Leaves of Grass*, and Comstock's censorious legislation grew pandemic. Prudery became brittle and anemic; repression, fanatical.

The literary movement that captured this mood and dominated the intellectual world during the late nineteenth century was naturalism. Zola's "realism" (as it was then called) filled the journals of the day, setting off a tidal wave of controversy. His work dramatized the national sexual tenor. His protagonists, left to the free expression of their passions, end exactly where Comstock's followers promised—in corruption, death, and sterility. And, like them, Zola was fiercely prudish. [14] His influence on Howells during these years was immediate and profound. Zola supplied an artistic framework for the dark sexual truths he wanted to treat "seriously" and "tragically," and corroborated the fears he was exploring. At the same time, the very extremism of Zola's prudery helped direct his imaginative sympathies away from the official ethic. Howells read him, then, with a blaze of enthusiasm. Certainly he was familiar with his work just before he began his "New Medea," [15] but toward the end he wrote John Hay ecstatically: "I read everything of Zola's that I can lay hands on." [16]

Zola's effect on his erotic art was revolutionary. The subjects he had concealed in fine print and comedy he learned to handle boldly, profoundly, and panoramically. "Every literary theory of mine was contrary to him when I took up *L'Assommoir*,"[17] he admitted and added that Zola gave him the courage "not to shrink from the things of dirt and clay."[18] By nineteenth-century standards, *A Modern Instance* was filled with "dirt"—scandalously so. Even after Howells had diluted the original version for *Century* magazine, an outraged reader complained: "[T]he whole thing from beginning to end is revolting."[19] He had dealt directly with such tabooed themes as sadomasochism, narcissism, and promiscuity and—even more incriminating—divorce.

Not only did Zola and his contemporaries encourage Howells to face these topics directly; they showed him powerful means of rendering them. The French "realists," first of all, reinforced the direction he was already pursuing. Their use of dramatic method, circumstantial detail, the physical surroundings to convey sexual passion, paralleled Howells's own practices of the past eight years. Beyond strengthening his approach, though, they—particularly Zola—taught him abundant methods of encoding sexuality and eliciting its power. The epic scale Zola employed to duplicate the magnitude of desire was one of Howells's most significant borrowings. For Marcia's and Bartley's tempestuous appetites, he utilized a canvas as large as *Nana's* and symbols as all-encompassing. Thus, animality, heat, food, horses, and clothes became central motifs in *A Modern Instance*, spanning the whole drama. Zola's erotic vocabulary was equally valuable. Howells not only found such euphemisms as "kiss" handled explicitly (with *baiser* as the French pun for intercourse) but found images that had special significance for his autobiography—alcohol, heat, dizziness, and suffocation. Through the continental novelists he was put in touch with an eroto-literary tradition of the highest sophistication. The large and deep range of sexual truths he wanted to convey became both possible and esthetically viable. Amidst his writing, he acknowledged his debt enthusiastically: "I am a great admirer of French workmanship."[20] Prepared by the naturalists, the sexual *zeitgeist*, and the upheavals in his personal life, Howells was ready for his "enormous"[21] study of undisciplined sexuality by the spring of 1881 after he left the *Atlantic*.

Just as Mrs. Farrell springs out of the erotic wasteland of West Pekin, Marcia and Bartley arise in a town bled dry by neopuritanism. Surrounded by "iron-grey crags" and "arctic quiet" (*MI* 1), the inhabitants live in houses that smell of decayed rats and peer through "funereal" (*MI* 2) blinds for signs of excitement. Marcia's parents are grim examples of the sexual desolation in Equity. Locked up in their silent house together, estranged, and dressed in permanent black, the Gaylords are caricatures of marital death. The Squire, with his "hawk-like profile" and "harsh rings of black hair" (*MI* 11), reigns over his wife like a Plutonian deity, and she sits embalmed in her rocker, listening to the clock tick. Her calcified and anemic puritanism and his skeptical negations have leeched their lives completely of Eros.

Marcia and Bartley enter this blasted landscape with the same show of life and brilliance as Mrs. Farrell. The connection, though, between Mrs. Farrell's deadliness and her apparent vitality is underscored from the beginning with the two lovers. Their first entrance foreshadows a fate for their undiscipline that is just as lethal as the Gaylords'. They dash into the dark, lifeless town in Bartley's redlined, "musically clashing" (*MI* 2) cutter behind a colt who is sure to "be the death" (*MI* 4) of them. Illustrating Darwin's two savage types, the possessive monogamist and expansive polygamist, they steadily substantiate every tooth-and-claw axiom of the age. Egged on by a corrupt purity cult, they regress into the sort of "fools" the Victorians most dreaded: bankrupt children who end in the "house of death."[22]

Their opening scene together—one of the steamiest in Howells's fiction—is freighted with portents of their ruin. As always, Marcia's and Bartley's appearance is revelatory. Marcia resembles a Southern beauty with the low forehead of "savage" races, who blushes and blanches, and dresses in red or black as her untamed appetites swing from ecstasy to deadly despair. The blond, debonair Bartley cuts an unabashedly sensual figure. He has long-lashed eyes that cast "deliberate look[s]" (*MI* 4), a "rich, caressing voice" (*MI* 5), and an appetite that equals Mrs. Farrell's. Signifying special gratification for Howells, his mustache sweeps up "like a bird's wing" (*MI* 3)[23] and his manner is casual, bohemian, and jocular. Yet his eyes are "clouded gray" (*MI* 4), the chin beneath his mustache recedes weakly, and he indulges his gluttony in "choking air" (*MI* 12) and gets sick afterwards.

During the midnight rendezvous with Marcia that initiates their courtship, the sinister side of his easygoing charm insinuates itself into his love-making. As their excitement rises before a smouldering fire (reminiscent of the laundry seduction in *L'Assommoir*), Bartley ominously threatens to strangle Marcia with his stylish coat; then forces her, in an adumbration of the sadistic power he will wield over her, to write Y-E-S on an imaginary note. In the context of their humid tête-à-tête, the "yes" comes with the force of Molly Bloom's "yes" in

Ulysses. The culmination of their interview confirms this sense of the word. Her brain filled "like wine" by Bartley's advances, Marcia reels "dizzily" (*MI* 10) into his embrace and kisses him (with clear sexual implications to Victorian readers) at the door. Afterwards, in a phallically loaded gesture, she kisses the doorknob behind him.

Similar omens surround their engagement. When Bartley's dyspepsia and egotistic self-pity prompt his love declaration, Marcia abandons herself to her passion in ways that are bitterly prophetic. Indulging her feeling of "foolishness," she playfully regresses to an infantility she will experience through her marriage. "There is something about this that lets me be as silly as I like," she exclaims, and begins to talk baby talk to Bartley. But her child's play grows inadvertently portentous. Her fevered caresses garrote Bartley, and she cries with delight, "You may kiss me—you may *kill* me, now!" (*MI* 30). Prefiguring that very fate, Bartley seizes her when he leaves and pinions her arms against her sides until she is "helpless": "I knew you were dead in love with me," he exults.

Their engagement celebration and marriage further elucidate their contrasting savage dispositions and predict their doom. After they have committed themselves to each other, they drive off in Bartley's cutter on a joyride that symbolizes the course of their romance. In an image of their runaway libido, they let the colt "open up" on a country road until they enter a forest which bears the same relation to their passion as Mrs. Farrell's primeval dell to hers. There, in the "wild and lonesome" (*MI* 43) woods, the Darwinian compulsions in their free sexuality come forward. As the colt picks up faster and faster speed, they run into another sled carrying the town spitfire. Bartley promptly engages in a torrid *à deux* with her, while Marcia watches "*almost killed*" (*MI* 47) from the sidelines. Afterwards, she clutches "herself tighter to him" (*MI* 47) and sobs, to Bartley's uncontrollable laughter.

Their wedding is an equally inauspicious occasion. Preceded by a quarrel and separation over Bartley's polygamous adventures, it takes place impulsively under dubious circumstances. With the undisciplined possessiveness that characterizes her, Marcia pursues Bartley on his flight out of town and captures him "at the touch" (*MI* 104). A five-dollar bribe buys their illegal license and their aphrodisiacal wedding supper of oysters and coffee is part of the same fraudulent deal. Later they consummate their union under a cloud of death imagery. They see "The Coleen Bawn," a melodrama about marital murder, which Marcia watches like a "savage" (*MI* 115) who witnesses her own execution. Bartley, in turn, roars with laughter, and cracks a joke as he turns off the bedroom light that changes the plot so that the protagonists are "both found suffocated in the morning" (*MI* 105).

In fact, they both suffer genuine and slow death as their marriage and personalities dissolve bit by bit. Rather than regulating their unbridled appetites, marriage only encourages darker, crueler, more pathologic expressions of them. When the charm of novelty wears off, they submit to the laws of their mutually incompatible primitive personalities. Bartley's libido expands outward in direct ratio to Marcia's tightening grip, until they propel themselves into a death-in-life entrapment. As Bartley's flesh swells on beer and oysters and his extramarital reveries with it, Marcia contracts into a mute, frigid recluse whose slammed door—earlier kissed—resounds fatally through their marriage. In their downward spiral, the negative powers of Eros have full vent. Bartley's egotistic sadism grows with the increase of Marcia's masochism and jealousy, and they both drift into the incoherence and amoral instinctuality of childhood. At last, like Mrs. Farrell, they lose their inner vitality with their outer sexual failure. With her disintegration, Marcia faces the "deadly unsympathetic stillness" (*MI* 232) of psychic emptiness. Bartley's robbery, similarly, is only a visible manifestation of what he has stolen from himself. Each layer of fat sinks him further into animal apathy, regression, and *néant*. Thus, amid Marcia's sobs and Bartley's laughter, they circle down to a pure center of death that is both internal and external. And in an elaboration of Mrs. Farrell's self-destruction, theirs infects and poisons the whole community.

Two episodes in particular illustrate how they tighten the noose around themselves. The first occurs after their entropic descent is well under way. They no longer do or "say anything" in their "dull" (*MI* 204) home and Bartley becomes so bored he tries to send Marcia away to visit her parents. A quarrel erupts; Marcia's jealousy flares; and Bartley walks out "with a sense of release" (*MI* 207) and embarks on a subtly coded sexual debauch. He begins with an aphrodisiacal plate of oysters and ends at a bar where he drinks himself into oblivion. Given the equation between alcohol and sex in Victorian America, his escapade takes on the value of an extramarital fling. His identification with a barfly who runs a girlie show and the horrified reaction of Ben Halleck, who finally discovers him, strengthens this interpretation of his binge.

Afterwards a deeper "quiet" (*MI* 264) settles over the Hubbard marriage as Marcia's jealousy and Bartley's promiscuous appetite increase apace. The adulterous implications of his barroom spree become explicit in their next major conflict. Bartley openly and maliciously escapes with another woman, leaving Marcia in a paroxysm of jealous rage. The occasion, aptly, is a picnic on a mountain named "Devil's Backbone," for there the evil in their lawless passion reaches a peak of destructiveness. When Bartley arrives in Equity for the outing, their estrangement is far advanced. They forget to kiss each other and immediately start to quarrel over Bartley's proposed jaunt with the flirt, Mrs. Macallister. At last, under Bartley's sadistic threats, she gives in, "moving her head from side to side like one that breathes stifling air" (*MI* 236). While she tags behind, he dashes off with Mrs. Macallister on a drive that ironically duplicates his engagement sleigh ride. They race to a wooded glen—another of Mrs. Farrell's wild pastures—where they enact a fiery flirtation before the suffering, choking Marcia. The marital bloodshed is not limited to the Hubbards alone. Marcia's guests are enmeshed, as well, in the Hubbards' web of evil. Brought to tears by Bartley's antics, Marcia takes Ben Halleck, whom she has enamored, to the top of "Devil's Backbone," where she vents her pain. His resulting anguish, as the site of her breakdown attests, is another evil Marcia and Bartley perpetrate through their indulgent, malign appetites.

From this point on, their tailspin into the vacuity of death is rapid. Marcia withdraws into frozen apathy and Bartley fleshes out to ever widening "raffish" (*MI* 242) degeneracy and insentience. On the eve of their final break, with Bartley deep in debt, peculation, and wanton dreams, they enter the last stages of inertia. Overcome by a funereal peace, they sit interred in their narrow, airless parlor "with nothing to say to each other" (*MI* 271). Marcia's climactic explosion, therefore, only sets the match to the dry husks of their marriage.

Deathly white and "whirled . . . beyond the reach of reason" (*MI* 274), she accuses him of infidelity and warns him (ironically invoking the "touch" which joined them) not to "*touch*" (*MI* 274) her again. The "Devil" (*MI* 275) takes possession of Bartley and the dark, hostile drives in his sexuality leap out. He rises up in all his sadism and confesses what has been figuratively true throughout—that he has been unfaithful. With smiling malice, he delivers the coup de grâce to their relationship: "[Y]ou certainly won't live with me again" (*MI* 276). The foreordained moment, their "death" arrives: Marcia storms off and Bartley meets his fatal crisis. Each separates from the other mutilated beyond recognition. Childish, irrational, fragmented, and violent, they have lost the *érotisme* that defined them, as well as their very identities. They have enclosed themselves in the Victorian "house of death."

Yet, at the same time, the Victorian remedies for their deadly passions offer no viable alternatives and are equally moribund. The social-geographical range is wider and the moral spokesmen wiser than in *Private Theatricals*, but ultimately the conventional sexual ethic proves just as defective. Not only does the purity culture breed sterility; it fosters a secretly prurient neoromanticism and sentimentality that promotes the Hubbards' tragedy. The Mrs. Grundys of Equity, for instance, make Marcia's and Bartley's romance the surrogate object of their ungratified libidinous drives, and therefore encourage the Hubbards' excesses. The Bostonians provide no normative values or support either. Benevolent and latitudinarian, the elder Hallecks break down when Marcia reveals the extent of her incontinence and read her a fundamentalist lecture. After they have left her to her own inadequate devices, Mrs. Halleck bristles priggishly: "I felt like a missionary talking to a South Sea Islander" (*MI* 203),[24] she sniffs.

Their son, Ben, brings even less help through his adoration. Just as Gervaise's limp in *L'Assommoir* symbolizes an inner sexual deformity, so Ben's suggests the sick imbalance of his neochivalry. Like the culture, his febrile romanticism is the perverse outgrowth of a denied sexuality. Through it, he both manages to destroy himself (as his defloration of his pear tree demonstrates) and injure the object of his devotion as well. His idealization of her "dependent and childlike" (*MI* 227) qualities only guarantees Marcia's puerile subjection to Bartley. When she asks for the religious guidance that might have saved her, he bridles like his parents and patronizingly evades her questions. He delivers the drunken Bartley to her with such chivalric delicacy that she mistakes the cause of the trouble and redoubles her marital commitment. On the "Devil's Backbone" he fails her more seriously. He squeamishly ignores her tears, strikes his phallic cane on the rock, and offers to bring Bartley back to her. The hint of a collusion and even an affinity between Ben and Bartley in this episode gains strength during the Hubbards' last days together. Suggesting a secret salacity in his sentimentality, Ben "nobly" lends Bartley his getaway money and acquires his inebriated walk (*MI* 230, 292, 295) as his "spiritual" ardors for Marcia increase.

The lawyer, Atherton, is the most morally sophisticated character in the novel and grounds Ben's romantic excesses with his pragmatic, level advice. His intellectual respectability, however, makes his prudery all the more dangerous, and his pieties turn shrill and hypocritical in the course of Marcia's and Bartley's downfall. Beside their sordid difficulties, his armchair preachments sound increasingly irrelevant and Draconian. Marriage, he declares, is the "realm of unreason." Yet he offers no ethic for it except a punitive Swedenborgianism which forbids separation at any cost, even "hell" (*MI* 229) on earth. In inverse ratio to the Hubbards' misery, his bachelorhood waxes happier and plusher, while his judgments harden. Moving further from Swedenborg's temperance, he insists on a Calvinistic repression so severe that Ben shudders after one of his speeches: "It's horrible!" (*MI* 224).

At the opposite end of the spectrum is the transcendentalist drifter, Kinney. Migrating from Alkali City to one bachelor camp after another, he illustrates the decay and final obsolescence of Whitman's erotic optimism. Without ever enough money to marry or meet his "Darling Minney" (*MI* 79), he falls prey to the postbellum purity cult and becomes a grotesque icon of sterility.

If Bartley "spends" himself into insolvency and Marcia's "child's play" (*MI* 145) budget grows manically tight-fisted, their surrounding milieu offers no sounder fiscal-sexual policy. In the "spermatic economy"[25] of the age, none of the characters is monetarily or erotically balanced. The Gaylords are stingy, the Hallecks backwardly lavish, their son unable to earn a living, and Atherton mercenary. When Bartley faces his tragic hour, then, there is no promised "moral" anywhere in the society: nothing but prevailing barrenness and a sick prurience concealed in the genteel culture. The normative figures in *Medea*, the chorus and exemplary Cruesa, never appear to deflect and drain off the pity and terror. Two overwhelming negations converge at the end of chapter 31. Marcia leaves Bartley with a debased, valueless civilization on the one hand and entombment in a dead marriage on the other.

His choice is either to remain trapped in a vacuum or escape his suppressive society for the West. Here Bartley meets a more tortuous fate than marital suffocation: he encounters all the wracking ambivalence in free, unmonitored sexuality. He fluctuates in an agony of indecision. Relishing his liberation, he feels "strangely hungry," then returns twice to the "hideous" (*MI* 276) heat of their cramped parlor before he leaves for the train. Once on the way, his conflict worsens. Intoxicated by the idea that "he was to be free of her," he nonetheless quails at the "vast . . . sterile and hopeless" darkness ahead of him and, for the first time in the novel, cannot eat. When the train stops in Cleveland, he collapses, short-circuits his maturity ordeal, and decides he "must return or throw himself in the lake"—with everything the lake of fire implies. But at the ticket office, he discovers he has been robbed (by his own imperious sexuality) and "reel[s] away" (*MI* 277) to his feared and desired freedom.

This was precisely the time during the writing that Howells fell ill. "Sleeplessness from overwork," was one reason he gave his father, but the second, his "long worry,"[26] must have been decisive too. His "new Medea" had taken an unexpected, "wholly tragic" turn. While Marcia and Bartley exhumed his adolescent fears with their descents into death and decadence, the restraints imposed by his superego disintegrated. Just when his "prudery" was most fervent in his criticism and letters,[27] his imagination invalidated it and returned him to his old Ohio terror. More than that, his imagination had thrust him into his neurotic conflict. When the ethical defenses collapsed and Bartley confronted his awful choice, Howells was cast upon his own ambivalence with a frightening immediacy. With his artistic distance weakened through self-portraiture, he may have been defeated just as totally as Bartley by contradiction.

The imagery in Bartley's escape scene is tellingly autobiographical and demonstrates how Howells's inner division overwhelmed him. The suffocation Howells endured in his hydrophobia attacks is avoided at the cost of drowning; the heat he loathed at the cost of a lake of fire; and the food, which always symbolized erotic gratification to him, cannot be eaten amidst sexual freedom. All the ambivalence in Bartley's character comes to a critical head: pleasure and its opposite merge in a hopeless deadlock. In the same way that Bartley gives out at this juncture, and reels away with a vertigo like young Will's in 1858, Howells broke down and relapsed into one of his neurotic symptoms. As in Cincinnati, when he could not bear the stress of sensationalistic newspaper stories, he could not stand the sight of the newspaper or "anything of a dramatic cast" (*MLP* 178) while he was sick. Hurled, like Bartley, into the irrational thicket of his conflict, he backed away from a deeper engagement with it and fell ill. With the characters in his novels, he had met and sidestepped a maturity test.

Feeling exhausted and eviscerated by his long illness, Howells took up the novel again with a weakened grasp. "I work feebly and ineffectually,"[28] he told Clemens, "every mental effort costs about twice as much as it used, and the result seems to lack texture."[29] Along with the normal fatigue of convalescence, he had the extra strain in the last chapters of reclaiming a "moral" and "distinct" meaning for his tragedy. The dramatic lull in the plot after Bartley's flight shows an enormous effort of will to extract a value from the ruins of the Hubbard marriage. The scenes circle around the Halleck family and Atherton in a desperate search for wisdom and perspective. Halleck realizes his "illness," decides to flee to South America (in an attempted maturity ordeal), and turns to Atherton for advice. Although Atherton intones sagely about virtue and encourages Halleck on his way, he, like the other protagonists, undergoes an even sharper reduction in the final pages.

Rather than cooperating with his conscious plans, Howells's imagination obstinately recurred to its old course. As though empowered by his breakdown, it followed Marcia's and Bartley's fate out to the core of the adolescent terror, and pressed harder toward pleasure. The suppressive Victorian norm suffers a greater devaluation and gratification erupts more intimately and powerfully into the text. The ambivalence escalates and the book ends in a deeper double bind: death weights both sides of the erotic equation and paradox rends its final meaning.

The climactic courtroom battle brings all of these themes to a head. In the chapters that precede it, each character drops further into disrepute, Marcia slips into a real "house of death," and the novel enters the intensely sensuous landscape of Howells's youth. Atherton's speeches, for instance, grow fanatical and openly hypocritical. With *Watch and Ward* histrionics, he warns Ben that his desire for Marcia is "ugly as hell and bitter as death" (*MI* 292). In addition, his lectures begin to wax Pecksniffian. When he next hectors Ben about "scoundrels" who legally "lure women from their duty, ruin homes, and destroy society" (*MI* 317), he himself has just appropriated Clara Kingsbury and her large fortune under the sanction of the same marriage laws. Halleck's remark that his "luxury" (*MI* 325) would have redeemed Bartley redounds on Atherton with devastating irony in his loftiest sermonette in the book. From the vantage of his opulent life, he makes a rare condescension to his wife and instructs her on the evils of the Hubbard tragedy. He lambasts Ben's criminal passion, damns Bartley as as "wild beast" who deserves his "hell" (*MI* 332–333), and concludes with a string of banalities on order and propriety. After the reduction he suffers here, it is no surprise that Ben uses his very arguments to spur Marcia toward her last insane grasp at Bartley.

Ben Halleck also loses stature. He comes back from his South American *rite de passage* uninitiated, "savage[ly] wasted" (*MI* 315), and more sentimentally abandoned to his passion than before.

Nor is Marcia's partial recovery while Miss Strong boards in her house long-lived. The malignant advance of her uncontrolled sexuality accelerates. She regresses into insanity and the dissolution of death. By the time she hears of Bartley's whereabouts, she has deteriorated into a "querulous, vulgar . . . middle-aged woman" (*MI* 320) who dementedly canonizes her lost husband. At the news of his plan to divorce her, she begins a sharp, rapid decline. Blanching with manic jealousy, she gasps for breath while her father mutters beside her, "Oh you poor crazy child" (*MI* 328). Her former passion transformed into hatred, she fluctuates between two kinds of death on her trip West for the trial. Either white with revenge or catatonically withdrawn, she bewails her fate to Halleck: "I feel like someone that has been called to a death-bed" (*MI* 338). When she arrives in Indiana, she has been reduced to a "frightened child," leaning "unsexed" (*MI* 344) on Halleck's shoulder. During the same journey the rest of the cast falls into greater disrepute. Olive Halleck snobbishly frets about appearances, Kinney appears en route to Leadville; Ben encourages Marcia's vengeance with Atherton's arguments, and Squire Gaylord, gnawing wood, presides with berserker fury over the whole retaliatory pilgrimage.

As the trip advances into the Middle West, the book enters a realm of positive experience countered by equally powerful negations. The contradictions in Bartley's character grow into a full-fledged ambivalence—on the ground of Howells's youth. Lyric passages of prose describe the spring landscape from the train window. The willows wear "their delicate green like veils," the mayapples "pitch their tents" (*MI* 340) in the woods, and the pink flush of peach trees (Howells's earliest memory of beauty) so enraptures Bartley's child that she shrieks for joy. At the same time, though, the Western forest is an infernal, "grime-blackened," "primitive wilderness" (*MI* 338), and the burning haystacks beside the corn fields leap past like a "trail of fiery serpents" (*MI* 343). Near the destination, the train derails in a Howellsian Arcadia. If darkness and snakes were the special incubi of his boyhood, images of his warm, informal home were always the "light of heaven" (*BT* 229) to him. The Dutchman's mill, then, which gives the group refuge and coffee "like a fellow's mother" makes, rises up on the prairie like paradisal vision. Surrounded by fields of wild flowers, the windmill towers "over the commonplace houses," and takes "the sun gayly on the light gallery that encircle[s] it" (*MI* 347). But Tecumseh—itself named equivocally for the Indian (another key image for the boy Howells) who brought war and a unified peace plan to the United States—restores the ambivalence in all its force. The town where the trial takes place is double-edged: at once more verdant than New England and dilapidated. In keeping with the "careless and unscrupulous" moral atmosphere, the fences wave drunkenly around the houses and show a "faltering conscientiousness of paint" (*MI* 348).

Under this pall of confused and discrepant imagery, the finale of Marcia's and Bartley's "undisciplined" romance takes place. There, at the divorce trial, the two negative principles of their tragedy reach a fatal juncture. The death wielding powers of orthodox repression collide head-on with the murderous influence of uncontrolled Eros. When Marcia walks into the courtroom, she looks like an allegorical representation of death. She is "heavily veiled in black" (*MI* 352), and Bartley appears just as reft of life. Paradoxically, he has regressed to a corpse-like infancy. Three chins descend to his chest and his complexion has turned a baby's "tender pink" beneath a white mustache. The sight of his father-in-law brings a "tallowy pallor" (*MI* 350) to his face and he wanes into progressive inanimateness as the Squire's accusation proceeds.

In his rigid, fierce indictment of Bartley, the Squire represents the collective force of the official morality. Looming over the courtroom in his black frock coat, he, too, embodies Thanatos. He distills the deadliness of suprarepression with his inhuman vengeance, and epitomizes its sensationalistic infirmity through his rhetoric. His "cavernous eyes" (*MI* 352) ablaze, he flails his fist in the air and makes meretricious, sentimental appeals to the tobacco-spitting audience. Playing on their voyeurism, he depicts his daughter's misery through the eyes of an imaginary Peeping Tom and exploits his wife's death with a bathetic graveside set piece. While Marcia and Bartley sink under this harangue into deeper insentience, he reinflicts on them what they have already visited upon themselves. In a perfect illustration of Marcuse's theory of "surplus repression,"[30] he pronounces the lifeless Bartley "dead to honor; dead to duty, dead to her [Marcia] . . . [and] dead to the universal frame of things" (*MI* 353). When he tried to double lock them into their death-in-life imprisonment by calling for Bartley's incarceration, the two lethal forces meet and implode in a slaughterous dénouement. Marcia flings herself at her father with stifled sobs and renounces her vengeance—her last remaining vital sign. He, in turn, falls victim to the Hubbards' very fate. He "fetche[s] his breath in convulsive gasps," and collapses into a state of paralysis, infantilism, and imminent death. Bartley escapes in the fracas to a dark, airless room and the "long, frightened wail of a child" (*MI* 355) sounds the requiescat to his and Marcia's tragedy.

On this note of helpless pathos, they go to their deaths. "I am very sorry," Howells told his editor, R. W. Gilder, "that I can't leave out the last chapter."[31] It is one of his most chilling endings. Marcia and Bartley fall to their dooms in diametrically opposite ways, the society sinks lower in credibility, and the ambivalence leaves the conclusion caught on the horns of contradiction. Bartley lights out once more for the West where he dies in a gunfight in Whited Sepulchre, Arizona, over a sexual scandal. Marcia withdraws to Equity and buries herself in her parents' empty house—becoming "dry, cold, and uncommunicative" (*MI* 358), and growing queerer, more infantile with age. The prospect of her future marriage with Halleck, who has turned into a hard-shell, unbelieving minister, Howells quelled in an interview: "Marcia did not marry Halleck"[32] he insisted. Marcia, then, meets a fate only qualitatively different from Bartley's: the deathblow is internal and self-inflicted rather than external.

There is no "distinct" meaning, either, amidst the devastation. The same Bartley who counters Halleck's angry sentimentalities with the view that he and Marcia were "incompatible" and should have parted, has also plunged into a moral "abyss." When he proposes a marriage between Halleck and Marcia, "nothing" (*MI* 357) shows his damnation so completely. Yet Atherton's censure of that union in the last pages is just as infernal. Opulently ensconced in his "place on the Beverley shore" (*MI* 360), he frowns priggishly at Halleck's request for permission to marry Marcia and decides that it would be an impossible "lapse from the ideal" (*MI* 362). While his wife punctuates his platitudes with criticism, he persists in his objections—casting a final, stinging irony over the book with his feigned indecision about what he will tell Halleck. To Clara's question about whether he will really dissuade Halleck, he flings his letter on the table (reaffirming his contempt for it) and mutters pontifically: "Ah, I don't know! I don't know!" (*MI* 362).

The concluding mood is that of the nihilistic, melancholy Jacques who lambasts well-fed prigs like Atherton with their "wise saws and modern instances"[33] and sees all lovers as "fools." Howells had inadvertently backed into the "impenetrable darkness" of pure tragedy—the realm, he later said, where man "cannot lift or shift or move."[34] He had wedged himself between two withering negations: the deadliness of uncontrolled Eros and the deadliness of the official ethic. "Divorce" became a larger theme than he realized. Besides the separation of men and women, he found a separation of mind and body in a critically strained culture. A ferocious sexuality had proved resistant to morality; and spirituality seemed leagued with another death through oversuppression. At the same time, Howells had discovered a division within his own psyche—an attraction and aversion to passion—powerful enough to strike him ill.

The Swedenborgian underlay to the novel dramatizes his dilemma. Swedenborg's negative, proscriptive doctrine dominates the theme of sex-terror in the book. Marcia has the "pallid countenance"[35] of the demon of self-love, suffers the "captivity and stifling"[36] of jealous love, and descends, as Swedenborg's sexual sinners do, into insanity. The "Devil," the *Conjugial Love* monster of lust who terrorized Howells's boyhood (*BT* 12), possesses Bartley in his evil hours and haunts his flirtations. Atherton voices this negatively perceived Swedenborgianism. His exaggerated and puritanically lopsided version of his teaching (so like Henry James, Sr.'s[37]) stresses all the horrors of sin—bestiality, brimstone, and eternal damnation—without mitigation.

The repudiation of Atherton's authority duplicates the larger indictment of suprarepression in the novel. Similarly, the contradictory registrations of Swedenborg point up the ambivalence. Spring, the season of his sexual paradise, contains the snakes, wild forests, and sterility of his hell, and Bartley is a conflicting blend of angel and demon. Like the blessed, he jokes, feasts, and dresses royally; but like the damned, he is a bloated egomaniac who inhabits abysses and exhales infusorial filth. Swedenborg's prohibitive and affirmative doctrines stand at extreme, opposite removes, with his positive thought uncomprehended and threaded secretly and paradoxically through the text. Later, the dichotomies would relax as Howells gave Bartley's pragmatism and Halleck's romanticism ethical validity. He would endorse Bartley's defense of divorce,[38] just as Swedenborg did, and ground Halleck's gyneolatry in the difficult and imperfect real world. What Halleck says sentimentally, Howells would say seriously, through the voice of tragic experience, at the end of his career: "Why a real woman can make righteousness delicious and virtue piquant" (*MI* 171).

Oscar Firkins has charged that after the dark turn Howells took in *A Modern Instance*, he veered off on a "diagonal course."[39] On the contrary, his future novels suggest that he worked out of and beyond the "wholly tragic" bind of his "new Medea." There was no "revelation" in such tragedy, Howells believed, no "light."[40] Instead, he opted to struggle toward an enlightened, pleasurable acculturization of Eros. Two years later Henry James called Howells the "great American naturalist," but reproved him, "I don't think you go far enough." Still, he encouraged, "[Y]ou are on the right path."[41] Zola's path, however, was wrong for Howells. Zola had galvanized him into confrontation with his hyperbolic adolescent fears. He had thrust him into the heart of the culture's sexual apprehensions and given him courage and means to discuss them. But ultimately Howells could neither accept that negative exaggeration of passion nor accept the prudish ethos behind it. He went further than James could have anticipated. Once pushed to a crisis by his erotic theme, he began to break away, gradually and at last radically, from the received sexual norms of the age. He refused to acquiesce in the wholesale Victorian terrors, penetrating past them to the real demonic bases of sexuality. His imaginative "will to cure" stopped at nothing less than the wail of the child in the courtroom, the dark, primal urges in the subconscious mind. He would seek a more difficult maturity test and emerge from it with an ethic that reconciled the erotic dualities in a sophisticated, pleasurable synthesis.

Worn out and "thoroughly broken up about [his] work,"[42] Howells wrote John Hay at the end of *A Modern Instance*: "I do work hard, and I know that I *aim* at the highest mark, morally and artistically."[43] Harder work still awaited him as his sexual theme expanded outward into a broadened concept of complicity and turned inward to the psychological mysteries. Yet, to reach his high "mark," this tragic low point of his career had been necessary. It became a major turning point in his quest for a positive Eros. Without the defenses of comedy, without the surreptitious arts of the miniature painter, he had brought his and his era's excessive sexual fears forward, had discredited the cult of repression, forged further into the domain of pleasure. That the terms were heightened and extreme only forced him with greater urgency to the next plateau of his erotic quest. Despite the pain and difficulty it caused him, Howells continued to call *A Modern Instance* his favorite book until the mid-nineties. If the chief function of the novel, as he claimed, was to "adjust the proportions"[44] this may have been his reason. The exaggerated doom Marcia and Bartley drew down on themselves through their undiscipline, the exaggerated cultural controls against it, and the crisis pitch of the sexual conflict may have shown him the depth of the need for proportion and erotic adjustment, both personally and creatively. Though he sank into the most "wholly tragic" mire of his literature and lost his "moral" and "distinct" meaning, he may have gained a vision of the "highest mark" as a consequence—the aureole of light around the windmill, the ideal of an associated sexuality—and pledged himself to strive for it.

The Rise of Silas Lapham: The sexual subplot | *Five*

While Howells was planning *The Rise of Silas Lapham* and jotting ideas in a "savings bank diary," he wrote R. W. Gilder: "It [the book] will involve more interest, I find, and be more of a love story than I expected."[1] This "love story" element—including the other sexual "interests" in the novel—has aroused more controversy than any other aspect of the book. At the time, reviewers accused Howells of "depravity,"[2] of "out Zola[ing] Zola," of promoting an esthetic of skin— "very dirty skin."[3] After his death, critics complained about the imperfect fusion of the love plot with the rest of the drama and charged that it was an embellishment for his female readers.[4]

Now such dispute has long since subsided. Several recent articles defend the intrinsic unity of the two plots,[5] and the excitement over the "shocking" physicality has so far abated as to be almost inconceivable. Except for quasi-Freudian speculations on the pine-shaving scene,[6] in which Irene Lapham pokes the curls with her parasol, the novel is thought to be tame, blandly Victorian, and devoid of sexuality.

Yet, the question arises: might there not be an unexplored level of sexual meaning that explains the old controversy? A reexamination of *Silas Lapham* suggests that there is indeed a sumberged erotic subtext which Howells's audience may have read and the next generation missed. By reconstructing this sexual dimension, the novel appears to be even more closely, intricately structured than is thought. To be sure, the sexual "story" is not the major story, but it provides a rich undertheme that deepens the texture, restores the vitality, and binds the book more tightly. At the same time, it offers a possible further explanation of Howells's breakdown in the middle of Silas's "fall" and shows how he began to work out of the deadlock he encountered in *A Modern Instance*.

Besides the obvious triangular "love story," in *Silas Lapham* a penumbra of sexual suggestion surrounds Silas's drama. Each of his overt "sins"—his egotism, greed, aggression, and intemperance—contains an implicit libidinal component which Hamlin Garland pinpointed when he called Silas the victim of "bad blood."[7] Instinctually, he is not only dissociated; he is immature, a "primitive" whose ordeal resembles a *rite de passage* as much as a spiritual death and rebirth. This tacit dimension to his career has an external dramatization in the erotic complications in his family. Persis, Irene, and Penelope provide specific sexual illustrations of his flaws, reflecting, amplifying, and clarifying them. Their tests, moreover, duplicate his and predict his final fate.

"Barbaric"[8] and "vulgar"[9] recur repeatedly in discussions of Silas's character. Silas supports the sexual sense of these terms through speech, gesture, and appearance. The impression he creates in the first chapter is one of roughhewn, elemental virility. Personifying his namesake, Silenus the Satyr,[10] he rises up out of his chair like "one of nature's noblemen" (*RSL* 2), pounds an envelope with a "great hairy fist" (*RSL* 3), and slams the door with his "huge foot" (*RSL* 4). Bartley Hubbard, the reporter, reinforces this sense of his sensuality. While he is ostensibly Silas's foil, there are libidinous similarities between them, which the readers of *A Modern Instance* would have picked up. Both have tell-tale red hair,[11] physical intimacy in conversation (*RSL* 14), a passion for fast horses, and a "bond" (*RSL* 19) that causes Silas to see "himself a young man again" (*RSL* 14) in Bartley.

In addition to his sexual exuberance, Silas's immaturity and dissociation also appear in the opening interview. He disproportionally dwells on his childhood (harping on his mother as Bartley yawns), and suggests an inner head-heart division when he talks about his "passion" (*RSL* 50), his paint. You should "keep [your conscience] as free from paint as you can," (*RSL* 12) he tells Bartley, and then praises his wife's "supernal" (*RSL* 13) virtue, as though he has displaced his moral maintenance to her. Bartley's similar view of *his* wife both establishes another parallel between them, and strikes a note of foreboding. The chapter closes on a quarrel between the Hubbards, sparked by Marcia's jealousy.

On his visit to Nantasket, Tom Corey notices that Silas only has three topics of conversation: paint, horse, and house. All are central symbols in the novel, and as such, give off a wide spectrum of meanings, one of which is libidinal. His paint is the most suggestive. Discovered in a hole in the earth caked to the roots of a fallen tree, it has the attributes of a life symbol, a procreative essence.[12] To Silas it is his "heart's blood" (*RSL* 105), his "poetry" (*RSL* 50), and when he enters the scented, twilit storeroom, he puts a hand on a keg "as if it were the head of a child" (*RSL* 12). The supporting characters corroborate the sensual significance of the paint; Marcia, by mistaking the "crimson mass" for "jam" (*RSL* 22), and Bromfield Corey, by calling it "delicious" (*RSL* 143)—the same adjective used for Irene's sexual allure.

The paint also mirrors Silas's psychosexual adjustment. His bragging, hoarding, driving competitors from the market, and rash overstocking reflect the sexual modalities of childhood. Buried in the psyche are impulses to narcissism, greed, aggression, and reckless gratification, which he has not yet subdued. Yet, in the main, he is eminently normal; his richest, fanciest brand of paint is named for his wife.

Silas's horse has sexual overtones as well.[13] In the same way that Bartley's wild colt personifies his undisciplined appetites in *A Modern Instance*, so Silas's high-blooded mare symbolizes his libidinal élan. Similarly, his horse gauges his immaturity. When he eulogizes his mare (his family calls his boasting getting up "on his high horse" [*RSL* 87]), hogs the Milldam, and "lets out" (*RSL* 35) with abandon, he exemplifies the untamed, presocialized id. Ecstatic with predatory glee, his "gaiety" perverted into "grim, almost fierce alertness" (*RSL* 35), he becomes a model of unalloyed infantile aggressiveness. Still, his orientation is fundamentally adult and average, for he rides best, with a "pretty tight fit" (*RSL* 34) with his wife. Her warning that his horse is a "fool" (*RSL* 233) and will "kill" (*RSL* 36) him is another crucial omen, adumbrating his downfall.

The house he is building, likewise, is more than just a visible manifestation of his material-social rise. With Spenser's "house of Pryde" in *The Faerie Queene*, it, too, contains a sexual dimension. Mythically and psychoanalytically, houses signify the bodily self,[14] and in that context, Silas is both richly sensual and undeveloped. Luxurious as his new mansion is, it nonetheless remains half-finished, crude, and rudimentary, with his passion for pile driving suggesting primitive, phallic propensities. Even the fetid smell, which emanates from the foundations, is libidinally significant, since Swedenborg, Howells's family prophet, equated putrid odors with sexual maladjustments. Like the paint and mare, his house becomes a vehicle for expressing them. Incessantly bragging about it, he squanders on decoration and design, and greedily, belligerently builds "not [to be] outdone" (*RSL* 29). The "normal" alloy is his equally strong desire to build for his daughters, and especially, his wife.

Money is a fourth index of his psychosexuality, and perhaps the most telling to a nineteenth-century audience. From a modern standpoint Silas's use of wealth—his irrational splurging, paint smearing, and sublimation of enjoyment into moneymaking, is a classic case of anality.[15] But he is better understood within the Victorian "spermatic economy." According to this doctrine, sperm and money were synonymous; wealth accrued through mature, stringent repression; bankruptcy, through immature, undisciplined indulgence. Silas's prodigal spending and overextending, therefore, was indicative of sexual incontinence, and his financial boasting, avarice, and competitive "crowd-[ing]" (*RSL* 47) were symptoms of unwholesome, dangerous child's play.

These symbolic registers of Silas's unschooled, dissociated libido are supported by his actions in the first part of the book and presage his tragedy. Unable to feel anything but an "easy" (*RSL* 46) conscience about edging Rogers out of his business, he atones by appropriating his wife's superego, and making an extravagant, quixotic reparation.

In Tom Corey, his "symbol of splendor" (*RSL* 92), his whole primitive disposition comes to a focus. He swells with vanity over him, challenges his superior social position, and overconfidently, rashly lets things ride when his calls begin. As they take the ferry together to Nantasket, Silas's psychosexual immaturity rises to the fore. Looking at the couples on board, he tells Tom that he can't "make any sort of guess" about whether they're engaged, just as he will not be able to divine Tom's romantic intentions. It is here the narrator interjects: "We are no more imposing than a crowd of boys" (*RSL* 80). When the ferry docks, Silas's callow obtuseness grows portentous. While he watches Penelope, the source of so much future discord, he imagines an "impending calamity" on the pier "as if it could not possibly include him" (*RSL* 81).

At the Corey dinner, the precise center of the book, his libidinous immaturity reaches a peak of expression, and comes into collision with the reality principle, Proper Boston. His anxiety beforehand resembles the "mounting panic" of Susanne Langer's "caveman" before "the toils" of civilization—the essence of manners' comedy.[16] Nothing illustrates this better than Silas's anguish about his gloves, and the final image of his huge, hairy hands trussed up like "canvassed hams" (*RSL* 188) before the party. During the first half of the dinner, his terror effectively obliterates his personality. He cannot "hold up his end of the line" (*RSL* 196) and relapses into torpid silence. However, as he drinks and eats "everything" (*RSL* 199), his fear dissolves, destroying his reserves. Recalling that inebriation and gluttony signalled licentiousness to Victorian Americans, Silas's after dinner performance is freighted with implied sexuality. In one condensed period, he narcissistically touts his horse, house, paint, money, and Tom Corey, and crows over his "charity" (*RSL* 293), Jim Millon. "Profoundly flattered" (*RSL* 202) by the attention, he describes Millon's sacrifice for him, conscious only of "having talked very well" (*RSL* 204). The other three strands of his untamed, primitive libido also converge in his drunken monologue. Greedily securing "the talk altogether to himself" (*RSL* 205), he aggressively hammers his chair, goads Corey about his loss of four hundred dollars, and assures Mr. Sewell he has "more money than he [knows] what to do with" (*RSL* 206). But the end of Silas's psychic "letting out" is the same as his anxious "holding in" earlier; when he steps in the cab after his "supreme triumph," he feels suffocated, his tongue "stop[s]" (*RSL* 207), and he sinks into unconsciousness.

The dinner party marks a turning point in Silas's affairs. The phallic swelling, pounding, seizing, and spending cease and reverse. He begins a descent back into the hole from which the paint sprang—the disorganized irrational subconscious—and the predominant imagery changes to deflation, flaccidity, slippage, and contraction. Psychosexually, his ordeal corresponds to a maturity trial, a passage through primal chaos to self-integration.

Irene's and Penelope's erotic crisis foreshadows and prepares him for his own. After his overatonement to Tom for his drunkenness he learns about the romantic misunderstanding and his chastening-in-miniature begins. During his daughters' ordeals, Silas suffers a forecast of what will befall him in the second half of the novel. His horse has an accident, he hears that Irene will "never live in" (*RSL* 245) his new house, and his bearing sags so badly that the druggist presciently thinks the sleep potion is for him. The predicament, he says, "is a perfect snarl" (*RSL* 259), like the tangle that will soon enmesh him. Without equating his semirobbery of Rogers with Penelope's, of her sister's, he assures her with an ominous lack of self-application that she "hasn't stolen anything" and that "whatever [she's] got belongs to [her]" (*RSL* 252).

Rogers, like the repressed unconscious itself, though, comes back to haunt Silas and pursues him back to the hole. If he is a devil figure, as Richard Coana suggests,[17] he is a Mephistophelean version, a "spirit that negates,"[18] a nonvital principle, who avenges Silas's exuberant, regressive sexuality. He bleeds him (*RSL* 274)—to use Silas's term—of his very life essence. As soon as he reappears, images of entrapment, suffocation, curtailment, shrinkage, and flaccidity accrue. Telling Persis that he "can take care of [himself]" (*RSL* 262, 284), he embarks alone on his slow, tedious downward passage. His initial aggressive defenses, his threats of "squeezing" (*RSL* 261) Rogers, gradually erode. With a "drownin' man's grip" (*RSL* 272) on him, Rogers leads him to an underworld that is the reverse image of his former one. Instead of expanding, his paint and money begin an "awful shrinkage" (*RSL* 272), and he withdraws, morose and humiliated, to "his own den" (*RSL* 283). He rejects the food he had gorged before (*RSL* 276, 288), his posture and features flag ((*RSL* 289, 309, 310), his mare breaks down, and the "net" (*RSL* 307) steadily closes about him.

As the meshes tighten, he confronts the underside of his charitable devotion to Jim Millon. Seen in the light of Howells's condemnation of charity,[19] Silas's encounter with the drunken Moll Millon represents the "debauch[ing]" (*RSL* 241) effects of self-sacrifice that Sewell warned him about.[20] In any case, what filled him with vanity at the Corey dinner, now transports him downward to the most sordid recesses of alcoholism. From this, he is cast upon the necessity of selling his house and enters the "depths of gloom" (*RSL* 310). Afraid of proving he was a "fool in some way" (*RSL* 308), he turns into a true "fool"—the embodiment of the powers of unreason.[21] Against his better judgment, he resists the sale of his "pride and glory" (*RSL* 310) and goes to Beacon Street where he indulges in one last bout of infantilism. He inhales "the peculiar odor of his own paint" (*RSL* 311), impulsively lights a fire in the fireplace, and decides—in a spasm of greed—that he can't part with the house. Among other things fire is a standard emblem of libido;[22] therefore, as it builds, Silas "lets out" more and more. He angrily challenges a policeman who mistakes him for a tramp, exults in his fantasized preeminence, and consigns the buyers "to the devil" (*RSL* 312). He achieves the same "perfect success" (*RSL* 311) of the dinner party and the result is identical: annihilation. With the house, which is reduced to a human skull in the flames, Silas is physically eviscerated by the fire. Still, broken as he is, he persists in his regression and, like a "perversely proud and obstinate child" (*RSL* 316), tries to save himself by buying out the West Virginia company.

When this fails, he finds himself "driven to the wall" and faced with his severest test. His narcissism wounded, aware that "he was not so rich and not so wise as he had seemed" (*RSL* 319), he begins his deepest descent. His moorings start to drift, and he follows the sinister Rogers through the night to an amoral subworld where the Englishmen tempt him with their unethical offer. He responds in the archetypal way of the sexual initiate: he refuses the alcohol he had consumed so voraciously before, and barricades himself alone in his study without wife or family, for an all night vigil. Surmounting his narcissism, "swallowing" his "self-pity" (*RSL* 329), he wrestles with his tempter, the demonic, until daybreak. Afterwards, after the railroad squeezes him out, [23] he can at last "feel like a thief" (*RSL* 332) towards Rogers. But he does not emerge victorious from his *rite de passage*. Unlike the classic pattern of growth from "savagery" through chaos to an integrated body and mind, he comes out physically defeated if spiritually redeemed. A reversal has taken place; the dissociation remains. He has incorporated a civilized, adult conscience at the expense of his body; his "spring" has weakened, his "animal strength," ebbed (*RSL* 349). He returns to the ground of childhood without surmounting division or attaining full psychosexual maturity. Although he overcomes his narcissism, greed, aggression, and extravagance, he loses his fleshly vitality and appropriately moves into a "plain" house without central heating or "luxuries . . . [except] . . . statues of Prayer and Faith" (*RSL* 363). All that remains of his paint is the monogamic Persis Brand, pursued on a "smaller scale" (*RSL* 354). He bows to the next generation, and exchanges his horse for a frisky "immature" colt behind which he drives a buggy "long past its prime" (*RSL* 363). As he tells Sewell, he has "crept" out of the hole (*RSL* 365). If he attains "manhood" (*RSL* 359) through his ethical rise, it is a partial, disembodied manhood, bought at too high a price. This very likely is what Howells meant in his synopsis, when he emphasized that Silas "*does not recover*"[24] from his bankruptcy.

The openly sexual "stories" in the novel repeat and elucidate the covert libidinal themes in Silas's. Persis, Irene, and Penelope each offer specific erotic examples of his sins and pass through the same maturity ordeals. Nor are they any more successful, despite the sexual ethic Mr. Sewell provides. Although Persis seems to be Silas's exact opposite, as wholly superego as he is id, she, too, falls prey to the very greed and foolishness she accuses him of. Her earthy remark about getting remarried if Silas were killed in the war, and the richness of her Brand, suggest an innate warmbloodedness. However, with her husband's material rise, she has become dissociated like him; her bodily life, severed from her moral life; her conscience, hypertrophied and hidebound. She warns Silas that he is "greedy" (*RSL* 47), that he is "bewitched" and "los[ing] his head" (*RSL* 129), but through her over-control, she is ambushed by these same lower impulses.

After inspiring his ruinous, surplus atonement to Rogers, her virtue begins to play "her false" (*RSL* 334). Her sexual greed, the destructive lust for possession in Eros, starts to build as soon as she sees the mysterious "Mrs. M" on a scrap of paper. While her moral sermons mount, she oscillates between bitter suspicion and "sweet[ness]" (*RSL* 299) until her conscience reaches a pitch of severity during Silas's crisis, and she breaks down. As the immature, tyrannical superego always does, it reduces her to "helpless[ness]" (*RSL* 329) and exposes her to the influx of real evil. Trying for still higher virtuousness, she goes to Silas's office to atone, sees Zerilla, and is engulfed by jealousy. She herself plays the fool. Unable to "fight the madness off," she succumbs to the forces of unreason, and becomes so "demoniacal[ly]"[25] (*RSL* 377) possessed that she reels and faints. During her seizure, she plumes herself on her worth and lusts for revenge, tapping the veins of narcissism and aggression in her own psyche. When she discovers her mistake, she enters the deepest level of her ordeal and wrestles with "shame and self-reproach" (*RSL* 342) in her darkened, shuttered room.

Yet, despite her chastening, her initiation is no more satisfactory than Silas's. Although she and Silas return to "their old united life" (*RSL* 351), she cannot help relapsing into her former severity. Back in Lapham, her "satisfaction [is] not so constant" (*RSL* 362). She lectures Silas about his former prodigality, and with a hint of still-unresolved jealousy, jibes that if he'd treated his paint as well as he treated the Millon women, he'd never have been ruined.

Irene, Silas's beautiful, headstrong daughter, sexually dramatizes his egotism and recklessness. High-pulsed like him, she has his red hair and a complexion that radiates her sensuality: "There is no word," says the narrator for her coloring, "but delicious . . . the tints of her cheeks and temples were such as suggest May-flowers and apple blossoms and peaches" (*RSL* 52). With her father, though, she is psycho-sexually dissociated and immature. Throughout she is called a "child" (*RSL* 27, 124, 235), and Bromfield Corey equates her with savages: girls like Irene, he exclaims, "ought to have been clothed in the skins of wild beasts and gone about barefoot with clubs over their shoulders" (*RSL* 117).

In her pursuit of his son, Tom, she supports the Victorian association of savages with unregulated passion. On the slim evidence of a newspaper clipping, she deduces his interest in her, and rashly sets her cap on him. That her infatuation is largely hormonal, Howells insinuates through her choice of Tom's attractions. After she sees him at the building site, she ticks off all of his bodily endowments for her sister's admiration, dwelling particularly on his nose, his phallic icon. With Tom she is equally physical and precipitant. During the famous pine shaving scene, she first maneuvers him onto a trestle beside her; then mimes the act of intercourse, taking the masculine role with her parasol, while Tom passively holds the wood curls in place.

Besides embodying her father's extravagance in her love affair, she sexually mirrors his egotism as well. Although the introductory chapters insist that she is not conscious of her beauty, the image of her before her looking glass runs like a Narcissus leitmotif through the book (*RSL* 59, 86, 123, 185). She devotes herself exclusively to preening and identifies with the arch-narcissist, Rosamond Vincy of *Middlemarch*, whom Howells accused of "deadly and deadening egotism."[26] So self-absorbed is she that she doesn't notice Tom's unresponsiveness, and after his visit to Nantasket, in which he talks about her sister all night, she congratulates herself on the "splendid call," and selfishly pushes Penelope's "things aside on the dressing case to rest her elbow and talk at ease" (*RSL* 153).

Both her immoderacy and narcissism come to a head at the Corey dinner. When she makes her eye-stopping entrance, she beams with the "knowledge of success" (*RSL* 188) and reigns in "triumph" (*RSL* 196) through the meal, unaware that she has not met Boston's sartorial or conversational standards. Self-intoxicated, she, too, believes it was a "perfect time" (*RSL* 207). At a fever pitch of passion the next day, begging for flattery, and "giv[ing] [her]self up" (*RSL* 232) to her imaginary romance, she encounters the same end of instinctual uncontrol as Silas. She learns the tragic news that Tom loves Penelope, and grows suddenly inanimate. Her floral complexion turns "snow-white" (*RSL* 240); her feelings, rock-like; her voice, icy. After her first angry thrust at Penelope, she locks herself in the kitchen, and paces out her agony like her father. Her parents comment that it is as though someone "died" (*RSL* 248) in the house. Her ritual death, however, brings only partial rebirth. Although she returns from Lapham (the source of her being) with new altruism and self-discipline, she has acquired "the cutting edge of iron" (*RSL* 347) and the accents of an "old maid" (*RSL* 344). For her spiritual salvation, she has sacrificed her sexuality, which, like her beauty was "very great" (*RSL* 52). "It had been a life and death struggle with her; she had conquered, but she had also necessarily lost much. Perhaps what she had lost was not worth keeping; but at any rate she had lost it" (*RSL* 347).

Penelope provides a subtler, but no less dramatic sexual expression of Silas's sins. Secretly, "sly[ly]" (to use Mrs. Corey's term [*RSL* 169]), she "squeezes" Irene, just as her father squeezes Rogers. The dark, competitive underside of Eros, the aggressive propensities Silas releases on the Milldam, Penelope vents on her sister through her "innocuous" funning. Warmblooded like the rest of her family, with her husky voice,[27] brunette coloring, and demonstrative gestures, she is also immature and dissociated. If Irene illustrates the classic id-tyranny of adolescence, Penelope exemplifies the second maladjustment—the displacement of the impulses into self-betterment.[28] Unaware of her sexual feelings, she expresses them semiconsciously through Freud's favorite defense mechanism, humor. Her comedy is not only another measure of her sexual élan; it is also a veiled, legitimate outlet for her rivalry with her sister and attraction to Tom. Her incessant teasing teeters on the edge of sadism, as the "cat and mouse" scene with Irene demonstrates. After Tom pays a surprise visit, she dangles the fact in front of her, snatches it away, and threatens to entertain Corey herself while her sister, "the mouse, moaned and writhed upon the bed" (*RSL* 85). On two other occasions, she jokes, only half-humorously, that she is edging her out with Tom (*RSL* 86, 121).

During his calls, she enacts this tabooed wish in the subtlest, most imperceptible way. Instead of promoting her sister, Penelope upstages her, through the same strategy of comedy. When she first meets Tom, she makes a jest so that he "looked at her" (*RSL* 52), and she serenades him later at Nantasket with her wit and charm. While the three sit in the moonlight (always a dangerous omen in Howells's love stories), she leans forward and "croon[s]" to him, softly "clucking" as he laughs, and "funning" until he reels away "fascinate[ed]" (*RSL* 133–34).

Concealed in the text are clues that point to Penelope's half-knowledge of her "squeezing." When her mother asks her if Tom loves Irene, she cannot meet her eyes, and replies acidly that he should perhaps find out whether her sister can "interest him alone" (*RSL* 151). Mrs. Corey's visit, as well, throws her into a suspiciously excited state. However, with a willed blindness to her impulses, she brags like Silas: "*I* don't intend to do anything wrong; but if I do, I promise not to be sorry for it" (*RSL* 148).

Tom's visit after the dinner party triggers Penelope's boldest, most blatant seduction attempt. She ties a coquettish red ribbon on her throat, and escorts him to a "cozier" room (*RSL* 215), where she sits beneath him on a low stool in a flattering drop light. Her first joke, aimed at his missing her, is succeeded by a series of provocative maneuvers: she blushes at the sight of his hat, laughs wildly, flirts her fan, and as much as forces his love-confession. She asks him how she should reform, which predictably prompts his declaration and her self-awakening. All of her passion for Tom—so long buried and subversively expressed—suddenly surges up, and she faces her underself. She turns "white" though the blood rushes "to her heart," and she springs away despite her "potential complicity" (*RSL* 220). She afterwards exaggerates what she had suppressed before, and dismisses Tom in a crescendo of contradiction: she forbids him to see her, seizing him in a tight embrace.

The ordeal that follows duplicates those of her family. She retreats without food to her darkened room and toils until daybreak with her demon, the repressed unconscious. Instead of integrating and mastering it, though, she segments herself further by adopting a suprapunitive infantile superego. At the same time that she admits her pursuit of Tom and resentment of Irene, she decides to punish herself and begins to rave about self-sacrifice. Her inner fragmentation worsens, until she regresses into a "fool" (*RSL* 230, 257, 307)—the soul of incoherence. She grows emotionally labile, redoubles her pleas for martyrdom, and feeling pushed against the "wall" (*RSL* 256) like Silas, thinks she is going "crazy" (*RSL* 255). Only when she awakens to her father's cries does she recognize—in unison with his confessions and in the same language,[29] that she has been at fault—an egotistical martyr.

Yet, despite her recognition, her passage to maturity is only minimally more successful than the others. She cannot wholly incorporate her libido into her adult identity. When she meets Tom's parents a year later, she behaves with "piteous distraction" (*RSL* 348) instead of her old pluck, and seems no nearer the resolution of her conflict. During her final interview with Tom, she vacillates between acceptance and self-repudiation until she takes him in a fit of indecision. By default, she chooses Sewell's "economy of pain" (*RSL* 241), the less punitive morality, but still does not fully recover. It is true that her humor (a gauge of her sexuality) is enough intact after a week with Tom's parents for her to quip that she won't "feel strange among the

Mexicans" (*RSL* 296). And she has also achieved enough intimacy with Tom to be honest emotionally. But in the final frame, as they drive off to Mexico, she has been psychically unhinged by his family. Neither able to accept their genteel ethic nor reach an integrated one of her own, she weeps on Tom's shoulder, and lets her competitiveness flare one last time. Explaining her tears, she whimpers "I only meant I should have you all to myself" (*RSL* 361).

It is at this point that the narrator makes the famous observation about the price of civilization being "too much" (*RSL* 361). Each of the Laphams has been unable to pleasurably assimilate value with passion; each has been libidinally lamed by "conscience," each left—fundamentally "normal" as they are—immature and dissociated. If their unmonitored passions lead to the Victorian "house of death," their mature accommodations are Victorian, too: they "kill" their sexual energy through overrepression. This was the dilemma Howells dramatized more drastically in *A Modern Instance* two years before. The Hubbards' lawless sexuality leads to untimely "deaths," while the surrounding society reflects the lethal effects of orthodox morality. The Boston the Laphams confront is also deadeningly suppressive, an "airy . . . graceful superstructure" (*RSL* 138), with the spirit attenuated to bloodless heights; the flesh condemned underground. The Corey women—the thin, chill Lilly, satirical Nanny, and their snobbish mother—epitomize this genteel norm. The daughters languish without men in a resort called Mt. Desert, and Mrs. Corey, a "block of Wenham ice" (*RSL* 128), stalks through the novel brandishing "decency" (*RSL* 266) and relegating love (her own included) to "nonsense" (*RSL* 128).

But, unlike *A Modern Instance*, there are gleams of potential relief within society. They are faint, flickering, and form no consistent pattern. They do, though, mark a departure in Howells's "love stories," a turn, albeit tentative, toward hope and amelioration. Bromfield Corey, for instance, seems at first to be another Atherton, a sybarite, who shudders at the "lower" passions from his comfortable eminence. Yet his is the wholly different perspective[30] of a transplanted Italian-American—cosmopolitan, loose-jointed, and sensuous. He buys an apple for the pleasure of holding it, and temperately advocates second marriages and a hedonistic solution of the love triangle. Nonpuritanically, pragmatically, he advises: "practically the human affections . . . reconcile themselves to any situation that the human sentiments condemn" (*RSL* 267). In the last analysis, of course, he comes down on

his wife's side, and draws off from the Laphams' "savageries" with pa-
trician disdain. He does, however, throw off sparks of sexual promise,
suggestions of redemption.

Mr. Sewell provides another positive glimmer. He not only repudi-
ates the surplus repression of Proper Boston; he offers a nonpunitive
alternative. To the shock of the assembled guests at Corey's dinner
party, he opens fire on sentimental prudery, attacking the swollen love
"ideal" and sick self-sacrifice of such novels as *Tears Idle Tears*. Later
when the Laphams consult him about their daughters, he extends his
condemnation of sacrifice into a positive theory. To suffer more pain
than is necessary, to suprarepress for the sake of "virtue," both "be
fool[s] and [pre-Freudianly seizing the connection between prurience
and prudery] debauch[es]" (*RSL* 241). Instead, he counsels common
sense, moderation, and an ethic of the least possible denial. Although
Silas and Penelope seem to take this course during their crises,[31] neither can effectively apply it intrapsychically. At the end, their libido
have both suffered immoderately; they have not been able to comfort-
ably meld heart and head. While Sewell, then, supplies a plausible
theoretical solution, it remains theoretical and incapable of demonstration. This is perhaps what Persis means when she exclaims after
they have left his study: "Yes, he talked sense," but she added bitterly
"I guess, if he had it to *do*!" (*RSL* 243).

The real "hope" of the novel centers on Tom Corey. "Sweet" (*RSL*
127), prudent, and moderate, he embodies Sewell's sober ethic, while
at the same time, exhibiting Silas's libidinous élan. He recapitulates
Silas's career, investing it with affirmation and renewal. He is the inspiration of Howells's note in his savings bank diary: "The young
trees growing out of the fallen logs in the forest—the new life out of
the old."[32] In striking contrast to rigid, sterile Boston, Tom is warm
and virile, an *homme sensuel* whose stylish clothes seem to "peel away"
(*RSL* 60) from his body and whose prominent nose, so pointedly emphasized, advertises his phallic drive. Unlike his mother who restrains
the corseted Silas on the way to dinner, Tom, with his easy physicality, pulls a chair closer to him when they meet, and doffs his jacket.
Silas's "instant pleasure" (*RSL* 73) at this highlights their compatibility, and, in fact, Tom bears a marked likeness to his mentor. Like him,
he has sought a fortune in Texas and returned home a prodigal (*RSL*
63), and is energetic, decent, and innovative. However, he corrects
Silas's tragic flaws. Free of narcissism, he is not interested in "shin-
[ing]" (*RSL* 127) and supplies "prudence" (*RSL* 118) for rashness

When Silas says his paint is the "best in God's universe," Tom quickly amends it to "the best on the market" (*RSL* 76). Having "nothing predatory" (*RSL* 70) in his nature, he takes a dim interest in Silas's aggressive driving on the Milldam, and is so lacking in greed that he offers to work for nothing.

On the other hand, he is not without faults, chief of which is his innocence. The same sexual naiveté that makes him recoil in disbelief from Walker's hint of a liaison between Silas and Zerilla, plagues his courtship of Penelope and helps promote the triangle tangle. By densely overlooking Irene's infatuation (to the point of assuring his parents that she is "transparent" [*RSL* 159]), by "dangl[ing]" (*RSL* 160) after Penelope and sanctioning the dinner party, he assures the tragic dénouement.

His erotic immaturity, though, comes in for a ritual harrowing. In miniature, and on a lower frequency, he repeats Silas's night passage. After the dinner party debacle, he is overwhelmed by his repressed, irrational self, his own impulses to "shine," and struggles with his snobbishness through the night. For three hours, he paces up and down, his pride "wounded" (*RSL* 211) like Silas's, his "savage" propensities rioting within him. Before his "chaos" (*RSL* 212) ends, he also finds himself psychically trapped, combating a "blight" he can't "escape" (*RSL* 264).

Of all the *rites de passage*, Tom's is the most superficially successful. He surmounts his prejudice through an inner, moral "girl's voice" (*RSL* 212), faithfully meets Penelope's tests, and gains courage from his trial. "I'm not afraid, and I'm not guilty" (*RSL* 256), he is able to say afterwards. As Silas sinks towards his material ruin, Tom's material-sexual rise begins: "a broad light of hope flashed upon him. It came from Lapham's potential ruin" (*RSL* 272). Yet, he remains disturbingly naive, portending difficulties for his future, and perpetuating his psychosexual immaturity. Almost as imperceptive as before, he mistakes Penelope's masochistic histrionics for "nobility" (*RSL* 345), and fatuously, "less judicially" (*RSL* 356) assures her that she and his mother will be friends. When she collapses on his neck after a grueling week in his home, he cannot imagine what is wrong and begins his married life with a "puzzled smile." As they head off to Mexico, the narrator comments: "[He] ought to have known better" (*RSL* 361). He is, then, an embryonic hero, at best, the core (as his name suggests) rather than the fruit of erotic hope. Despite his positive recapitulation of Silas's career, despite the apparent union of opposites in his personality—sweetness and force, sense and sensuality—he is still a boy, the colt behind Silas's buggy "which [has] not yet come of age" (*RSL* 363).

Of Howells's novels, *The Rise of Silas Lapham* was uniquely autobiographical.[33] He told Henry James that he had used "all of his experiences down to the quick,"[34] and the writing grew so intense that he suffered a breakdown somewhere in the middle of the book. Suddenly, with no apparent reason "the bottom dropped out."[35] It is generally believed that the novel represented a crucial juncture in his career, an ethical-sociological moment of reckoning. Having just moved to the water side of Beacon, the argument runs,[36] Howells faced a critical, ultimately debilitating conflict between Proper Boston and his social conscience, a contest that ended in the next decade in favor of his conscience. However, the sexual subtext suggests that the conflict went much deeper, beyond the moral question to the neurosis at the crux of his personality.[37] This neurosis involved the psychosexual tug of war, the love and terror of the flesh, that caused three breakdowns in his youth and sporadic, milder relapses throughout his life. The tense prudery of his early prose was the visible scar. Yet, beneath the overt squeamishness was an aggressive exploration of sexuality—his conflict especially—via his fiction. According to Ernst Kris and others, creative work has the advantage of providing access to unconscious tensions while simultaneously permitting ego control and the possibility of resolution.[38] Through the oblique route of narrative art, then, Howells imaginatively revived his neurotic difficulty over and over, gradually unknotting it.

Silas Lapham both illumines the difficulty more clearly than his previous novels and registers a breakthrough. The Laphams, named significantly for a family in Howells's first hometown,[39] are a locus of his intrapsychic tension. Embodying the instinctual attraction and fear, they are equally sensuous and self-destructive. Their "tremendously good" (*RSL* 99) living, country informality, and "funning" duplicate Howells's own boyhood home, and Irene's coloring, mirrors his earliest memory of beauty. "All his [the author's] life," he recalls in *A Boy's Town*, "he has never seen a peach tree in bloom without a swelling of the heart, without some fleeting sense that 'Heaven lies about us in our infancy'" (*BT* 7). But Silas most intimately registers the sensuous pleasure of his youth. The childhood idyll Silas paints for Bartley—the barefoot country rambles, the mother who doted on him, the kind father—echoes, sometimes verbatim, Howells's reminiscences of his Ohio boy-life.

But if Silas and his family contain the pleasure-pull of his psyche, they also project the competing terror with that gratification. Their infantile, lawless libido leads them to the very horrors that haunted Howells during his breakdowns: "death," darkness, insanity, vertigo, and suffocation.[40] Again, Silas captures the sex fear in an intensely autobiographical way. He is a composite of the bad boy self in *A Boy's Town*—egotistical, acquisitive, combative, and extravagantly un-curbed—and he experiences Howells's neurotic symptoms most acutely. Before they assail him, at the floodtide of his "savagery" at the dinner party, Howells is supposed to have suffered his "vastation."[41] Since the party is the pivotal point in the book, when libidinal excess and the available ethical options meet head-on for the first time, this is a tempting hypothesis. There, the Corey women are at their frigid worst, and the other guests, still without their redemptive proposals. Bromfield Corey's armchair liberalities wilt under the prospect of damage to his possessions, Tom fades into snobbish passivity, and Mr. Sewell provides only negative criticisms of sentimentality, rather than a positive alternative. There are, then, no viable ethical checks to con-tain Silas's runaway instinctuality, no ego controls to prevent a resur-gence of the conflict Howells had tapped so directly. When the bot-tom began to drop out for Silas, when Rogers got his "drownin' man's grip" on him, the bottom may also have dropped out for Howells,[42] and plunged him back in his old, asphyxiating, terrible neurosis.

If something like this did happen, as it had happened before in *A Modern Instance*, the rest of the novel signals a psychic as well as an artistic advance. He was able to strike a partial accord with his demon, to bring up from his "vastation" the materials for a compromise be-tween the engulfing fear and secret ambition for pleasure. Although Sewell's nonpunitive ethos cannot be implemented, although Brom-field's insights are dilletantish, Tom is still a naif at the end. Howells had found the raw data of a sexual affirmation. Out of Silas's psycho-sexual and financial destruction, which the age and Howells's exces-sive qualms demanded, arise the shoots, the "young trees" of a new stage in the resolution of his neurosis.

It is perhaps such a deep, inner shift rather than a sociopolitical or esthetic change of heart which prompted the upheavals of the next dec-ade. Ironically, just when Howells moved to his Beacon Street home, he began to drift away from the dominant beliefs of the society he had been so anxious to join. The submerged longing for equality, modera-tion, and gratification apparently broke into his Boston idyl in the same way that the sexual theme had unexpectedly taken over his business novel. He turned to Christian socialism and realism—effectively alienating himself from the "right people." To be sure, the break was not entirely clean and a prudery seeps into his early realism credos, as though his critical thinking had not caught up with his imaginative discoveries. But his allegiance to the "red tides of reality"[43] had been released in *The Rise of Silas Lapham*, never to be completely suppressed again.

An attractive hypothesis is that the low visibility of the sexual themes permitted this germination, allowing room for growth outside the glare of a primary love story. In any case, his gains become consolidated in the next major erotic novel. Strengthened by realism and inspired by Tolstoy, he fashioned an ethic in *April Hopes*, which solidified the hypotheses of 1885, all the while continuing the investigation of the demonic. The characters grow even more "average"; their interlocking sexual problems, more extensive; Sewell and Bromfield, erotically reliable; and Penelope and Tom, *almost* mature: integrated, temperate, easygoing, sensuous, and (appropriating Tom's "girl's voice" and Penelope's husky one) slightly androgynous. Eventually the lovers will not have to flee to Mexico for a real "marriage" nor Silas return to his bodily origins without incorporating joy into conscience.

Here, though, the tonic note is still, psychosexually speaking, failure. Despite the affirmative germs embedded in the book, the society remains bound to an infantile, severe, sentimentally corrupted superego; the Laphams remain dissociated, and Tom and Penelope, imperfectly happy and developed. After all the maturity passages through disequilibrium, darkness, entrapment, and psychic chaos, none of the characters have achieved an associated, adult sexuality.

But if a sexual reading sees the novel in a less optimistic light,[44] it also enhances the artistry and exposes the inner design. The incidents are both more closely woven—with the subplots repeating the libidinal shades in Silas's story in primary colors—and more profoundly autobiographical than has been realized. Beyond the level of sexual reference in the book lies a deeper stratum that reveals Howells's neurotic conflict and suggests a transition in his "cure."

An examination of the sexual subtext also helps explain the reaction of Howells's contemporaries. With a symbolic vocabulary drawn from literary tradition, nineteenth-century euphemisms, and his own innovations, he infused the novel with a distinct, palpable sexuality. Yet what seems to have disturbed his readers as much as this linguistic dimension, was his incipient ethic. Shocked and puzzled, they targeted the germs of his sexual synthesis for special abuse. The primitive Laphams were uninspirational, they protested, Penelope, "unnatural"; Tom, "extremely tepid"; and the whole moral drift, "not elevating, degrad[ing]."[45]

As the Folletts have said, the novel was preeminently a "drama of transitions,"[46] a moment of departure from the orthodox culture. Perhaps sensing this, Booth Tarkington ended his introduction to the centennial edition with a tributue to Howells, the "iconoclast . . . who pulled down a thing not merely to pull down; [but to] . . . set up a better."[47] With *The Rise of Silas Lapham*, he had begun pulling down the edifice of suprarepression, and had started assembling the building blocks of a new positive morality that would not require the Laphams and newlyweds to "rise" so high, that promised a moderate, mature Eros, midway between "letting out" and holding in, between savagery and Victorian civilization.

April Hopes (1888) is another novel about two sexually undisciplined, incompatible lovers who make a tragic match. Like Marcia and Bartley Hubbard, they are polar Darwinian opposites, a possessive monogamist and an expansive polygamist, who bring misery to themselves and others through their ill-starred marriage. But there are important changes. In *A Modern Instance* the mood was critical. The Hubbards' sexual excess led to dissolution and death; the respectable mores proved death-directed, and an unintegrated, contradictory subtext of pleasure divided and destroyed the final "meaning."[1]

With *April Hopes*, however, the crisis lifts and the ambivalence resolves. After the partial breakthrough in *The Rise of Silas Lapham* and the "black time"[2] of the late eighties, Howells effected a major realignment in his sexual theme. Ego and id strike a compromise. The pleasure that his imagination had been trying to reclaim achieves a tentative, partial union with morality. The tension relaxes. A less drastic and more temperate vision of sexuality emerges. Undiscipline does not doom the lovers to degeneracy and death. Instead, passion is a volatile impulse, whose negative powers are freely chosen and nonfatal. Alice and Dan oscillate in their mixed desire for each other, and sentence themselves to a death that is only a death to life's possibilities.

By the same token, the society seems less bound to unconscious service of the death instinct. There are gleams of value and a "distinct"[3] villain. What had been implied in *A Modern Instance* and *Silas Lapham* becomes overt. Orthodox prudery is the agent of destructive sexuality. All of the evils in intemperance, all of the "savage" appetites, breed and multiply under the rule of genteel repression. On the other hand, a rudimentary, positive Eros takes root in the unconventional world. The "outsiders" in the book contribute the beginnings of a sexual ethic that brings reason and goodness into a relaxed accord with the truths of the body. Their chief emphases, like Mr. Sewell's, are negative, and they are unable to implement their principles, but they form the firm baseline of a nonrepressive morality in the novel. They accomplish a detente between gratification and the "higher" values. While they counsel selflessness, compatibility, and moderation, they provide a heroine who begins to assimilate the pleasurable impulses. Julia Anderson has Mrs. Farrell's bohemian élan, beauty, charm, and sensuality and *almost* succeeds in ethically integrating them. When the lovers, then, finally damn themselves to one another, there is a stable plane of erotic value beneath the ironic reductions. Howells had found a temporary equilibrium, a reprieve from strife and divorce.

The tumultuous years following *A Modern Instance* brought him to this new plateau in his sexual theme. Toughened by the "realism war," inspired by Tolstoy, and sensitized by personal suffering, he was able to break openly with respectability and move to an alternative sexual morality. In 1886, after weathering the criticism surrounding his *ballon d'essai*, *The Rise of Silas Lapham*, he started his "Editor's Study" in *Harper's* and launched his famous defenses of realism. The resulting warfare cemented his aversion to the genteel establishment, moderated his drastic sexual vision, and directed him to the sources of his ethic. Within the realist philosophy was an underlying allegiance to the flesh[4] and to the average ranges of experience that repudiated the extreme negative sexuality of *A Modern Instance*. At the same time, its democratic sympathies pointed him back to the lenient Middle West—the wellspring of his sexual value.[5]

Tolstoy solidified the revolt against "respectability" which had been latent in Lapham's drama and strengthened by the critical battles of the eighties. His teaching, which affected Howells like an "old-fashioned religious experience,"[6] indicted the lasciviousness of civilized society and espoused, instead, an unconventional humanism similar to Swedenborg's.[7] The selflessness, complicity, and equality of his ethic in *April Hopes* are Tolstoyan, but its relaxed sexuality reflects a reaction against his asceticism. Just as Zola's prudery indirectly steered Howells away from suprarepression, Tolstoy's fanaticism fostered Howells's amelioration of sexuality. In his criticism he labeled Tolstoy's obsession with purity, "good gone wild."[8] Both in the transfer of sexual destructiveness to the orthodox world, then, and in the formation of his ethic, Tolstoy was instrumental. He gave him, as Howells summed it up later, the "heart to hope" (*MLP* 188).

Paradoxically, the personal tragedy that ought to have deepened the pessimistic stranglehold of *A Modern Instance* worked to release it. His

daughter's hopeless and tantalizing disease, worsened by the severe an-
tidotes of the age, secured his distrust of official solutions and pushed
him to seek new ones. The need for remedies became urgent. Possibly, too, his suffering highlighted the folly of surplus repression and
recalled him to his temperate origins. The "impenetrable darkness" of
tragedy, he once said, demands "a play of sunshine."[9] At this "black
time" in his life, his imagination may have demanded a compromise
with pleasure, and Tolstoy and his realism war supplied a temporary
answer.

During Dan's and Alice's romance, the same negative truths that
accompanied Bartley's and Marcia's *mésalliance* unfold. Sadomasochism, narcissism, and promiscuity fill their benighted courtship until
they, too, regress into childishness, psychic disintegration, sterility,
and death. But these truths now take on a more complex and insidious
expression. Instead of a slow, downward spiral to death, their undisciplined libido leads them on a zigzag path to a proximal, "realistic"
ruin. Their characters are less flawed, their self-direction greater, and
the evils in their relationship, muted and variable. Savageries alter-
nate with decencies, pain with pleasure, regression with glimpses of
maturity.

What makes the destructive forces an even subtler presence in the
text is the fact that they are part and parcel of the society's "highest"
values. The implied connection between prurience and genteel puritanism in the earlier novels becomes explicit. Rather than existing outside proper Boston, as the Hubbards and Laphams do, Alice and Dan
are part of it and indulge their fatal impulses through its express sanction and encouragement. Moreover, the frigidity which obliquely af-
fects previous heroines is now the direct result of sentimentality: like
an archtease, the respectable sublimations foster sexual excess but
deny gratification. While a hormonal whirlwind sweeps Marcia and
Bartley to their doom, an intricate combination of culture, appetite,
and imperceptible evil draws Alice and Dan to their mundanely lethal
marriage. Because of this increased sexual difficulty and their greater
control over it, their story ends where the Hubbards' begins. Theirs is
a drama about a fate they might have avoided. They are "fools" of a
more highly evolved order—less easily and thoroughly duped.

The chief "fool" is Dan Mavering. His shuttle-like movements in
and out of immaturity, in and out of the clutches of the neurotic Alice
and the romanticistic illusions that mask the evils of their affair, create
the primary tension in the book. His career is one long, episodic matu-

rity test. Unlike the heroes of other erotic novels, however, his ordeal is more inward, and he fools himself as much as he is fooled by Alice and the genteel world. In addition, he comes closer to manhood than anyone before him—with an opportunity for salvation literally pressed in his hand—and has the benefit of a ministering band of wise counselors. That he nearly saves himself, that he bamboozles himself, and loses his head in a rash hour, only adds a deeper poignancy to his *rite de passage*.

Howells's distinctive erotic imagery registers this evolution in his sexual theme. Darkness, money, entrapment, hell, and forests still convey negative sexuality, but now they are subtly entwined with respectability. During a genteel picnic in the woods, Dan woos Alice in the deepening fog and high-mindedly alludes to the "Inferno" and Browning's "Gold Hair," in which the heroine buries herself with her gold. The disequilibrium associated with sexual imbalance becomes internal as Dan pitches back and forth on a sea of shifting emotions. By the same token, certain images which were negative or ambivalent before acquire positive meanings. Bartley's desired and feared freedom, and the intoxication, food, and savagery that go with it, are Dan's salvation. The "highs" he feels at home amidst his family's feasts or in Washington surrounded by Blacks are indices of sexual health and maturity. Likewise, the sunshine around the windmill, which diffuses erotic hope in *A Modern Instance*, encircles and defines the belle of "broad daylight" (*AH* 324), Julia Anderson.

Joined to these developments in his erotic idiom was an overall elaboration and enlargement of Howells's sexual artistry. As he read the book, Henry James was overwhelmed by Howells's craftsmanship. "Your literary prowess takes my breath away," he exclaimed, "you write so much and so well. I seem to myself a small brown snail crawling after a glossy antelope." [10] In his old age Howells reread the book and was equally impressed: "I am often amazed at the quality of my stuff." [11]

Three influences were responsible for his high finish: Tolstoy, realism, and his concentrated playwrighting between 1882 and 1886. Tolstoy's techniques may have been too close to his own realistic ones for Howells to have consciously registered their impact, and his remarks on the subject are inconsistent. [12] But the Tolstoy he read while he wrote *April Hopes* is everywhere evident. Permeating the novel is the same "astounding" [13] subtlety he praised to T. S. Perry. Alice's smallest hand movements, like Anna Karenina's, transmit her sexuality; Dan's association with Blacks,[14] like Vronsky's with horses, transmits his; and their tragic future is as delicately foreshadowed. Tolstoy also showed him, through his "psychological eavesdropping"[15] and montaging of private with public scenes, how to render the inner truths of sexuality and the outer ones of complicity. His famous life-likeness, his fidelity to the flux and texture of reality,[16] gave Howells, too, important means of conveying the density and open-endedness of his altered sexual vision.

Realism provided other important ways. Its emphases on veracity and "God-given complexity"[17] added both explicitness and deeper dimensions to his erotic fiction. Dan's and Alice's love scenes reach a high watermark of physical candor, even after they have been toned down for *Harper's*.[18] At the same time, they are richly laminated with somber submeanings. The romantic pieties that inspire the sex play, for instance, expose an unholy alliance of sentimentality with prurience, and the embraces vibrate with evil omens. With the new richness in meaning comes a new and parallel richness in figurative language. Such strikingly original metaphors as photography embody sexual truths and they give off double, even triple meanings. Julia Anderson's apple in the "Judgment of Paris" farce simultaneously evokes discord, temptation, and fertility and suggests the pleasures of sensuous love when she bites it hungrily. Symbols evolve and metamorphose within the text, inverting malignly. The flowers that signify phallic exuberance in the first chapter grow overripe, acquire thorns, and at last emit a cloying, vapid scent. Allusions, too, expand in *April Hopes*. They incorporate all the arts—popular, visual, and literary—and relay intricate, sometimes sinister, messages.

The seven sexual farces Howells wrote after *A Modern Instance* also honed and empowered his erotic art. The lovers' trysts are so pointed, compressed, and beautifully paced they crackle with sexual tension. Whole discussions pivot on a euphemism, and speech disintegrates at times under the pressure of desire. In addition to an increased boldness in dialogue is a concurrent growth in texture. The same surcharged conversations resonate with acid revelations about the lovers. Their endearments betray their fatal incompatibilities; their rapturous promises of self-sacrifice presage the terrible sacrifices ahead; and their debased language dramatizes the "lower" attraction they feel for each other.

Howells, then, came to his fourth and most elaborate tale of undisciplined sex at the full tide of his artistic powers. In the first chapters, the major themes unfold with the momentum of a musical overture. The couples' immaturity, incompatibilities, and their pernicious support from the genteel world all emerge in their introductory meeting, while hints of impending disaster play beneath the surface like a minor motif.

As usual in Howells, the physical appearance of the two protagonists is all-important. Alice is a statuesque brunette with a sharp nose, narrow face, and grey, immobile eyes, who looks like a Louis Quinze portrait, passive and stylish, amidst the graduation celebrations. Dan, by contrast, bursts on the scene in a blaze of motion. Perspiring, laughing, and gesticulating, he introduces himself to the guests with dancing blue eyes and a flash of brilliant white teeth.

Their names, as well, are significant. Alice means noble and Pasmer is the Spanish verb to chill, to frostbite. Dan, on the contrary, is the name of the Assyrian sun god and leader of the tribe that worshipped the golden calf.[19] The maverick overtones in Mavering suggest, as well, his nonconformity and sexual vagrancy. During their preliminary flirtation, these oppositions come into high relief. Alice's hat ribbons tremble in response to Dan's breezy, gregarious attentions, and she seizes his comic bouquet from the class tree (a Harvard version of the phallic maypole) with intense, speechless gravity.

The society's conspiracy in this immature, mismatched romance also surfaces in the opening pages. Although Dan's personality is a complex, largely benign mixture, he has real flaws which are endorsed by his "respectable" environment. His evasiveness and vain passion to please[20] demonstrate his "artistic temperament" (*AH* 34) and the vein in his forehead tells Mrs. Pasmer that he is a "genius" (*AH* 31). Ironically, the book begins with his "genteel" graduation to manhood. Alice's faults, too—intermixed as they are with average amounts of girlishness—receive the express sanction of her proper colleagues. Her snobbish hauteur passes for "repose" (*AH* 46) and her egotistic quixotism for nobility. The assurance her friends give her that she will meet her "fate on Class Day" (*AH* 14) is perhaps the most deadly encouragement of all.

Contained in the prologue of Alice's and Dan's love story are murmurs of difficulties ahead. Do not "bite off more than you can chew" (*AH* 24), a guest warns Dan as he walks off with Alice, and his father jokes about women who get the upper hand in marriage (*AH* 8). The facts that Dan is an avid reader and Alice "very romantic" (*AH* 51) ensure us of their ability to live up to these dark presentiments.

Their romance begins appropriately on the island resort of Campobello. Wrapped in mists (a recurrent "dark" motif of their courtship) and romantic legend, it symbolizes perfectly the prevailing mood of their affair. And, like the sensuality disguised in their lofty sentiments, a savage, tangled forest lies at the center of the island. Ensconced in the resort hotel are the two rival factions in the forthcoming drama: the romanticistic[21] majority, who idolize Alice and supernal love conventions, and the sexual heretics. The nervous spinster, Miss Cotton (whose name evokes the Victorian epithet "cotton-top,"[22] for a respectably dressed loose woman) speaks for the first group and to some extent for the dreamy Alice. At the exact opposite pole are the eccentrics, Mrs. Brinkley and Julia Anderson, both of whom try to salvage Dan with their sane insights.

The Campobello picnic is the scene of his capture. It also brings the lovers' incompatibilities into keener focus and shows how their romantic playacting conceals their differences and promotes their lust. As they perform their sentimental charade, amidst a cloud of evil portents, the Boston vacationers watch with mounting excitement and approval. Significantly, the picnickers drive in a "silvery" (*AH* 81) fog, through a blighted, snarled forest, to their destination and there abandon themselves to "nature" (*AH* 84) on the beach. Reverting to his natural sensuality, Dan launches into a Black song and dance routine, which strikes the first warning note of the day beneath its gay frivolities. Not only does Alice disapprove, but the part she will play in Dan's future appears ominously in his song about a giantess whose footprint leaves a hole in the earth. Afterwards, beneath the fascinated gaze of the guests, they escape to a blueberry patch where they have one of their most intense romantic encounters. Their "poetic" antics during this interlude provide a prime example of the way in which sentimental conventions camouflage and excite their purely hormonal attraction. While Alice plays wood nymph to Dan's Pan—she supine on scented fern, he chivalrically attendant—their *tête-à-tête* grows more and more impassioned. Under the pretext of decorating the blueberries, they engage in one of the most scintillating sexual encounters in Howells's fiction. As Dan holds his blueberry stalks before her, Alice tremblingly binds them with withes of sweet grass until they both flush and laugh uncontrollably.

In the excitement, they ignore the disagreements that punctuate their conversation. Almost like the unrelated crosspatter in a Pinter play, Dan laughs and compares life to a picnic, disregarding Alice's laments for perfection and martyrdom. She, likewise, glosses over his differences and envisions him romanticistically as a happy satyr out of a storybook. Once they return to the open air of the picnic, however, their personalities stand out in sharp, irreconcilable opposition. Alice retreats to the back of the crowd, where she looks at the bay with her hands in her lap, while Dan circulates gayly among the guests, extending his "hospitable hands" (*AH* 96). Through his continuous movement he becomes covertly associated with the visiting fishermen who will not keep still for the fashionable photographer. Yet he persists in his pursuit of the prim Alice for the rest of the excursion, even though the poem he recites about a greedy girl who buries herself with her gold[23] presages her character and his doom. Throughout their drama these references to death recur repeatedly, as do the hell allusions which first appear in their walk back from the picnic. Borne up on a tide of sensual bliss, they wander into a "savage woodland" (*AH* 101), which seems like a picture from *The Inferno* to the love-drunk Dan. Delirious, they ride off to the hotel in the thick, enveloping evening fog.

But the erotic spell soon breaks. At an amateur play that evening, Dan's sensuality, in all its natural vagrancy, comes to the surface and their idyll ends. The chief skit, appropriately, is an improvisation of the apple of discord story, in which Dan, as the weak Paris, has to choose between the contending goddesses. Wearing only a tablecloth and tennis shoes, he and Venus (Julia Anderson) exchange racy sallies and afterwards fall into a flirtation that may or may not have been Dan's "fault" (*AH* 121). But Alice's innate possessiveness flares up and she dismisses him, with "properly" disguised jealousy, as "ungentlemanly" (*AH* 122).

Against the sobering commentary of Mrs. Brinkley, who condemns all young and incompatible alliances, Dan sets off on his first maturity test of the novel. Like the ship that takes him to the mainland, his mind heaves back and forth between sense and sentimentality, immaturity and maturity, never achieving equilibrium. Yet amidst his fluctuations, the voyage provides him with a series of stiff warnings. As he alternately melodramatizes and reproaches himself for a "fool" (*AH* 135), the ship runs into a storm which both deflates his levitations and darkly prophesies his fate. Giving a mordant turn to his "picnic" and "inferno" rhapsodies, an officer looks at the approaching gale and tells Dan dourly: "Looks like hell . . . I guess we're going to have a picnic" (*AH* 136, 137). His subsequent dream predicts the

whole course of his affair with Alice. He sees her face outlined sur-
realistically in the storm and although he wants to cry "Horrible!," he
says, "I love you" instead, and ends up unsuccessfully protecting her
(the miserly girl of the poem presumably) from a burglar. In an ominous reference to Alice's best friend, Miss Cotton, Dan's fists fall like
"cotton" (*AH* 137) on the thief.

But despite these prophecies and lessons, Dan leaves the ship in the
same state of mental oscillation as before. He postures; he calls himself
an "ass" (*AH* 138); he canonizes Alice, and vows to abandon women;
then steps directly out into the bright sun with two lively ladies from
Boston.

The mists, however, descend again. No sooner does he begin to recover than he meets Alice at the Boston Museum on her way to the
"Joan of Arc," and their ill-starred romance starts up once more. Their
enchanted walk back through the hazy October day duplicates, in its
subtle choreography, the very pattern of their future courtship. In defiance of Alice's commands to leave, Dan follows her all the way to her
respectable address, agreeing to each of her progressively superlative
and masochistic ultimatums. Lost in their "transport" (*AH* 155), they
ignore the important social cues in their path: the women Dan has
jilted at the museum, the park hobos, and, significantly, the children's
fort that blocks the sidewalk. They end their reunion on even darker
ironies. With Dan's promise to put "his life in Alice's hands," and
hers, to keep everything "clear" (*AH* 163) between them, they retreat
into the obscurity of a stairwell and embrace in total darkness.

During the first feverish flush of their reconciliation, the sensuality
beneath their sentimentalizing becomes increasingly manifest. At the
same time, the negative side effects of their romantic affectations begin to accrue. Egotism, deeper immaturity, and blindness to their incompatibilities are the initial consequences; but they gradually increase to include the whole gamut of evils that plagued Marcia's and
Bartley's union in *A Modern Instance*—with the addition of frigidity.
As these destructive forces mount and Alice and genteel love conventions grow proportionally debased, Dan develops more and more reserves. In the last resort, however, he cannot rub the romantic gum
from his eyes and goes down to a fate tragically foreshadowed in his
most delirious excesses of lovemaking.

The wooing that takes place after their reunion beautifully illustrates the physical basis of their attraction and how it is fanned by the
erotic idealisms of proper Boston. Right in the middle of one of their

loftiest duets, in which Dan raves about self-sacrifice and Alice about God, they forget what they are saying and kiss passionately. Symbolically, the flowers he brings her on this visit are slightly overblown yellow roses (traditionally expressive of jealousy) instead of the "natural" bouquet of Harvard Class Day. Their second meeting makes the tie between their lust and sentimentality even more explicit. Here, while Alice soars off into pseudo-religious sublimities, Dan stares at the "fluffy silken balls" on her dress with an excitement that reaches a pitch when she says she has been praying: "Dan wanted to fall on his knees to her. The idea of Alice in prayer was *fascinating*" (*AH* 183) (italics mine).[24]

Yet a note of foreboding cuts through Dan's highest transports. Walking back from an ecstatic tryst with Alice, he meets his newspaper friend, Boardman, on the way to the scene of a suicide. "What have I got to do with him?," Dan fatuously asks, and Boardman retorts: "Both mortal!" (*AH* 177). His climactic parting scene with Alice before his visit home contains another loaded allusion to death. After a steamy session in the same darkened stairwell, during which Alice slips her photograph in his pocket, Dan sails entranced into the street: "He seemed to float down the stairs. . . . 'I shall go mad,' he said to himself in the excess of his joy, 'I shall die!'" (*AH* 186).

Once in the presence of his family, Dan's passion not only takes an unexpected turn but the negative aspects of the love affair gain sharper clarity. Faced with his warm, unconventional parents and sisters, he suddenly cannot recall his adoration for Alice and becomes ashamed of it. In a perfect demonstration, though, of his self-ignorance and the regressive effects of his sentimentality, he hymns her incessantly and breaks down at one point into tears of self-pity like "a little child." After this very scene, he assures his mother bathetically: "I'm not quite a fool" (*AH* 199).

When Alice and her mother come for a visit, more negative symptoms appear and their incompatibilities rear up menacingly. Their torrid reunion, for example, outside a hothouse of roses under the stars touches for the first time on the problem of frigidity in their romance. To the "wild kiss" that consummates their endearments, Alice responds with fretful objections, and the narrator interpolates: "[I]t seems to be only the man-soul which finds itself even in this abandon. The woman-soul has always something else to think of" (*AH* 216). At their introduction just afterwards, the keen Mrs. Mavering comments instantly, "Why, child, you hand's like ice!" (*AH* 217).

The interview that follows brings their personality differences into a light as "intense" (*AH* 217) as the one that illuminates Mrs. Mavering's bedroom. While Dan's eyes sparkle gayly during his sisters' musical entertainment, Alice stares with increasing coldness and disapproval, especially when they encourage Dan to sing his Black song. Yet each walks away from this encounter into a romanticistic cloud-cuckoo-land, oblivious to their incompatibility and fatally self-intoxicated. Alice luxuriates in her success as she gazes at the moon and Dan, mindless of his mother's warnings, reels off "to sleep, to dream upon his perfect triumph" (*AH* 224).

The next stage of their engagement provides a sterner test for their passion. As the luster of novelty wears off, the malign qualities in their romance multiply thick and fast. Simultaneously, the sentimental conventions that nourish them grow increasingly discredited and Alice begins to deteriorate further and further into neuroticism. Her performance after the reception she and Dan attend in Boston is a demonstration of her advancing psychological disintegration. There, at an elite party where everyone seems to be "posing for a photograph" (*AH* 252), Dan befriends the two women he had abandoned in the museum, and Alice explodes. Raving about her generosity and Dan's "happiness" (*AH* 234), she sends him back her ring with the injunction to enjoy himself with the women.

Dan, though, disregards how "silly" (*AH* 254) she behaves and refuses to see past the romanticistic flummery to the truth. He ignores Boardman's advice in his sunny apartment and recites instead a string of genteel clichés—Alice's freedom from jealousy, his death without her, their eternal love, the impossibility of another woman—as he egotistically hurls his friend's clothes on the floor.

Nevertheless, he embraces Alice with a new sense of holding a thorny rose in his fingers when they reunite and his reserves, secretly, start to build. Alice's ardor, now, takes a decidedly perverse turn. Her jealousy—still unadmitted—becomes so engulfing that she asks Dan to renounce his friends; her masochism so heightened, she seeks "the most distasteful" (*AH* 256) sacrifice possible. Yet both of these perversions masquerade under an "engagement ideal" (*AH* 253) blessed by the orthodox morality, as does the frigidity which continues to haunt her love play with Dan. In contrast to his simplehearted pleasure in sitting with his arm around her waist, she has "to think, to struggle to recall things beyond it, above it" (*AH* 272), and besieges Dan with a torrent of "morbid doubts" (*AH* 271). Although he objects, and steadily mounts his guard, Dan is too besotted with romance to realize his danger. Alice's jealousy flatters his ego; her masochism proves her "nobility of soul" (*AH* 256); and their antipathies dissolve in the passionate clinches that end their high-flown dialogues. Added to this is his chronic flightiness which makes him sail over every difficulty with comic disregard. After one particularly exasperating interview with Alice, for instance, he laughingly (and ominously) confides in Mrs. Pasmer, "We will die together . . . Alice will kill *me*" (*AH* 266).

The storm clouds gathering over their romance, though, finally break, and Alice rejects Dan for the third and last time. Reaching new heights of romanticistic inanity, she condemns Dan for a peccadillo and casts him out with a misquotation from *Romola*.[25] Even mawkish Miss Cotton questions her behavior, and Mrs. Brinkley frankly reviles her. But Dan's reaction is more complex and signals the beginning of his severest maturity test in the book. While his "good angels," the group of noncomformists, beseech him with wisdom, he struggles between his real feelings and the manufactured romantic ones. The poignancy increases as he moves nearer and nearer self-knowledge and happiness yet persists obstinately in his sentimental delusions. Unable to pull his volatile and uncoordinated personality into focus, he continues fooling himself until the end, when Alice and Proper Boston finally have the last laugh.

From the first moment of his rejection, however, the normative figures in the novel flock to his rescue. Boardman assures him he is "out of a scrape" (*AH* 284), and fortifies him with a practical lecture on tragedy and the therapy of mailing Alice's mementoes back in a stiff, subtly symbolic photographer's envelope. Nonetheless, Dan abandons himself to Wertheresque fantasies on the train home, despite the fact that his actual feelings run counter to his imaginary pangs. In reality, his sensations are a complicated mixture of remorse, indignation, and guilt, surmounted by a powerful sense of relief. But he convinces himself that he suffers a "fatigue of the soul" (*AH* 291) like a popular romance hero and theatrically staggers off to his room when he sees his family. At the same time, he slowly begins to come to his senses. He tries "not to pose" (*AH* 309) and listens to his father's astute advice about women, marriage, and his future happiness. The objections he makes—that he cannot get over his guilt or love—not only ring false to him after a while, they begin to dissolve when he goes to Washington on a business trip.

The sky clears, the air sharpens, and Dan enters a world that is the

exact antithesis of the one that nurtured his love affair. In the "gay,"
informal atmosphere, surrounded by sympathetic "kind black faces"
(*AH* 315), he forgets his despair and cheers up in spite of himself. Appropriately, the guardian spirit of this oasis is the plucky Julia Anderson, whose role in Dan's maturity drama appears in their first meeting. Discovering her in a Washington hotel, Dan hands her a sprig of
forsythia,[26] the flower traditionally associated with graduation, but
tells her inauspiciously that it means "expressive silence" (*AH* 310).
For despite the progess toward manhood he makes in her care, he will
not be able to speak his heart, thanks to his combined immaturities
and romantic bad habits. Julia, though, introduces him to a totally
new sexual universe. Unlike her antagonist, Alice, she is gay, warm,
flexible, relaxed, and generous, and shares Dan's sympathies with
Blacks. "I *adoye* [*sic*] them" (*AH* 318), she exclaims in her offbeat ac-
cent, as she escorts Dan through a party that is the complete reverse of
the Boston reception. Rich, poor, young, and old, all jostle together in
perfect ease and equality and Dan finds himself "intoxicat[ed]" (*AH*
320) with freedom. After several more meetings with Julia, in which
they stroll in the bright, soft (her name means soft-haired) sun and
agree on everything, he discovers he has lost his broken heart. His
sexual interest kindles, and on their "habitual ground of frankness and
reality" (*AH* 327) a romance starts to bloom.

But Dan's sentimental fixations and boyishness conspire to foil him.
As soon as he realizes Julia's attractions, he strikes up an imaginary
dialogue with Alice, whom he still fancies is his "one and only." Even
Mrs. Brinkley's efforts to promote his affair are to little avail and Dan
wanders away from a fiery tête-à-tête with Julia, envisioning himself
as her Platonic, inconsolable friend for life. When his desire finally
dawns on him, his romanticistic ideals trip him into a pratfall and renewed entrapment. During his declaration build-up, he tells Julia
about his engagement to Alice and abruptly ruins the effect by mouthing conventional pieties that he does not feel. He glorifies Alice and
blames himself, and then shakes his head in bewilderment when Julia
cools off: "[S]he was laughing at him; and he could not console himself
with any hero of a novel who had got himself into just such a box"
(*AH* 331). He tries to speak a second time, but the letter he writes is so
noncommittal, so perfect a reflection of his inner disorientation, that
Julia rebounds to her old fiance with the exclamation: "*You* are a *man*,
anyway" (*AH* 335).

On his third attempt, fate jinxes him. Alice has already preceded him to the resort where he pursues Julia and his doom is sealed. At the "Hygeia" at Old Point Comfort, ironically named for the goddess of community health,[27] the mists collect again and Alice appears in a state of mental and physical regression inversely proportionate to Dan's growth. Thin and pale, she paces in the "soft, heavy sea air" (*AH* 339) and feeds her pain with imaginary atonements for imaginary crimes and a cultivation of Mrs. Brinkley whom she hates. Her hands have grown "very cold" (*AH* 343), her egotism obsessive, and her sentimentality "tawdry" (*AH* 345). Hearing of Dan's visit, Mrs. Brinkley tries to save him but "abandon[s] him to Providence" (*AH* 351) in disgust when he arrives unexpectedly and denies, with characteristic evasion, that he has come to see Julia. He fools himself, though, for the last time. At that moment, Alice walks in and makes him her permanent fool.

The wedding that follows brings their romance to a crescendo of acid ironies. All the motifs of their love affair converge in one of the most spine-chilling endings in Howells's fiction. In keeping with the soft-focus atmosphere of their courtship, a stained-glass glow suffuses the respectable Boston church and the flowers, which have metamorphosed so diabolically since they met, emit a "delicate" (*AH* 352) noxious scent. Miss Cotton, of course, has the last word. Through her we hear, like pistol reports, the final developments of Dan's and Alice's passion. Caroling their "promise of happiness," Miss Cotton ticks off the grim facts to Mrs. Brinkley: Alice has made Dan go to Europe against his mother's wishes, made him drop Boardman in a best man trade off, and made the Maverings "idolize" (*AH* 353) (read "detest") her. The discrepancy between appearance and reality is further heightened by the general consensus that Alice's father, an impassive drone, seems "deeply affected" during the service. But the consummate touch is the terrible finality of the line: "The ceremony proceeded to the end" (*AH* 354).

The novel concludes on an equally devastating fade-out of Alice and Dan in the bridal coach afterwards. With her "cold clutch" on Dan's wrist, Alice assails Dan once more with ideal sentiments and once more he absently concurs as he passionately kisses her behind the curtains (the curtains of genteel romance?) of the dark carriage. He swears he will be completely honest with her in the future, then reflects with typical evasiveness and self-ignorance that he will tell her about Julia sometime when he understands the situation. Presumably this is not the last time his words and thoughts will contradict each other, nor will this be the widest gulf between them. And on that note they ride off into their romanticistic sunset, with the narrator providing the final trenchant assessment: "If he had been different she would not have asked him to be frank and open; if she had been different, he might have been frank and open. This was the beginning of their married life" (*AH* 354).

But beneath the caustic ironies of the ending rests a solid ground of erotic value. Unlike the infinite false bottoms of *A Modern Instance*, the group of nonconformists provides a stable sexual perspective from which to view Dan's and Alice's romantic debacle. The insights of each are fragmentary and partial; yet, combined, they create the beginnings of a nonrepressive ethic in Howells's work. To be sure, their primary emphases are negative. They puncture the prevailing romanticistic sanctities one by one with sharp, common-sense barbs. Mrs. Mavering, Mrs. Brinkley, and Julia all deflate Alice's pretensions with their perceptions of her morbid egotism; and Boardman consistently topples Dan from his sentimental heights. From Mrs. Brinkley comes a larger critique of the whole courtship ritual: the immaturity of the participants, the covert sensuality, and engagement inflexibility.

But in addition to their reductive insights, they also contribute the rudiments of a positive sexual morality. Dan's father and Boardman both champion what William James called the "Gospel of Relaxation."[28] In place of romantic intensity, they counsel tolerance and an appreciation of moral and emotional "degrees" (*AH* 238) rather than absolutes. Mr. Mavering encourages Dan to find a wife who is easygoing and "wordly" (*AH* 312), while his mother cautions him—in an extension of Howells's complicity theory—that he sins "against the peace and comfort of the whole community" (*AH* 203) if he does not marry happily. Compatibility, not the glamorous oppositions of love stories, is the best path to that happiness, Mrs. Brinkley insists, and she elaborates a creed of marital generosity to help insure it: "Marriage is a perpetual pardon, concession, surrender; it's an everlasting giving up; that's the divine thing about it" (*AH* 306). Sexual relaxation, complicity, compatibility, and selflessness: these are the cornerstones of Howells's erotic ethic and here provide the firm foundation beneath the book's merciless ironic demolitions.

If the secondary characters have acquired more authority since *A Modern Instance* and *The Rise of Silas Lapham*, they have also become more involved in the lovers' fate. In a direct illustration of Mrs. Mavering's complicity theory, they not only affect Dan's love affair but are permanently affected by it. The Maverings, Boardman, and Julia each hasten Dan on his path of retreat from Alice, and Mrs. Brinkley, with her praises of Julia, nudges him into his liaison with her. By the same token, they become the immediate victims of his capitulation to Alice. Mrs. Brinkley suffers a fruitless moral upheaval at Old Point Comfort. Boardman loses a friend, and Julia flings herself on her old, unloved fiancé and thus into an improvident marriage. Dan's parents, meanwhile, must live with their son's certain unhappiness and his antipathetic, demanding bride.

Yet among these characters exist embryonic versions of the heroine and hero Howells would later create to redeem this endless cycle of sexual pain. Contrary to the Victorian sexual stereotypes of business baron and lily maid, his two potential erotic models are heterodox mixtures who seek to bridge the "abyss of inequality."[29] Mrs. Mavering playfully calls the humane, unselfish Boardman a "she" (*AH* 300) and Julia Anderson is a shrewd businesswoman with a "bold deep voice . . . like a man['s]" (*AH* 68). Both are social outsiders, versed in common-sense wisdom, and at one point Dan fantasizes a marriage between them. But Boardman's short, plump physique and cynical detachment disqualify him for the romantic action and they never meet.

Julia, however, represents Howells's closest approximation to a sexual heroine. Bohemian, relaxed, stylish, and sensuous, she is as much a *charmeuse* as Mrs. Farrell and just as ravishing in her private theatrical. Like her, she has the "simpler, freer" (*YOMY* 149) manners of Howells's midwestern girlfriends and a comic repartee that is irresistably seductive. Yet she blends her *volupté* with virtue. The spiritual values dear to Howells's youth merge with her sexual allure. She is hospitable and giving, and the hotel room where she captivates Dan is softened to . . . a domestic effect" (*AH* 329) by her ministrations. The "light of heaven" (*BT* 229) of Howells's home, which shines from the windmill in *A Modern Instance*, begins to glimmer in her character. As Mrs. Brinkley says, "She always ma[kes] me think of broad daylight" (*AH* 324). Ultimately, of course, she cannot resist her romantic conditioning and martyrs herself to her fiance, but she is the prototype of the realistic goddesses who would dominate the erotic fiction after the turn of the century. Given a maturity trial and Dan's warm blood, Boardman, too, would reemerge, transformed into a sexually awakened, disciplined adult.

Although the nonconformists cannot finally provide a working model of their beliefs, although they must watch passively as Dan goes to his doom, they at least envision the possibility of a sexual synthesis. After one of her elevating speeches, Mrs. Brinkley says insightfully, "One can afford to be . . . [wise about love]—in the abstract" (*AH* 80). Yet she and her friends supply the groundplan for a sexual ethic which would have a concrete expression in the future novels.

Within the bitter ironies of the title lurks a sense of this new sexual mood. Ostensibly, *April Hopes* refers to the stormy future, so darkly foreshadowed, that awaits the two lovers. Like April weather, they are in for stern surprises. With sharper irony, it evokes Dan's boyish fluctuations, which insure his fate and make him the archetypal April fool. But there is a suggestion of real hope, too. If the title casts a sardonic eye on Dan's and Alice's "respectable" love affair, it casts another on a pragmatic sexual universe, which, like April, is variegated, open to change, and charged with generative promise. In a letter to Hamlin Garland, Howells said that he had written the novel from a faith in men and a genuine "trust in them." [30]

As a result, the positive erotic ideals of Swedenborg's *Conjugial Love* enter his work unambivalently for the first time. The negative proscriptions are equally prominent and, mirroring the incorporation of Dan's and Alice's evils within "society," are byproducts of gentility. Their Campobello forest is a replica of Swedenborg's hell and Alice's chic pallor a reflection of the Demon of Self-Love. Her elite rigidity, moreover, duplicates the inner stiffness Swedenborg "saw" in jealous lovers, [31] while her neuroticism illustrates a *Conjugial Love* precept Howells had never openly acknowledged before: "[E]xcessive restraint . . . [causes] diseases of the body and disorders of the mind." [32]

At the same time the positive ingredients of Swedenborg's love ethic appear—unmixed with contradiction. His discriminating, relaxed attitude toward sex shows up in Mr. Mavering's and Boardman's doctrine of "degrees" and colors the thought of all the unconventional witnesses in the book. The beliefs that marriage is the seminary of human existence and that compatibility guarantees its success—two Swedenborg axioms—both emerge in Mrs. Brinkley's lectures. But Julia Anderson is the best exemplar of Swedenborg's sexual ideals. She begins to approach that union of flesh and spirit, beauty and truth, men and women, enjoyed by the blessed in in his heavenly visions. Her virtues—common sense, generosity, and gaiety—are precisely those Swedenborg celebrated; and, like his angels, she combines them with beauty and sensuousness. Like them, too, she is a coquette, who skillfully keeps Dan's interest at full pitch. But just as the roses (the flower of Swedenborg's paradise) metamorphose diabolically in the novel, so Julia's potential excellences, along with her romance with Dan, go the way of all reality and she remains a heroine *in posse*.

Even more than *The Rise of Silas Lapham*, *April Hopes* created a critical uproar. "Dreary,"[33] "depressing and uncharitable,"[34] "an exercise in morbid anatomy"[35] were the outcries and the abuse became so strident Howells said he felt like a "literary Ishmael."[36] It was, it is true, sexually bolder than his earlier book, but the real cause of the outrage went deeper. He had exposed what D. H. Lawrence called "the dirty little secret"[37] of Victorian puritanism. He had pried up the gilded lid of genteel prudery and revealed its alliance with prurience. His "Editor's Study" columns of the eighties hinted at the same thing[38] and created a similar storm. In addition, he had shown—decades before Freud—the illness and destructiveness that attend sexual suppression.

Such an easy explanation of the sexual enigma, however, would not long satisfy Howells. Libidinal evil could not be explained by suprarepression alone; the larger "secret" of sexuality, the demonic in everyman, would lead him to recesses of the subconscious. Nor would his imagination settle permanently for compromise. As "restful" (*AH* 325) as this tentative fusion of soul and sense might be (as Mrs. Brinkley calls Julia), his creative mind insisted on recovery of the highest pleasure seized from the deepest tragic knowledge. His next sexual drama would surprise him again, overturning his temperate solution, and casting him into the infantile, irrational heart of his conflict.

April Hopes, though, was a crucial step toward his final goal. Racked physically and intellectually by his "black time," he had managed to break through the norms of his age. He had openly repudiated the orthodox cult of purity, exposed its uncleanliness and mendacity, and moved beyond its exaggerated fears. Instead of a tripwire to "anarchy" as his friend, Twain, continued to believe,[39] sex was a multifaceted, complex impulse with equal possibilities for happiness or destruction.

He had been able to get past his culture's wholesale sexual terror and his own adolescent one, and also discover a ground of potential value beyond the official pale. His "sneaking fondness" (*MF* 184) for Mrs. Farrell and "perverse sympathy" (*MI* 325) for Bartley Hubbard had led him back, with a magnetic-like pull, to his pleasurable, informal, origins in the Middle West. On the bases of gaiety, gratification, selflessness, and equality, he would erect his great turn-of-the-century love ethic.

The interior emphases of Dan's maturity rite and the thickened web of complicity, point to the directions his sexual theme would take before the light of a positive sexuality appeared again. The inner subterranean journey he avoided in *A Modern Instance* still awaited him, with its harrowing intrapsychic and universal truths. While the furor over *April Hopes* raged around him, Howells protested: "People take me so viciously awry . . . when my whole trouble has been to sugarcoat my medicinal properties."[40] He had wrapped the painful sexual realities of Dan's and Alice's affair in his finest artistry and sweetened it with both the rudiments of sexual value and a scapegoat—the genteel world. Yet he may have intuited, then, that he would take his next dose of negative sexuality straight. Perhaps he knew that he would have to confront the blackest reaches of the human heart—the demonic that inhered in sexuality—before he could reclaim the highest sweetness: a perfected Julia, a matured Dan, and a society joined in sensuous peace and fulfillment.

The Shadow of a Dream: Howells and the demonic | *Seven*

Howells, always a prolific dreamer, sent a comic account of one of his nightmares to Mark Twain in 1884. After a bedtime snack of a potato and onion "horror," he said, "the wife of *two* of [his] friends" approached him and forced him to "escape from her premises with the ignominy and virtue of Joseph." [1] Five years later this was to be the subject of one of his most merciless, probing sexual tragedies. A man's dream of his wife's infidelity in their *ménage à trois* household becomes so imperative that no one—not even the temperate narrator—can escape its chthonic power. The moderate, "realistic" erotic solution of *April Hopes* dissolves before the demonic[2] truths of *The Shadow of a Dream* (1890). The darkest, most primitive secrets of the unconscious well up, and impelled by the libido, topple every value and deliver Howells's sexual theme once more to Thanatos.

As in *A Modern Instance*, Howells did not originally plan it that way. He told Howard Pyle he had intended his "romantic"[3] novella to end happily.[4] Again, though, his imagination surprised him, swerving back like a compass needle to his buried neurosis. Within Faulkner's dream, within the primitive well of the psyche, it divined the heart of his sexual fear. As the story evolved, his imagination progressively confirmed, instead of disclaimed, the anarchic, destructive truths of the nightmare. Douglas Faulkner, the centerpiece of the novel, is the quintessential "fool"—the repository of the irrational. His character and dream are a composite image of the classic dark side of Eros. He not only contains the evils that had surfaced before—jealousy, narcissism, polygamy, sadomasochism, and disintegration—he incorporates new perversions as well. And as the plot advances, the characters progressively crumble before him. While the group of nonconformists in *April Hopes* puncture sentimentality and counter its negative sexuality with a rudimentary ethic, the protagonists in *The Shadow of a Dream* themselves come under the sway of Faulkner's morbid, neo-romantic presentiments and collapse morally. Sentimentality is no longer the scapegoat; the dark powers it releases are common to every man.

The first-person narrator, Basil March, provides the best instance of this. Democratic, relaxed, rational, and happily married, he personifies the erotic compromise of *April Hopes*, yet finally resists Faulkner's chthonic power no better than the others. Within his narration is a covert subdrama that moves in counterpoint to the major one. If Faulkner's dream plumbs the essence of Howells's sexual fears, Basil's response reveals Howells's conflict. Like a "shadow self," Faulkner lures Basil, despite his reasoned defenses, to his repressed unconscious where attraction and fear vie with equal intensity. He not only experiences the very tabooed impulses Faulkner shadowed forth, he experiences a pleasure-terror toward them that brings Basil to an intrapsychic crisis. Amidst his maturity ordeal, he looks for a non-repressive way to resolve his conflict (coming closer to success than ever) but falls back at last on the old, invalidated strategy of denial, qualified by one last, ironic query. The injury he causes, through his failure and dissociated sexuality, becomes worse as the web of complicity tightens: indirectly he promotes the deaths of the two lovers.

At the end of *The Shadow of a Dream*, then, the negations that enclose the book have grown deadlier and more serious. Rather than an exaggerated, adolescent vision of sexual darkness, Howells's imagination had penetrated its chthonic core. In the absence of a controlling ethic, his only recourse becomes suprarepression—long since proved death-directed and salacious. The slaughterous finale, therefore, only dramatizes the sexual dilemma. If the lovers admit the validity of the dream, they surrender to the untutored, destructive powers of Eros. If they deny it, they yield to a different death, tainted with prurience. Thanatos crushes the love story from both sides. At the same time, the invocations of pleasure reach a peak of power, increasing the tension of ambivalence. Just as Basil's ultimate recourse is to quell the contradictions by suppression, so the annihilation of the lovers is also an escape from that excruciating tension. Never had Howells's sexual theme sunk so deeply into death.

The "wholly tragic"[5] outcome came at a time, so far as the matter was conscious, when Howells could least sustain it. "Beaten into the dust"[6] by his daughter's death, he wrote the book while he was still stunned by her loss. Guilt and grief overwhelmed him, leaving him for weeks without the will to live or work. Combined with his almost

suicidal mood, was a severe conflict in his critical ideas about sexuality. On the one hand, he encouraged his readers to read Zola,
Ibsen,[7] and face the "facts of life";[8] on the other, to eschew illicit
themes in fiction and "keep off the grass"[9] of passion. When his imagination, then, plunged back into the infantile, unconscious recesses of
his neurosis and gave him no means to integrate it, his conflict and
mood of denial were exacerbated. His psychic breakdown during *A
Modern Instance* adumbrated the long, dark night of the soul he was to
endure after *The Shadow of a Dream*. Yet, as with the harrowing he endured then, he emerged from this lengthier, more focused period of
suffering with a new synthesis of Eros.

Howells's erotic artistry gathered a poetic intensity in his psychological study of love. As in a dream, the prose becomes condensed,
symbolic, and mythic. Compressed into three chapters, the action unfolds with the precision of a sonata. Faulkner's section states the romantic problem; Hermia's develops it, and Nevil's recapitulates and
concludes it, while Basil's first-person narrative weaves contrapun-
tally through the whole in a minor key. Erotic symbols that had appeared in Howells's novels before, elaborate, move to the foreground,
and acquire an archetypal resonance. The femme fatale, Hermia, is
a "goddess" (*SD* 82) with a horse's gait who lures two men to their
deaths. Basil's trip West (in a telescoped version of Marcia Hubbard's)
is a psychic night sea journey which leads to the hearthfire, food, and
domestic "luxury" (*SD* 83) of Howells's youth. Imagistically, Faulkner's ruined garden cants, with the imbalance of sexual error, toward
the weltering ocean of death. So too, the dark-light contrasts assume
poetic economy and force. Imperceptibly the light dims, from the
chiaroscuro in part one, to Hermia's evening visit, to the dark Western
town, to the pitch night of Nevil's death, as the shadow of the dream
steals over the book.

Along with its symbolic power, the story is also one of Howells's
most subtle.[10] Minute gestures, such as Faulkner's furtive glances, reveal his suspicions, and the lovers betray their secret attraction to each
other through the finest nuances. The connection between prurience
and sentimentality, which Howells highlighted in *April Hopes*, now
takes on a more muted, covert expression. When Nevil neochivalric-
ally leaps off the cliff to rescue Faulkner, he tumbles down the rocks
into a refuse pile left by an ancient "revelry" (*SD* 27) on the beach.

Subtler still is Howells's management of point of view. The whole
subdrama of Basil's psychic life is contained in the contradictions be-

tween his stated intentions and action, in the shifts of narrative voice from irony to lyricism. His philosophic speculations, therefore, which give a higher ideologic content to the sexual theme than ever before, are not fortuitous but ironically, bitterly apposite. Point for point, they, like so much that Basil says, run exactly counter to what he does.

Even more than *April Hopes*, *The Shadow of a Dream* benefited from his lifelong interest in poetry and theater. Literary allusions achieve the status of metaphor; and dialogue, with its intellectual play and ironic complexities, reflects his recent discovery of Ibsen. As his narrative erotic quest pressed forward, then, into unknown terrain, Howells's style expanded with it into progressively newer, subtler, more sophisticated forms.

Douglas Faulkner, the moonstruck midwestern lawyer, galvanizes the tragedy. He, even more than Don Ippolito, is the archetypal sexual "fool."[11] He personifies the dark powers of Eros, and his twisted dream eventually blights the lives and moral defenses of everyone in the book. Through his agency, the deepest, worst tendencies in passion come to the surface and irradiate malignantly into the plot. His first appearance sets the stage for the sexual tempest he will raise. As Basil remembers him, he incarnates sensual undiscipline. With "stooped" (*SD* 5) shoulders, trembling fingers, restless eyes, and sallow complexion, he is a textbook exhibit of the symptoms of masturbation and incontinence in Howells's culture.[12] Further incriminating are his compulsive cigar smoking and "humiliating" (*SD* 5) dreams.[13] What is more, all of this libidinal "indulgence" is actively cultivated through a smokescreen of exalted romanticism. Through his lofty adulation of De Quincy, he luxuriates in his shameful dreams, and through a sentimental mother worship, remains Oedipally attached to her. Equally perverse is his obsessive devotion to his schoolmate and later priest-companion, James Nevil, which masquerades as a "very romantic" (*SD* 4) friendship. In a distinct suggestion of homosexual attraction,[14] Faulkner eulogizes the "girlishly peachy" (*SD* 5) Nevil, praising him in phallic terms. Nevil, he rhapsodizes, rose up before him "tall and straight" when they first met in college and saved him by his high "example" (*SD* 6). By the end of Basil's reminiscence, Basil has left no doubt about Faulkner's disturbed sexuality. Even his name, in characteristic Howellsian fashion, conveys it: "Douglas" both evokes the romanticistic hero of Scott's novel and means "dark stream."[15]

When the curtain opens on the present drama and Basil sees him again in middle age, Faulkner's incontinence has reached a malign and sick fruition. His estate at Swampscott, with its connotation of a moral swamp, is a world mired in the destructive powers of Eros. There, during Basil's and Isabel's visit, the chthonic truths, which will shroud the book in shadow, make their first tragic and insidious appearance. At this stage, Basil's commonsense and Dr. Wingate's sunny materialism are enough to keep them at bay, but they will prove mysteriously hard to subdue.

The scene Basil and Isabel encounter on their mission to Swampscott is one of total sexual malaise. The expanse of wizened elms and neglected lawns that greets them is an outward and visible symbol of the erotic ill health they discover within Faulkner's home. Isolated from all human society, Faulkner, his wife, and James Nevil live together in a triangular household that festers with forbidden sexual feelings. Faulkner himself is in the last stages of psychic and physical decay. In a fulfillment of the Victorian prognosis for intemperance,[16] Faulkner's complexion has grown livid; his eyes, dull, his hands "languid" (*SD* 13), and he totters on a cane,[17] crippled by heart disease. With his disintegration, his sentimentality has turned saccharine and decadent. A tawdry Mariolatry masks his maternal dependencies, and Byron, who exemplified prurience to Howells and the age generally,[18] has remained his literary ideal. His shameful dreams, similarly, are not only nightmarish and obsessional; they have become objectively, grotesquely real to him. Instead of eulogies to Nevil, he harps on him with manic insistence, and jealously eyes his wife as he autoerotically fondles "the crook of his stick" (*SD* 17). So delivered is he to dark sexual forces that he seems to slouch through the first chapter like an embodiment of Eros the Destroyer.

His garden epitomizes his disordered libido and is one of the key symbols in the book. After lunch he ushers the Marches to a desolate spot beside the sea, and "as if he had invented the place" (*SD* 29), escorts them through a ruined, overgrown garden. Allowed to flourish unrestrained, the walks and fences have sagged "out of plumb" (*SD* 26); the fruit and vines have succumbed to disease and overgrowth; and weeds, with such sinister names as "witch-grass and Black Hamburg" (*SD* 29), have invaded everything. Like Faulkner's sterile immaturities, the berries moulder in "never-ripening decay" and roses, the traditional flower of erotic love, stand neglected and "skeletoned by slugs and blight" (*SD* 27). Surrounding the dilapidated beds is a row of box-bushes whose two opposite meanings, death and erotic truth,[19] come together with beautiful aptness. They bear eloquent testimony to the impotence, chaos, and final fatality of uncontrolled Eros.

Douglas Faulkner is not the only unbalanced member of his *ménage à trois*; Hermia and Nevil are themselves sexually unhinged. They, too, are sentimentalists whose high-flown pieties conceal secret, illicit desires. The desire gathering increasing validity and ultimately giving Faulkner's dream such power over their lives, is their covert, suppressed attraction to each other. Their good looks, in dramatic contrast to Faulkner's, create immediate suspicions, which they confirm through the first chapter.

The voluptuous Hermia, who has the walk of a "two-horse carriage" (*SD* 22) and the name of an earth goddess,[20] attends her wasted husband too apprehensively for conviction. She plies him with superfluous services, watches his every movement, and at one point rushes to his side so histrionically after a walk with Nevil that Basil bristles with irritation. More suspiciously, she bursts into hysterical tears when she sees Nevil fall down the cliff and laughs wildly as he recovers himself. There are other signs of trouble. She is frankly "uneasy" (*SD* 28) in the garden and convinces Isabel, through her sentimental overemphasis on Faulkner, that she does not love him. Corroborating these hints is Nevil's story about Hermia's early marital indifference to Faulkner and her present devotion, which is not, he says, "love in the usual way" (*SD* 41).

Nevil himself betrays suspect inclinations. When Basil first meets him he confesses a compulsive, irrational attachment to the Faulkners: "I'm neglecting . . . my proper work," he blurts out, "and yet I can't tear myself away from him—from them" (*SD* 26). For the rest of the visit he talks feverishly of them both, especially Hermia, whom he idealizes as the perfect wife and innocent victim of her husband's wrath. Symbolizing the "lower" desires concealed in his grandiosities, he tumbles down the cliff into a pile of garbage when he heroically tries to rescue Faulkner. So aware is Basil of his aberrancies by the end of the chapter that he labels the whole "three-cornered" relationship Nevil has become involved in, "disgusting" (*SD* 42).

When Faulkner, then, suddenly glowers at Hermia and Nevil, clutches his heart, and dies, the nature of his obsessive dream is self-evident. Through his subliminal sexual knowledge, he has been able to intuit the deepest, most tabooed impulses in his two companions. As the first act of the tragedy draws to a close, almost every negative truth of Eros has been suggested: perversion, aggression, promiscuity, jealousy, and the death impulses. Importantly, though, Basil and Dr. Wingate, whose name means "friendly guard,"[21] are still capable of dispelling these black intuitions with their "reasons."

In part two, their authority begins to slip, while Hermia progressively accords the dream more power and at last submits to it altogether. Her heroics after Faulkner's death begin the process of self-betrayal which continues unabated through part two. As though trying to punish herself for feared sins, she sacrificially goes to live with her mother-in-law and refuses to hear her husband's dream. Her four letters to the Marches, though, give her away. Basil's opening hints about her attachment to Nevil gain increasing substance with each letter. The first announces Nevil's engagement and attributes such hyperbolic "pang[s]" (*SD* 53) to her mother-in-law and such distress to Nevil, that Basil says he hopes his fiancée never sees the letter. The next, with news of the broken engagement, is even more incriminating. In the perfervid strains of sentimental romance, she tells of Nevil's rejection by his "vulgar" (*SD* 57) fiancée and flight to her home for comfort. After concluding ambiguously that his presence is "awkward" (*SD* 58) in the house, she writes a third time to hymn his virtue, manliness, and "joy in their affections" (*SD* 59). When Basil sees him in Boston a few weeks later, her exaggerations become plain: Nevil is as prosaic as ever and even "a little cold" (*SD* 60). The Marches' shock at the fourth letter, which proclaims her engagement, measures strength with which they have sensed her secret preference all along.

With the open admission of Hermia's and Nevil's love, Faulkner's demented dream bulks large again. And in a guilty frenzy to learn its contents, the newly radiant Hermia arrives at the Marches to demand the truth from Dr. Wingate. It soon becomes apparent that self-punishment is the real goal of her visit. Her demands for censure mount furiously through the climactic scenes of the chapter. She insists that the Marches "judge" (*SD* 66) her in a mock trial which she makes as damning to herself as possible. Wildly repeating that the dream killed her husband, she says she will have "no peace" (*SD* 66) until she hears it and accuses herself of fault after fault until Dr. Wingate finally explodes: "You wish to condemn yourself" (*SD* 67). First involuntarily, then, and at last consciously, Hermia steadily empowers and reaffirms the dream's dark divinations. When the actual disclosure comes, she capitulates completely to the chthonic truths and, as if hypnotized, grows as lifeless as she was revitalized before.

Basil and Wingate, meanwhile, can no longer counter the dream effectively. Wingate fails to convince Hermia of her delusion, bungles the revelation, and beats a retreat from the Marches in confusion. Basil proves equally inadequate. Defaulting on his own ethical principles of compassion and complicity (the reliable values of *April Hopes*), he recoils from Hermia's suffering with aversion and himself succumbs to nightmares.

In part three the dream continues its chthonic advance, successfully eclipsing the plot in tragedy. Nevil, this time, gives the nightmare its final crushing authority, while every attempt at ethical mastery disintegrates. During the interval before he appears, several peripheral characters add further credence to Faulkner's intuitions. His mother's shrewd comments about Hermia's morbidity and Nevil's efforts to make things "hard for himself" (*SD* 90) merely reinforce their guilt. Basil's friend, the sibylline old lady, contributes to the dream's veracity as well. She not only clairvoyantly envisions a romance between Hermia and Nevil but speculates that she was unhappy with Faulkner.

It is at this point that old Mrs. Faulkner reveals the full force of the chthonic irrationality that struck Faulkner down and is stalking the other characters. Taking Basil aside, she tells him the fearful apparition that has intuited the lovers' collusion and slain her son. Its setting is nothing less than the very wedding at which Nevil, the priest, officiated. Says old Mrs. Faulkner:

> "The doctor told [Hermia] that Douglas had been having the dream almost a year before he died; at first every month or so, and then every week. . . . He dreamed that she and James were—attached, and were waiting for him to die, so that they could get married. Then he would see them getting married in church, and at the same time it would be his own funeral, and he would try to scream out that he was not dead; but Hermia would smile, and say to the people that she had known James before she knew Douglas; and then *both* ceremonies would go on, and he would wake. That was all" (*SD* 92–93).

Nevil himself, however, builds the best case for the dream. In his ongoing debate with Basil through the chapter, he progressively mounts his own prosecution, despite every appeal to reason and restraint. Insisting on the mysterious origins of his love, he contends that he always wanted Hermia in the "guilty inmost of [his] heart" (*SD* 107) and subconsciously picked a fiancée who would reject him.

He then brings all of his and Hermia's actions in the book under review, and concludes fiercely: "I teach submission, renunciation, abnegation . . . what heart should I have to counsel or admonish others, when I was all rotten within myself?" (*SD* 111).

Faced with Nevil's self-surrender to the powers of darkness, Basil casts about frantically for an ethic to surmount them. His moderate, "civilized" sexual answers fail him. And as a last resort, he leaves Nevil not with a value to contain the demonic forces, but with two types of denial: either Nevil's own self-denial or a denial of the subconscious. His one attempt to incorporate the dream's truths in a relaxed, nonpunitive ethic ends in embarrassment. When he proposes that Nevil and Hermia marry in spite of their previous attraction, he flushes and presses even more strenuously for suppression. His arguments, however, ring hollow in view of his own experience with unconscious reality and he just narrowly convinces Nevil to reconsider his decision. The death Nevil meets afterwards by clinging too long to Basil's hand, then, is thematically right. To renounce and repress the demonic energies is always fatal.[22] As Nevil clutches Basil for final, farewell reassurance, the train (one of Howells's favorite symbols of the libido)[23] picks up speed and crushes him against a stone pillar. In consummation of the chthonic victory, Hermia dies swiftly behind him of heartbreak. Thanatos rules the day at last; and, when the epilogue fades out on Basil's futile and ironic generalities, the book is deep in the shadow of Faulkner's mysterious dream.

Though less conspicuous, perhaps the strongest support for the validity of the dream is Basil. Seen as a "more-or-less reliable narrator,"[24] Basil tells a story about himself that parallels and enhances the main one. Inadvertently, against all of his reasonable precautions, he, too, slips into the realm of the repressed unconscious. It is he, significantly, who supplies the title for the book. Ushered into Faulkner's garden, he exclaims inwardly that it is "as familiar to [him] as any most intimate experience of [his] life," yet as insubstantial as the "shadow of a dream" (*SD* 28). With the advance of the plot, the libidinal truths of the garden gradually assume an all too palpable substance in his life. While Hermia and Nevil experience what to them are the negative, tabooed passions, he experiences a rending ambivalence. Faulkner represents more to him than Eros the Destroyer; Faulkner is Basil's "shadow self," his denied infantile half, who takes him back to the conflict at the base of his psyche. His divided feelings toward Faulkner (reflected in his prose style) become, with his descent into the psychic underworld, the neurotic tension between gratification and fear in his deepest self. As he is drawn towards the lovers' forbidden desires, he suffers an inner ordeal, another of the maturity tests in Howells's erotic fiction. Twice, when his superego dozes, he almost finds a way to resolve his neurosis but in the end retreats despairingly to repression. The effect of his failure is wide-reaching. Through his moral and psychic evasions, he indirectly precipitates the tragic conclusion. Either the Keatsian or Shakespearian source for the title, then, is appropriate:[25] his *rite de passage* is an ironic parody of Endymion's and his ethical impotence before chthonic knowledge, the same as Hamlet's.

Faulkner from the beginning is an image of Basil's buried erotic life, in all its negative and positive potential. He is, as Basil once called him, a "demoniac presence" (*SD* 78)—a personification of the primal "lower" energies, which classically must be met and mastered in a maturity drama.[26] He is midwestern, "poetic," sentimental, sexually immature, and hopelessly backward in his tastes—precisely the childish identity Basil has rejected. And yet Basil shows an ambivalence toward him that suggests an unresolved, inner conflict. In the introduction he remembers how he and Faulkner stood together with linked arms beneath a full moon and recited Wordsworth in unison, "smitten into ecstasy by the beauty of the scene" (*SD* 7). The language is richly poetic and, on the same occasion, he tells Faulkner that he envies his politic "ability to mingle with . . . people" (*SD* 5). Another "voice," however, is juxtaposed with this lyric one. With cold, defensive irony, he describes Faulkner's unsavory appearance, his overintimacy, his saccharine sentimentality, and concludes that he "rather bored [him]" (*SD* 4). Basil ignores this tension, though, and concludes that hostility and time had finally separated them.

But when he sees him again, the old ambivalence returns. Although he assures Wingate afterwards that he never "cared for him" (*SD* 45), and reacts primarily with boredom and exasperation at Swampscott, he reveals a curious attraction to Faulkner during his visit. As soon as he approaches his estate, the prose gathers a poetic luxuriance and Faulkner's voice thrills him with "the charm of old associations" (*SD* 15). He staunchly defends him against Isabel's criticisms and talks of a private bond between them: "We men and we Westerners," he says conspiratorially, "have a civilization of our own" (*SD* 21). In the ruined garden, his contradictory feelings come to a focus. His description portrays both the sordid squalor of the place and its "poetry" and "disordered loveliness" (*SD* 27).

With the reemergence of his conflict, Basil begins a descent into the irrational. He feels involuntarily attracted to Hermia and Nevil and senses "disgusting" (*SD* 42) truths in the Faulkners' "three-cornered household" (*SD* 19). Like Ferris of *A Foregone Conclusion*, though, he fights off these impulses—the attraction and fear alike. He peppers Hermia with ironic raillery, discounts his *déjà vu* experience in the garden, and tells Faulkner to defy his dream in the interests of civilization. Supporting and protecting him throughout is the authoritative figure of Dr. Wingate, whose "robust and clear" materialism gives him "comfort" (*SD* 35) amidst the sinister upheavals at Swampscott.

His defenses, however, grow desperate in part two and start to erode as the irrational encroaches more and more threateningly. In the process, he commits moral offenses that violate his human preachments and secure the tragic issue ahead. While he records Hermia's four letters, his behavior runs counter, almost fuguelike, to his lectures on complicity and compassion. With every letter, his humor grows more sarcastic and misogynistic, until he finally tries to retreat altogether from the dilemma. "The affair was really none of my business" (*SD* 55), he protests nervously.

But irrational reality continues to intrude. Unwittingly, he finds himself duplicating Hermia's sentimentalities when he sees Nevil in Boston, and slowly and semiconsciously he assimilates the nature of the dream. Through "ghastly adumbration[s]" (*SD* 55), he intuits the dark vision and recoils with unexpected violence at the news of Hermia's engagement: "[I]t brought up again with dreadful vividness all the experiences of that day Faulkner died. It was as if he rose from the dead . . ." (*SD* 62).

Hermia's surprise visit draws Basil still further into the domain of unreason. The claims of his subliminal, buried self become alarmingly insistent and with it his defenses climb—widening the breach between his practice and principles, and causing a series of ethical lapses. The sight of Hermia on his doorstep "quell[s] and overawe[s]" (*SD* 63) him and he instantly begins to stockade himself against her. Complaining of her presence, he carps that her problems are "not [his affair]" (*SD* 64) and tries to evade them by not telling Dr. Wingate about her engagement. As a result, Hermia hears the dream unnecessarily and decides to immolate herself.

In the scene that builds up to the revelation, Basil's actions are in sharp contrast to his stated ideals of sympathy and brotherhood. He superciliously labels Hermia's arguments "childlike" (*SD* 66), laughs inappropriately, and with a misogynistic quip about feminine exaggeration, leaves her alone to learn that the dream is just as terrible as she imagined. Barricaded in his parlor afterwards, he continues his defensive retaliation. With an "increasing sense of injury" (*SD* 70), he impugns Hermia's decency and for "no reason" grows sardonic and "cheap[ly]" (*SD* 70) cynical. Humor, Basil's chief protective weapon, has failed. Dr. Wingate, too, has proved unequal to Hermia's dilemma and deserted him. His defenses weakened, he can no longer withstand the forces of the irrational. After more moral platitudes, another denial of the dream, and a last assault on Hermia, he begins his own descent into oneiric reality. His remark beforehand that he would not "like to shoulder . . . responsibility for [his] dreams" (*SD* 73) portends the outcome of the ordeal he is to endure.

By the time it begins, he has grasped the full extent of Faulkner's dream and falls into a "tormented" (*SD* 77) sleep at the "atrocious" (*SD* 78) prospect of having to escort Hermia home. In his dreams, Hermia's predicament assumes monstrous proportions and when he tries to escape, he sees a ghastly apparition: "Faulkner appeared to me a demoniac presence, at the end of a lurid perspective, running back to that scene in the garden—implacable, immovable, ridiculous like all the rest, monstrous, illogical, and no more to be reasoned away than to be entreated" (*SD* 78). Despite his attempts to avoid them, the unconscious powers have erupted and demanded a reckoning. Basil will have to return to the garden of the anarchic, repressed libido and be tested.

His trip West to the town where he "spent the happiest years of [his] young manhood" (*SD* 81), takes the form of an interior journey in which he travels backwards to the deep, infantile strata of his psyche. During this immersion he touches the source of his erotic conflict, but, instead of further exploration and integration, he shrinks from it in terror. When his efforts at reconciliation end unsuccessfully, he recurs to even sterner repressions, accelerating the tragic outcome of the story.

As he enters his subjective voyage, Basil sinks, like Hermia, into a twilight state of consciousness. He feels as though he is "something in a dream" to her and suffers nightmares[27] throughout the "strange journey" West (*SD* 80). In the smoke-dimmed town of his youth, he slowly descends to the foundations of his psyche, to his lawless wishes and the crux of his conflict. His first sensations are the pleasurable ones of the "lost body of childhood."[28] Enveloped by the "sumptuous comforts" of Hermia's home, he delivers himself "up to the caresses of . . .

velvety ease" (*SD* 82) and allows his imagination to roam amorally. If he were Nevil, he fantasizes, he would let nothing keep him from "this material bliss" and at dinner he has an "unruly sense" of Hermia. Regally presiding over her "exquisite" (*SD* 85) meal, she inspires him with intense sexual feelings. He notices her "perfect splendor of . . . womanhood" and "perversely" wants to flirt with her: "I wished to tease, to mystify her, to keep her between laughing and crying" (*SD* 84). Although he wonders whether Hermia is testing him to determine if Nevil, too, unconsciously desired her, he lazily discards the idea. Again, he works, without intending it, to secure her tragedy. After dinner, warmed by her hearthfire, he drops still deeper into unconscious realities. He has "long dreams" (*SD* 85) in which he envisions pleasant solutions to the lovers' problems and relaxes his ego control to such an extent that he does not know whether he has disgraced himself or not.

During the next day, his intrapsychic dive continues, bringing him to the lowest level of his repressed unconscious and thence to his conflict. After a night of dreams that counsel him to take everything "as naturally as possible," he walks in "pensive confusion" into the grey morning and "inhale[s] [his] glad youth" (*SD* 86). The description of the autumnal landscape that follows is one of the most sensuously lyric in the book. But the scent of boxwood (the sexual truthteller) interrupts his reverie and transports him back to Faulkner's garden. With that quintessential image of chthonic Eros before him, he reenters the house and recoils at two tokens of Faulkner's perverse, infantile sexuality: his madonnas and cigars. The dark side of his "glad youth" abruptly rears up: "It brought back my youth . . . not bright and warm, but cold and dead" (*SD* 87). Presumably Basil has glimpsed his own Oedipal and autoerotic impulses, and they terrify him. Rather than face the source of his libido-ego conflict, though, he begins a swift, frightened retreat. He fends off old Mrs. Faulkner's account of the tragedy with criticisms and when she reveals the dream, he oscillates wildly between belief and denial before he decides to "escape" (*SD* 98) from town on the night train.

Yet he does not leave without making two attempts to mend his ambivalence. Letting his guard down, he playfully broaches an ethic to his sibylline friend strong enough to defy chthonic sexuality and reclaim pleasure. Love, he teases, is wholly physical and "supersensuous" moral scruples should not keep Hermia and Nevil from plunging "through [Faulkner's ghost] into each other's arms" (*SD* 101). But his friend laughs at this notion and he speeds up his plans to get out of town. On the threshold, though, he is arrested by a sight that dashes all of his resolves. He sees Hermia and Nevil in a torrid embrace and his sexual self rushes to a rapturous defense of their passion: "She locked her arms around his neck, and wildly kissed him again and again, with sobs such as break from the ruin of life and love; . . . I felt that there would be only one good in the world, and that was the happiness of that woman" (SD 103).

His interview with Nevil is a last, frantic attempt to procure that end. It is also the culminating scene in the novella, when his drama fuses with Hermia's and Nevil's like a musical coda. Basil speaks "vehemently . . . beyond any explicit right" (SD 108) during their talk because his integration and salvation are as much at stake as the lovers'. Auspiciously, he turns the key in Nevil's lock for him, but, once inside the church study, he cannot fulfill his tacit sexual promise. Dark and lugubrious, Nevil's "protestant confessional" symbolizes the prohibitive ethos which ultimately defeats Basil and which he seems to sense at the time: "The place was not favorable to a judicial examination of [the] . . . case" (SD 106).

He launches his argument with a lame denial of the dream in the name of sanity, "character" (SD 108), and male superiority; then desperately tries to incorporate it morally. He impulsively suggests that the lovers marry anyway, even it they *were* as guilty as Faulkner's dream implied. But he draws back in horror when he realizes what he has said: "The words, when I had got them out, shocked me: they certainly did not represent my own feeling . . . I felt myself getting hot and red" (SD 109). Once again, his libido has caught his censor napping and almost redeemed him. But he retreats repentantly, and, as if to atone for his audacity, redoubles his repudiation of unconscious sexual realities. With greater vigor, he reiterates his first arguments, becoming hyperbolic and misogynistic and even hypocritical. To believe the dream, he hectors, is "mere madness of the moon" (SD 110)—a womanly impulse—and he thanks heaven (with glaring irony) that his conscience does not disturb him with his subliminal sins.

At last, he is unable to offer Nevil anything but the old drastic, genteel solution of denial which he had urged on Faulkner earlier and which had been surpassed in *April Hopes*. He harangues Nevil puritanically: "In the interest of human enlightenment, from the duty of every educated man . . . [you must] resist the powers of darkness that work upon our nerves through the superstitions of the childhood of the world, . . . you ought to act in defiance of it" (*SD* 111–12). Instead of a positive alternative, Basil leaves him with a repressive, dissociated strategy that is just as punitive as Nevil's own. Nevil must deny the deepest truths of his psyche or admit them and deny gratification. Either way requires the amputation of Eros. Basil, however, prides himself on his success as he escorts Nevil to the train station and can merely shake his head at the "meaninglessness of events" (*SD* 113) after the accident. Yet the final catastrophe could not be more apropos: Nevil has been literally crushed in the vise of two life-denying options.

Basil's epilogue cinches the book in a crescendo of bitter ironies. Although he admits that Nevil's death was "no true solution of the problem," Basil persists in his attitude of denial despite his own experience with subconscious reality. He calls Hermia's and Nevil's belief in the dream sheer morbidity and decides (in contradiction to everything he intuited throughout the story) that they were "guiltless" of Faulkner's charge. He has grown so alienated from his sexuality that he says (what Dan thinks in his silliest sentimental reverie)[29] the lovers could have enjoyed a "dramatic friendship" (*SD* 114) if they had lived. Only in the last four sentences does he entertain the possibility of an irrational, unconscious sexuality. Perhaps Faulkner's dream was true, he speculates; and Hermia and Nevil, unfaithful in their deepest hearts. But, as usual, he discards this notion and dispels it with a double-barbed irony. His wife, he quips, especially hates that idea and labels anyone who countenances it "worse than Faulkner" (*SD* 115).

In view of Basil's involuntary attraction to Hermia and his descent into Faulkner's irrational underworld, her antipathy is all too well-founded. Basil, then, thickens the texture of the tragedy and darkens its hues. Moreover, his "fairly reliable" commentary adds an immediacy to his dream ordeal that had never been present in Howell's "erotic" novels before. The reader is tricked into an identification with him, and thus, potentially, into a subliminal encounter of his own. Basil's failure, therefore, has larger ramifications than that of any previous protagonist: he not only mortally injures the lovers through his defenses and inadequacy; he trips the reader into an ethical void.

The Shadow of a Dream mentions Swedenborg by name for the first time and registers (although still imperfectly) his teaching on the deepest level yet. His childhood prophet suddenly acquired a "fresh attraction" for Howells after his daughter died. He told the minister, R. W.

Newton, that he had always thought about Swedenborgianism in a "loose and stumbling way"[30] and a year later was writing Howard Pyle for doctrinal advice. Faulkner, the apotheosis of the destructive powers of Eros, comes closest to the damned of *Conjugial Love*. Hump-backed, livid, with eyes that flash with jealousy, he incarnates the final fate of the accursed in Swedenborg's hell—insanity.

The evocations of pleasure, likewise, approximate most nearly the New Church heaven. The sensorium Basil enters as he travels West duplicates the paradise of intensified sensual delights enjoyed by the sexually blessed. More specifically, the beautiful, highly sexed Hermia and her house filled with delicious food and material luxury mirrors the women and rewards there. The critically heightened ambivalence also has a Swedenborgian reflection. The central image of *Conjugial Love*, the garden, is both aflower with roses and vines like Adramandoni (the home of ideal couples) and infected with putrescence like the fens of hell.

It is in the quest for a nonrepressive ethic, though, that Swedenborg's thought seems most prominent. The "mystic[al] and matter-of-fact" (*SD* 90) Swedenborgianism that old Mrs. Faulkner preaches, defying her son's insanity and leniently endorsing the lovers' marriage, is what Basil twice tries to grasp and affirm in his search for value. His "perverse amusement" (*SD* 100) and embarrassment each time is like the "sneaking fondness" (*MF* 184) and "perverse sympathy" (*MI* 325) for Mrs. Farrell and Bartley. The secret ambition for an ethical recovery of sensuality and joy was deep-rooted and destined for fulfillment.

After *The Shadow of a Dream*, with the wound of his neurotic conflict opened afresh and his failure to mend it upon him, Howells's imagination entered a period Howard Pyle called "the dreadful valley of shadows."[31] His novella had returned to the heart of his psychosexual division: to the intensest pleasures—his mother, her hearthfire, food, and the sensed beauty of childhood—and to the accompanying terror, without defenses or ameliorations. A lesser but similar dilemma had faced him in *A Modern Instance* when he tapped the adolescent level of his "neurosis." Then he fell ill and experienced one of his early symptoms. This time, the death-fixated mood of his mourning intensified. Even the vertigo that had incapacitated him during his 1858 nervous breakdown recurred.[32] Like Basil, his response for the next five years was denial and repression. If Faulkner's dream was a trapdoor to his repressed unconscious (as Bergson said of dreams), Howells kept it firmly bolted down. In an essay on dreams in 1895, he ambivalently called them clues to the "mystery of the universe"[33] and emanations from hell, and concluded that they should be rejected in favor of the conscious will. Some of the poems in *Stops of Various Quills* express a mood of extreme self-denunciation, targeting his sexuality with special wrath.[34] And his letters form a long litany of mea culpas and death wishes.[35]

Like Basil, too, Howells withdrew—although not as radically and never completely—from sexuality. After a companion novella, *An Imperative Duty*, in which the heroine, a mulatto (with all the oversexuality that implied), tries and fails to come to terms with her libido, he wrote Charles Eliot Norton despondently, "I doubt if I shall ever write another story in which mating and marrying plays an important part. I am too old for it, and it does not interest me."[36] He progressed, or perhaps grew roots, slowly. The breakthrough, when it came, would have a long foreground. If his novels of the next fourteen years do not pursue the sexual enigma as aggressively, the quest for erotic integration went on uninterrupted on another creative plane. In 1890 he began a series of autobiographies which consciously explored the "neurosis" his fiction had unconsciously exhumed. Division and denial dominate the first ones, but as he came closer to the bottom truths he had creatively intuited in *The Shadow of a Dream*, his conflict started to resolve. His criticism liberalized,[37] his letters spoke of new self-knowledge,[38] and in *The Son of Royal Langbrith* (1904) he achieved the erotic synthesis and conquest of chthonic evil, for which he had striven so long. His "cure," then, was accomplished in two ways, imaginatively and intellectually, each complementing and strengthening the other. The autobiographical project was sometimes excruciatingly painful for Howells, and he said presciently at the beginning: "Perhaps we can only suffer into the truth."[39] As in psychotherapy, he had to bring to consciousness those anarchic impulses Basil had glimpsed and fled. Although sexual tragedy had ambushed him again in *The Shadow of a Dream*, the novella proved pivotal in his erotic theme. He had discovered the negative half of the "truth of the secret" (*FC* 241) which Ferris tried to fathom in *A Foregone Conclusion*; he had seen what there was to fear. He had confirmed the meaning of "fool" in Douglas Faulkner and presented a heroine, of the highest sexuality and beauty, to ethically inform. At the same time, Basil's "perverse" solutions, which slip past his censor and embarrass him, had given him the key to the positive half of the "secret"; he needed only the courage and conviction to unlock it. On Freud's *via regia* he had reached the quick of his sexual theme, the demonic and redemptive essences.

It is true that Howells did escape from Faulkner's dream at the end, just as he had run from the woman with two husbands in his 1884 nightmare. The deaths of the lovers, apart from reifying the victory of Thanatos, evaded the ambivalence which had grown strained beyond endurance. But the sequel to the nightmare forecasts the direction he would take in the nineties. As Howells was fleeing from his dream-temptress, she handed him a human head rolled into the shape of a huge phallus which he could not manage to get rid of. At first he was able to accept it as "the head of a cadaver,"[40] but finally had to reject that explanation. In the same way, Howells would not be satisfied with the victory of Thanatos over Eros in either *The Shadow of a Dream* or his private life. Burdened with a sexual quest he could not drop, he would continue to struggle toward an affirmation, insisting that Hermia and Nevil find happiness together, and that Basil (and ultimately himself) learn self-integration through more sustained encounters with Faulkner, in which the shadows dissolve and a positive passion comes to light.

The Shadow of a Dream (1890) was a marker event in Howells's sexual quest. After the infantile bases of his neurotic conflict had been exposed—his earliest pleasure and its parallel terror—in his psychological love tragedy, Howells began an imaginative retreat from Eros. So searing must the encounter have been, so crushing, the renewed repression, that for the next fourteen years his novels cease to pursue "the secret" with the same energy. With his search transferred to the autobiographies, his sexual themes start to flag, dwindle or retrace old ground.

The Hazard of New Fortunes (1890), which preceded *The Shadow of a Dream*, forecasts the direction of the nineties' fiction. Although Howells had already branched into socioeconomic issues in *Annie Kilburn* the year before, *The Hazard of New Fortunes* was his first sustained examination of economic conditions. It launched a trend which continued through the decade, and which effectively demoted sexuality to a secondary status. The erotic subplots in *The Hazard of New Fortunes*—vivid as they are—serve more to corroborate the truths of the marketplace than advance erotic knowledge. Angus Beaton's exploitation of women, Christina Dryfoos' feral passion merely illustrate the competitive ferocity acted out on the larger social stage. They are examples of March's law of "having and shining" (*HNF* 396).

There is, at the same time, a trace of sex-weariness in the novel that would later solidify and strengthen. After all the sexual quadrilles in the plot, Basil March sighs at the end: "Why shouldn't we rejoice as much at a nonmarriage as a marriage? . . . By-and-by some fellow will wake up and see that a first-class story can be written from the anti-marriage point of view" (*HNF* 434).

A third tendency of the turn-of-century fiction was the repetition of earlier problems without relief or resolution. Angus Beaton and his counterpart, Christina Dryfoos, are two sexual "savages" like Bartley

Hubbard—sensual, seductive, yet wholly unreconciled to morality. The "good" spokesman, by the same token, cannot be reconciled with sexuality, although Alma Leighton contains all of Julia Anderson's erotic potential. The free-spirited Alma whose "shining ease and steely sprightliness" (*HNF* 114) anticipate the sexually integrated heroines of the future, nonetheless cannot find a match. One minor figure who does, Miss Woodburn, locates another feature of these interim novels. Amid the sexual failures appear occasional glints of progress, germs (like the "blooming, bubbling, bustling" [*HNF* 101] Miss Woodburn) of the final synthesis to come.

Howells, of course, had aligned sexuality with the tooth-and-claw natural order before—notably in *Private Theatricals*—but in his socioeconomic fiction, he explicitly denounced and codified what he had earlier dramatized. Love plots in these novels are contrapuntal variations on the major theme of commercial savagery. The two courting couples in *The Quality of Mercy* (1892) are as instinctually, irrationally attracted to each other as the protagonist, Northwick, is to pelf. They come together like "cats in the dark," (*QU* 326) and in one case, separate through insuperable social/economic differences.

The World of Chance (1893) articulates this alliance between Eros and the rule of the marketplace. Kane's "hard sayings" (*WOC* 293) assail the triumph of "the evil and foolish" (*WOC* 99, 396) in love and link it expressly to the "tremendous game played in New York" (*WOC* 100). Embodying his maxims is the young writer-hero who cannot remain constant to his ideal girl, but flits capriciously and greedily to others and finally leaves her in the lurch. Both the business and sexual realms have become "camp[s] of embattled forces" (*WOC* 155).

Mr. Homos, the visitor from utopia in *A Traveller from Altruria* (1894) sets these dark realities into sharper relief through the brilliance of his own example. A man whom all the women "follow with their eyes" (*TFA* 11) he preaches a marriage ideal and condemns a society "where you postpone and even forego, the happiness of life in the struggle to be rich" (*TFA* 67). Arrayed around him are casualties of that punitive society. The women languish in frustrated invalidism or idle snobbery like Mrs. Makely, while the battle of the sexes rages on with all the injustice of the marketplace. Just as the poor are squeezed by the rich, the natives are excluded from the dance (or marriage in the case of Lizzie Camp) by social-economic barriers.

If the sexual drama had been reduced to a subtheme, it also began to sour in the mid and late nineties. Cutting through the romantic complications is a sharp backtaste of sexual ennui—even despair. After the "unpractical doctrine of celibacy" (*WOC* 225) had been reemphasized in *The World of Chance*, the lovers of *The Day of Their Wedding* (1896) leave the Shakers to get married; then return to their celibate lives with relief. Basil's "anti-marriage" story reaches fulfillment. Suppressed as Althea and Lorenzo are as Shakers (Althea is compared to a "rabbit in a hole" [*DTW* 17]) they are so repulsed by the carnal, material bases of sexuality, that they decide to cancel their wedding. In a reverse striptease, Althea dons one alluring article of clothing after another, until the two realize the physical essence of their relationship and part.

Basil articulates this sex-weariness in two following novels. Amid a courtship in *An Open Eyed Conspiracy* (1897) which the young hero has already scripted beforehand in his novel, Basil provides a running fire of sardonic commentary. After assessing the immaturity of the heroine and egotism of her boyfriend, Basil explodes impatiently: "How sick I am of this stale old love-business. . . . It is curious . . . how we let this idiotic love-passion absorb us to the very last. It is wholly unimportant who marries who, or whether anybody marries at all" (*OEC* 86). When the couple do marry at the end, Basil drops a last acid aside: the heroine's girlhood will go, his wife says, and he adds, "And the girl will remain" (*OEC* 181). Intershot with his acrimony is a strain of nostalgia, which he and Isabel both share. While Isabel mourns the loss of "all the easy gayety" (*OEC* 39) between the sexes, Basil dreams that there are no women's wraps for men.

By *Their Silver Wedding Journey* (1899) two years later, Basil has grown even more weary, bitter, and nostalgic. The lovers now literally duplicate the romantic fiasco of *April Hopes*, even as they discuss the novel together. The bystander, Basil, is unsparing: "We're in love, we're out of love twenty times," he groans (*TSWJ* II 161). This time Isabel joins him in his spleen—though not as vehemently. She impugns the "hypocritical passion of love" (*TSWJ* II 217), and seconds his marriage sentiments: "It isn't all it might be," she quips, "but it's all there is" (*TSWJ* I 156). While the two youngsters go through their tired, predictable mating dance (doomed to end so drearily), the Marches' yearning for pleasure continues. Isabel dreams of the time when "it was delightful for girls—the freedom" (*TSWJ* I 130); Basil, of the "free, friendly manner of the West" (*TSWJ* I 276). He even re-experiences some of the old extramarital stirrings he felt in *The Shadow of a Dream*, pining at one point to join a band of bachelors beneath his window.

The Story of a Play (1897) is another novel in which love's tediousness is dramatized through a book-within-a-book device. The writer, Maxwell Brice, is so sexually disenchanted after a half year of marriage that he decides to write a play "without a love-element" (*SOP* 13)— only able to imagine a "man hating a woman with all his might" (*SOP* 43). He reflects on his marriage: "He had known moments of exquisite, of incredible rapture [but] he had been as little happy as in any half-year he had lived . . . [he felt] an obscure stress upon him" (*SOP* 217, 218). However, when his sponsor demands a sexual interest, he obliges—all too ardently when he meets the voluptuous leading lady. Although he models his newly eroticized heroine on his wife, she grows angrier and angrier, until he finally, haggardly caves in. Either way, in life or the play, sex is a turbid, exhausting affair—unreconcilable with happiness.

A third course in the decade was a tendency to repeat the erotic problems of the earlier fiction (as the lovers do in *Their Silver Wedding Journey*) without coming any closer to a solution. *The Story of a Play*, for instance, replays the whole drama of jealous wife versus polygamous husband, and ends with a *deus ex machina* exit of the rival, instead of a new explanation. The rival, in this case, sets off a sexual time bomb like Faulkner did in *The Shadow of a Dream*. More than simply an attractive woman, the star of Maxwell's play symbolizes all of the erotic subtruths denied by the Victorian age. Her abandoned swimming at the beach embodies this (the way Edna Pontellier's did in *The Awakening* a year later) as does her impassioned acting. Before she is forced off the stage and out of the plot, she exhumes almost all of the demonic powers of Eros: jealousy, inconstancy, violence. Maxwell has to admit that he doesn't "seem to know" (*SOP* 84) whether one wife is enough and injects a violence into the character of his heroine/wife which makes her not "mind killing a man to carry her point" (*SOP* 295). Meanwhile, his wife becomes unhinged with jealousy and dogs her rival like a crazed animal. At the test, neither she nor Maxwell can cope with these chthonic realities. To Maxwell's question, "Can't we grapple with this infernal nightmare, so as to get it into the light somehow, and see what it really is?" (*SOP* 279) Louise can only answer when she sees the play: "Horrible, horrible, horrible" (*SOP* 295). The issue, ultimately, is not faced, but shelved—as it had been before. The vamp is replaced by the insipid Miss Pettrell, who knows "how to subdue character to the interests of the domestic hearth" (*SOP* 300).

The Landlord at Lion's Head (1897), one of Howells's strongest novels about sex, in fact, takes the theme of Eros little further than the earlier fiction. Nothing new happens. Jeff Durgin, "the prehistoric man" (*LLH* 230), is a less inhibited version of Bartley, and his counterpart, the fiery Bessie Lynde, an understudy of Mrs. Farrell's. They demonstrate the identical truths of the past novels—sadism, perversity, polygamy, egotism, and greed—and offer no counter or palliative. Jeff is a powerful incarnation of the savage libido. "A young Hercules" (*LLH* 73) with bulging calves and brash manners, he magnetizes the women at his mother's resort, and is identified with wild natural forces: his fierce dog, Fox, and the "primatively solitary and savage" (*LLH* 2) Lion's Head mountain. His *sexualité* is thrice-underlined. "It was as if," the narrator remarks, "he were about to burst out of his clothes . . . there was somehow more of the man than the citizen in him, something native, primitive . . ." (*LLH* 127). Like Bartley Hubbard, Jeff is frankly selfish and self-pleasuring, with a dash of sadism in his makeup.

When he first appears as a boy, we watch him torture a local girl with a growling dog. His "savagery" becomes plainly sexual in maturity. His courtship with Cynthia, his early childhood victim, is no more than a genteel Punch-and-Judy, with Cynthia threatening to take "the whip hand" (*LLH* 154) while Jeff "digs" (*LLH* 152) and taunts her.

At Harvard, paradoxically, Jeff's id-self has its fullest expression. Although officially engaged to Cynthia, his eye strays to the wild Bessie Lynde, who joins him in one of Howells's most combustible, daring *à deux*s. Bessie, a "fascinating creature" (*LLH* 321), whose "rich mouth" (*LLH* 212) proclaims her sensuality, captivates Jeff at a party.

They no sooner meet than begin a heavily innuendoed, racy dialogue. She jibes him about his ambition to open a hotel, punning on a still-current slang word for coitus: "Oh, I understand now," said the girl. "The table will be the great thing. You will stuff people. / Do you mean that I'm trying to stuff you? / How do I know? You never can tell what men really mean" (*LLH* 211).

Their flirtation rapidly moves into deeper waters. Puffed with vanity, Bessie and Jeff both begin to let themselves go sexually, and the results are nasty. As Jeff's "will to dominate" (*LLH* 220) swells into naked aggression, and the "excitement" (*LLH* 232) mounts, Bessie's self-mastery disintegrates, and she succumbs to his cynical embrace. Their kiss, which climaxes a parry-and-thrust around the word "fascinating," comes with all the force of a rape. Afterwards Jeff "brutally exult[s]" (*LLH* 332) and states the essence of their relationship: "It's been a game from the beginning and a question of which should win. I won" (*LLH* 341). When he is horsewhipped, he returns to Lion's Head where he breaks his engagement, marries an heiress, and prospers.

During his whole demonic crusade—as he spreads sadism, egotism, greed, and incoherence in his path—not one counterforce is capable of resisting him. The artist, Westover, who observes him from the wings, is too sexually pallid to approach his inamorata, and significantly, can never find the right word to describe Jeff. He keeps painting Lion's Head Mountain each year unable to plumb its mystery. Neither is Cynthia Whitwell any match for Bessie Lynde. If Bessie cannot integrate her high-strung sexuality with virtue (her joke being that she'll try something "really difficult" next year, like "being very very good" [*LLH* 242]), Cynthia cannot yoke her spirit to her body. As exemplary as she is, as thoroughly good and maternal, she lacks vitality. Her "pure, cold beauty" is recessive and pale: she is a "hermit thrush" (*LLH* 61) "stopped to fly" (*LLH* 444)—rather than flying.

Yet even while the powers of chthonic sexuality ride triumphant through the novel, there is a covert attraction to Jeff. Just as Jeff's "mind stray[s] curiously to that other girl" (*LLH* 236), so Westover and the others cannot help an involuntary gravitation toward Jeff. Westover remains intrigued by Bessie, and unable to dispel his "illogical liking" (*LLH* 279) for Jeff. As Cynthia's father says in the end, summing up his daughter's and Westover's feelings, "He may have a knife in your ribs the whole while, but . . . you can't help likeing him" (*LLH* 446–47). It is the same ambivalence that runs through other novels time and time again. It is the Marches' recurrent nostalgia for freedom and pleasure—still unintegrated with morality. The stalemate between unvirtuous sexuality and unsexual virtue persists.

On the other hand, there were fragments of progress within the larger failures that prepared the ground for the erotic ethic at the turn of the century. The physical primacy of love which March was afraid to utter in *The Shadow of a Dream* becomes an established fact by *The Day of Their Wedding*. Even though the lovers cannot act on their insight, they realize the carnal essence of love: "'It's the body that contains the soul,' Lorenzo announces, 'and it comes first, and it has a right to'" (*DOW* 139). Similarly, the issue of multiple attraction is faced and accepted in *Ragged Lady* (1899). No longer the province of id-villains or semiconscious wishes, pluralistic sexual feelings become a legitimate human impulse—impractical but not condemned. Clemnetia, the heroine, is both good and sexual (her sensuality expressed in her passion for dancing) and is drawn to two men at once. Not only is this dual attachment recognized, but her second marriage to the man she liked before becoming engaged to the first is sanctioned. After Clemnetia becomes tragically educated in loss and moral complexity, her wise friend tells her: "Life is a struggle at best, and it's your duty to take the best chance for resting" (*RL* 273). With the awareness that "We're all fools" (*RL* 338), a tentative ethic of pleasure has been envisioned. The book is too slight for *Ragged Lady* to be a breakthrough, but the ingredients for one had been assembled; only the catalyst was needed.

The Kentons (1902) did not provide that catalyst, but it brought the realization of an erotic ethic much nearer. The demonic id reappears in the form of the "fascinating" (*K* 60) Bittridge who ravishes the heroine and reduces her to confusion. This time, however, he is trounced by an equally virile suitor, while Bittridge's appeal is accepted in all its power. "'It's a kind of sickness,' Mrs. Kenton says, 'and you can't fight it'" (*K* 26). Her daughter, Ellen, concurs, realizing that "you can't control feelings" (*K* 26) and goes on to redirect her affections to the sexy, humorous, easygoing Hugh Beckon. If Ellen's erotic coloring were slightly higher, if she weren't quite so "meek" (*K* 221) and submissive, a real sexual comedy—with a union of spirit and flesh, discipline and freedom—might have materialized.

As it was, it took two more years for the brilliant summation and celebration of *The Son of Royal Langbrith*. The period, then, between *The Shadow of a Dream* and 1904 was both less and more fruitful than it appears. Although the novels flag from an eroto-literary standpoint, they were a necessary phase in Howells's development. They permitted a quiescent period before the great spurt of energy at the turn of the century and they nourished the piecemeal discoveries which made his ethic possible. His defenses of the pluralism and physicality of passion, which lie scattered through these books, were the missing pieces required to complete the mosaic of his erotic affirmation.

The true advances of this period, of course, took place in the autobiographies, where Howells emotionally accomplished the return to his lenient, sensuous background. In 1902, he advised the aspiring writer to certainly accumulate "experience and observation" but most of all to achieve "knowledge" of "his own heart."[1] Howells had just recently struggled to that end, to the "black heart's truth,"[2] which permitted the forgiveness and reconciliation that transformed the sexual theme in his fiction—taking it from sexual darkness and despair to harmony, light, and life.

The autobiographical journey:
The rounding of the circle | *Nine*

By the end of *The Shadow of a Dream* Howells had reached a sort of psychic impasse. For many reasons the confident, resilient mood of the eighties, which characterized the early "realism war" and the temperate erotic compromise of *April Hopes*, had darkened. He faced a great divide in his life, a "valley of the shadows,"[1] in which the meaning of his life and work eluded and defied him. The theme of Eros in his fiction had led to a negative deadlock that seemed unbreakable. Faulkner's dream had revealed sexuality's deadliest secrets, destroyed every ethical defense, and forced a return to the lethal strategy of denial. Simultaneously, the ambivalence had built to a climax, leaving the deaths of the lovers as the only escape valve. Thanatos had caught and double-blocked Howells's erotic quest.

His personal life also seemed to feel the pull of the death instinct after *The Shadow of a Dream*. He complained of a world-weariness and despair during the early nineties similar to William James's "anhedonia."[2] He turned a fierce moral wrath on himself and again and again spoke of a yearning for peace and oblivion in his letters: "[A]t fifty-three," he wrote his father, "I want to coil up on the lounge and go to sleep."[3] With his dejection was a persistent, but unformulated nostalgia (as in the novels) for his sensuous past. He grieved to his brother that he was "cut off from all . . . simple delights and . . . long[ed] for the Western woods"[4] and later said he "felt a curious longing . . . [to] go back to Jefferson and live there."[5]

This "curious" pull towards his past perhaps explains the project he undertook in the nineties, which transferred his erotic quest to a new plane. He started the first of series of books that were to be harder to write than "three or four novels"[6] put together. Using a method similar to free association,[7] he began to investigate the intuitive discoveries of his fiction in what became six major autobiographies. Like Basil, he embarked on a "strange journey" (*SD* 80) into his childhood. He subjected himself to a maturity ordeal more arduous than any his fictional heroes had endured. Yet, for his imaginative theme to come to maturity, his own ordeal was first necessary.

His autobiographies proceeded in three stages, each drawing nearer the crux of his neurosis. The first group, four reminiscences which end with *Literary Friends and Acquaintance* (1900), records the primary data. Although each book enlarges the clinical picture, none escapes the self-division and despair of the early decade. To reach the unconscious levels of conflict, he needed the fictionalized approach of the next set. The turning point came with *The Flight of Pony Baker* (1902), a fantasized version of childhood that both penetrates the Oedipal stratum of his problem (the truths Basil grazed in *The Shadow of a Dream*) and witnesses the beginnings of a self-integration which continued until his death.

By 1916, when he completed the last fictionalized memoirs, he was ready to directly confront his past. *Years of My Youth* conflates all the stages of boyhood, adolescence, and young manhood, and turns on them the unsparing light of critical intelligence. It was his most painful autobiography to write. But his purgations permitted a triumphal affirmation of health and synthesis. He conquered his fears, welded the warring halves of his personality, and recovered the sensuous vitality of childhood in his adult identity. Nowhere is his achievement more evident than in his fiction, where his characters, after the discoveries of *The Flight of Pony Baker*, attain the sexual strength and happiness that had been the covert goal of the novels for twenty-five years.

Almost without a break, Howells moved from *The Shadow of a Dream* to his first autobiography, *A Boy's Town* (1890). In it he documents his infantile conflict and supercontrols and symptoms, without, however, relating or interpreting them. At the end, he complained that he did not have a chance to "give more than a glimpse of the heart of boyhood."[8] So barely did he scratch the surface of his neurosis that the narrator duplicates the maladjustment he describes in the child. But he had taken the hardest step: he had started a project psychiatrists call the "equivalent of the labors of Hercules."[9]

The book begins at the storm center of his difficulty, at the tension between sensuous beauty and pain and death in his earliest infancy. As the reminiscing author, he recalls the images of lovely peach blossoms and a pet deer beside two nightmarish ones—a drowning man and the deer's death through a dog bite. The rest of the book chronicles this paired "doom and horror" (*BT* 18) and pleasure. A fearful darkness always lurks beneath the joys of his informal town and home. Yet the conflict is treated in isolation, wholly independent of the accounts of his tyrannical conscience and symptoms. In a separate context he tells of the Indians, ghosts, and madmen that haunted him; the death that threatened, the homesickness that wracked him.

He had merely assembled the pieces of the puzzle; not fitted them together, and his "voice" in the memoir reflects his still segmented consciousness. As in *The Shadow of a Dream*, the realm of the senses and the realm of morality are at opposite removes and uniformly punitive. The child, the instinctual self, is a greedy, egotistical "savage" whose world is a "prison," whose vision, "distorted and mistaken," whose behavior, "cruel" (*BT* 6, 1, 49). On the other side of the equation, the prospect is no brighter. Adulthood is a universe of "toils and cares" where sins "insist on being paid for" and "there is so much misery" (*BT* 151, 35, 216). The same ruthless conscience of the child presides over the man's existence.

Beneath these two negations, however, runs an unassimilated and subterranean sympathy for pleasure. Juxtaposed against assertions of the child's imprisonment and savagery, are lyrical celebrations of the "free life of the woods" (*BT* 149) and the delights of the primitive state. He hymns swimming in the canal and writes rhapsodically of the opening of spring: "Life has a good many innocent joys for the human animal, but none surely so ecstatic as the boy feels when his bare foot first touches the breast of our mother earth in the spring. Something thrills through him. . . . His blood leaps wildly . . . the day will not be long enough for his flights" (*BT* 83).

Unable to assimilate this sensuous undercurrent, Howells falls back on redoubled repression. Going beyond condemnation of his boy-self, he denies his very identity. "If you have anything that seems quite your own," he admonishes, "it is from your silly self" (*BT* 205). His repudiation both demonstrates the psychoanalytic argument that self-image derives from the primal emotions and locates the source of his "fool" motif. The final mood is one of deep sadness. The past is "gone forever" (*BT* 246), and the last two sentences perpetuate the contradictions that have rent the book. The boy's town, he comments paradoxically, was "hemmed in" by ignorance and inexperience, yet "large with vistas" (*BT* 247). S. Weir Mitchell caught the spirit of the autobiography when he called it "full of terror and 'haunting melancholy.'"[10]

The next, *My Year in a Log Cabin* (1893), assumes a more neutral attitude to the boy and the pessimism abates. The conflict leaves the narrative voice and becomes absorbed into the account of his early adolescent year in a family utopian experiment. The libido-ego antagonism occupies the center of the tale and a reason for it begins to appear. During his Xenia year, the primitive conditions and surrounding wilderness provided unparalleled range for sensual enjoyment; but at the same time, the repressive forces were unusually strong. And their locus was his mother. Just when his sexual feelings were awakening, his mother reacted violently against the instinctual, natural world. "All this was horrible to my mother," he says, ". . . who *justly* [italics mine] regarded it as a return to a state which, if poetic, was not far from barbaric" (*MYLC* 15). The mother's embattled disapproval and the boy's "long delight" (*MYLC* 23) build in counterpoint through the first half of the book until the tension finally culminates in a series of symptoms. Although the repression and symptoms remain unconnected, they follow directly on the heels of the mother's exasperation in early summer. The phobias, in keeping with the intensification of his conflict, are now more numerous (including fears of a horse, the gristmill, and a dead man) and the homesickness assumes a sexual aspect. During a brief visit upstate he became so miserable, tortured by the laughter of schoolgirls in the boarding house and plagued by memories, "above all . . . of his mother" (*MYLC* 51), that he dissolved in tears and had to be taken home.

The fuller documentation of his difficulty, however, and closer approach to an answer still do not suffice. Howells's concurrence with his mother's view of Xenia as "justly" barbarous testifies to his continued bondage to his past and his attitude to his child-self is as alienated as before. The book closes with a bleak vignette of the author on a "sterile track of sand" yearning toward his youth and stranded in a present haunted by "real ghosts" (*MYLC* 59).

My Literary Passions (1895) seems at first a retrospect of Howells's reading experiences, but obliquely it continues his psychic history. Through the filter of his literary life, he follows his neurosis from Xenia to early adulthood, tracing the growth of his conflict into three nervous breakdowns. Both sides of his struggle reached intolerable levels during those years. The next two moves, which took him to Dayton and Jefferson, removed him from the emotionally charged wilderness but exposed him to a social environment full of new temptation and new forces for repression.

The story of his adolescent reading indirectly records these developments. In his Jefferson literary experiences is a covert account of the approach of desire and the fierce sublimation he used to quash it. "The look of type," he recalls, "took me more than the glance of a girl, and I had a fever of longing to know the heart of a book, which was like a lover's passion" (*MLP* 141). The overstrict superego of the child, already strengthened by his mother's Xenia anxieties, resurfaced with a vengeance. He brutally overworked himself, burying himself in studies that betray the extent of his sexual suppression. Amidst the survey of books read at the time are at least four digressions on "the streams of filth . . . in literature" (*MLP* 110).

With a better grasp of the psychology of repression, Howells puts these revelations of self-tyranny next to those of his nervous collapses. The same symptoms of childhood—the ghosts and death fears—reappeared, with the addition of an imaginary hydrophobia and real vertigo. He felt a hideous, suffocating entrapment, he says, like the hero of a Scandinavian romance, walled in by the fjords.

But even these elaborations of his adolescent attacks fail to alter the despair and dissociation of the mid-nineties. Like *My Year in a Log Cabin*, *My Literary Passions* preserves the divorce between spirit and sense, man and boy. The narrator's digression on the "monkey and goat" in us replicates the nineteen-year-old's disgust with literary "grossness" (*MLP* 109, 119). The breach, likewise, between his mature and early identities gapes wide. He begins and ends the memoir with the confession that his "own youth seems to [him] rather more alien than that of any other person," and decries his "troublesome and wearisome self" (*MLP* 2, 226).

In the same year he wrote an essay, "I Talk of Dreams," which offers an almost fluoroscopic vision of his conflict. Revealingly, his dreams are intensely sexual and enact the identical scenario: the passions run rampant and result in death, violence, and terror. A hunchback chases a "swarthy beauty" up a tower where she plunges to her death; a runaway fire engine creates a scene of "horror";[11] a sled loses control and hits a train. Although he isolates the key polarities of his neurosis—sensuality and death—Howells stops short of the deeper truths he plumbed in *The Shadow of a Dream*. He never taps the infantile, maternal levels of his conflict.

Yet he denies the validity of the unconscious even more strenuously than he did in the novella. The dreamer, he protests, is a "dog" (recalling the dog of the deer's death),[12] a soulless savage, whose hallucinations reveal the "state of the habitual criminal . . . the lunatic, the animal, the devil. . . ."[13] Across Freud's *via regia*, Howells throws up a blockade; art and the unconscious, the waking and sleeping man must be permanently, irrevocably separated. With the victory of division this time, though, are glimmers of promise. Embedded in his dream life are two visions of potential health. In one, his father, the paragon of relaxed, ethical Eros, stands silently over his bedside waiting for him to wake up; in the other, the figure eight, the archetypic emblem of integration,[14] looms up as though it contains "the revelation of the mystery of the universe."[15]

At the turn of the century, just when his interior transition began, he completed the last in the first series of autobiographies, *Literary Friends and Acquaintance* (1900). An update through the Boston years, it recounts the victory of his punitive superego over his libido. His literary mentors, who provide the occasion for the book, ratified and reinforced the suprarepressive strategies he had adopted as a child and young adult. When the Boston literati received him into their genteel, elevated circle, they augmented his mother's "respectable" ambitions and fulfilled the "dream of [his] life" (*LFA* 164). But it was his mother's dream, not the child's, which was to be Apollo, the god of light *and* underworld wisdom.[16] For that reason, a covert revolt against the Brahmin solution threads through the memoir. Side by side with the praises of Boston are left-handed criticisms of the snobbery, sexism, and coldness that well from his democratic, lenient childhood. This he would gradually incorporate into his mature identity over the next decade and a half. For now, though, his protest is incipient and the mood of sadness for "earlier and happier years" (*LFA* 207) predominant again.

Howells once observed that "no man unless he puts on the mask of fiction can show his real face" (*YOMY* 110). Accordingly, this next approach to his past, the approach which was to reach the deepest, root causes of his neurosis, was through fantasy.

At the time he started this group of semifictionalized autobiographies, there were signs of major shifts in his personality. His criticism seemed to make a volte-face. His lecture, "Novel-Writing and Novel-Reading," retracted his reticent realism dogma of the eighties. Instead of "decency," he advocated the "grossest material honestly treated," and insisted that "the truth may be indecent but it cannot be vicious."[17] Realism, he argued, must take all experience as its province. His view of censorship also changed. In 1902, he announced that young girls should be allowed to read whatever they wanted, adumbrating a more complete condemnation of literary suppression fourteen years later.[18] While "civilization" became "hypocritical" and a "carrion of false-hood," the sexual impulses ameliorated into "instincts [that were] not more vicious than virtuous."[19]

Indications of a psychic breakthrough emerged as well. After a "dreamy fumbling for [his] . . . identity" through the first years of the new century, he spoke of the discovery of a "black heart's truth" about himself. To his sister he admitted a renewed kinship with his father and exclaimed: "What a pity that we learn everything in life too late!"[20] Another alteration was an apparent accord with his unconscious. Re-considering the subject of dreams in his review of James's *Psychology*, he praised them as bonds between the inner and outer man and de-nounced the "old desolating doctrine of denial."[21]

Set amidst these developments like a centerpiece is *The Flight of Pony Baker* (1902). A fantasized *Boy's Town*, this deceptively slight book reaches into the maternal matrix of his childhood and divines the heart of his neurosis. With the license of fiction, Howells splits his in-fantile personality into at least three different "boys." Pony (the horse of his Xenia fears?) enacts the Oedipal drama in his conflict; Frank plays the part of his tyrannical conscience; and Jim, the "bad" boy.

In Pony's story, the child's struggle with his mother occupies center stage. Pony has a particularly difficult relationship with his mother. An only son, he both loves her excessively—prizing her attentions and frequent caresses—and has a hard time pleasing her. She is de-manding and volatile, to the point of boxing his ears for a flirtatious prank. She is the "afraidest mother in the boy's town" (*FPB* 103), a pillar of respectability, who makes Pony a laughingstock to his friends with his prissy clothes and rules. Hence his repeated attempts to run away from home. The strain, however, between his desire for the sen-suous pleasures of boyhood and the need for her approval is too in-tense and before every "flight" he collapses.

Instead of the conflict and symptoms coexisting independently, they now follow in sequence. Twice, when he can neither escape to savage freedom (personified by the boy-gang, Indians, and the circus) nor escape his mother dependencies, he falls ill, has nightmares, and feels "as if he never wanted to get up again" (*FPB* 160). The only flight that semimaterializes is a thinly veiled retelling of Howells's homesickness attack. After a night in the barn before his circus geta-way, like the night away from Xenia, Pony has a crying fit and must be rescued by his mother. The sensuous reception she gives him—not only here but whenever Pony is sick—suggests an added difficulty in his relationship. His mother lavishly rewards his neurotic symptoms and breakdowns.

The motivating force behind each of his flights is the villainous Jim Leonard, the projection of Howells's bad boy-self. A scapegrace and ne'er-do-well, Jim is an anathema to Pony's mother and an object of intense ambivalence to Pony himself. Just after he has fled from his friend's Bacchanalia in fear and trembling, Howells comments: "Pony liked Jim as much as his mother hated him" (*FPB* 77). Jim's story, though, presages a solution of the child's dilemma. The "rude, fierce" (*FPB* 9) part of Pony, against which all of his mother's respectable energies have been directed, becomes displaced onto Jim. He is a "fool," an irrational power who has "bewitched" Pony, and with his banishment the controls and moral strictures loosen: "They let him do more things, and his mother did not baby him so much before the boys. He thought she was trying to be a better mother to him . . ." (*FPB* 210, 222, 223).

The interpolated tale of Frank Baker's adventure extends and concludes Pony's drama. Frank, in contrast to Jim, is Pony's superego, his wholly good and socialized self. So honored is he by the adult community that he is entrusted with a daring mission: he must deliver two thousand dollars to an owner twenty miles away. With his habitual superconscientiousness, Frank worries about the money the entire trip until he finally contracts symptoms. After a frightening ride on a runaway horse, he cannot eat or sleep and becomes terrified by imaginary Indians and madmen on a bridge he must cross. Irrational guilt feelings assail him: "It seemed to him that he must be to blame, somehow, but he could not understand how . . ." (*FPB* 182–83).

Given the nineteenth-century equation between money and sexuality, Frank's overcontrol and anxieties symbolize Pony's internalization of his mother's sensuous prohibitions. His fears, for that reason, consistently focus on instinctuality and its anarchical release—food, sleep, the unbridled horse, the Indian, and madman. The episode, however, charts a victory for the first time in the memoirs over the suprarepressive self. When Frank successfully accomplishes his mission, he loses his fears, feels jubilant, and falls asleep after his father warns him against overvaluing money.

Having made these discoveries, Howells rises to a new narrative plateau. He had sighted the Oedipal origins of his neurosis: the extreme love for his mother, her high demands, his exaggerated internalizations of them, and breakdowns under the strain. Moreover, he had envisioned a solution. Consequently, the authorial "voice" grows hopeful and warmly accepts the boy. The joys of dancing nude in the rain, the lush woodland, and the heaped bounty of his mother's dinner table are now paramount and the mood of fear almost lost. With the incorporation of the sensuous impulses, the gloomy sense of alienation vanishes. The ghosts, which haunted the narrator at the end of *My Year in a Log Cabin*, metamorphose into an apparition of a boy who smiles on the gambols of the other boys and looks as though he wants "to play" (*FPB* 128). A positive affection for the boy pervades the text. As a proof of his recovery, Howells benignly equates boys with dogs and commemorates Pony's first triumph in a reunion with Trip, his pet mutt.

If *The Flight of Pony Baker* launched the deeper explorations of the next autobiographies, it was also decisive for his fiction. After his recognitions, after diagnosing Basil's mysterious conflict, he was able to return to his erotic theme and master it. *The Son of Royal Langbrith*, which followed, resurrects sexual evil in all its ferocity, surmounts it, and achieves an erotic harmony that reconciles sense to spirit, body to mind.

The second fictionalized memoir picks up the unfinished story of Xenia and supplies the missing pieces. In *New Leaf Mills* (1913) the adolescent tensions of *My Year in a Log Cabin* receive a more penetrating, sexually informed explanation. As in the previous book, Howells imaginatively splinters his early identity into several characters, each of whom enacts a major role of his psyche. The dreamer, the younger brother who suffers homesickness and visitations from a ghost that looks like a clown (a "fool"), is the ostensible Howells persona. He drifts around the margins of the story in a naive trance, unaware of the central action. But there is another Howellsian figure crucially involved in it. An older incarnation of Jim is the principal player in the piece and touches off more than a conflict with the mother. This time husband and wife are also at loggerheads over the issue of the "lower" versus the "higher" impulses. To the mother's dismay, the father cannot defend the family against libidinal danger, specifically against Captain Bickler, a rakish impersonation of the *Boy's Town* "bad" boy. He is an egotist, a dandy, a shirker, and a "miserable boy" (*NLM* 43) who swaggers around on a dashing horse. Not only Bickler, but a drunken miller as well (perhaps indicating the source of the gristmill fear) present impossible challenges to the father. While the miller storms and Bickler works his dark designs on the family's pretty servant, the father stands by helplessly and the mother's fury mounts.

Through the "mask" of fiction, then, Howells has shown how his soma-psyche conflict became sealed in adolescence. At thirteen he not only had strange, new urges to deal with, which his mother seemed to abhor; he had the added burden of parental friction. Because of his father's failure to satisfy his mother's respectability needs and govern the son (the miller, Bickler), he had extra pressures to discipline himself. He had a twofold obligation to please his mother, along with unusually strong passions to tame. Thus the overtense prudery of his teens and early twenties.

Like Pony Baker, though, the book's conclusion suggests a successful resolution of the problem. Bickler collapses when the mother berates him and, in a paroxysm of tears, vanishes from the plot. The miller, on the other hand, moves from sin and guilt to a qualified redemption. In a drunken orgy, he climbs on the roof, wheels dizzily, and pitches to the ground. When the father comes to his bedside, as he did in Howells's dream, the miller tells all. He blurts out that he expects to die within the year and by the father's hand. Since his symptoms (the vertigo and death fear) so closely parallel Howells's, the confession may well be of Oedipal castration terror. In any case, the father's explanation absolves him and the miller leaves a humbler but happier, wiser man: "He was like a man who had been dignified by the vision of a specter and then cast down by finding it a shadow or a dead tree" (*NLM* 143).[22]

A small quasi-autobiographical story three years later continues and crowns the imaginative conquest of his neurosis. A seemingly slim account of a fantasized theft and its consequences, "The Pearl" (1916) provides a parable of excessive sexual guilt and its mastery. The boy, nineteen now, mysteriously discovers his cousin's missing tie in his suitcase and experiences irrational throes of "shame and horror."[23] At last he becomes sick with the "nightmare [of the] thing."[24] This is the same morbid conscience and pathology of the boy in *A Boy's Town* and *The Flight of Pony Baker*, but the sexual symbolism, if Freud is right about the tie as a key emblem of the phallus,[25] is plainer. The crime is more nearly sexual. Meaningfully, too, the story takes place on a trip away from home in a city, the precise circumstances of Howells's two breakdowns.

But "The Pearl" brings the boy's crisis to a brilliant denouement. As the experience continued to haunt him through adulthood, it became a "grain of sand . . . keep[ing] him a kind of sick oyster" until it metamorphosed through patient industry, into a "pearl of great price."[26] His sexual "sin" and overatonement have been imaginatively transcended. Fictionally Howells has depicted the sexual bases of his neurosis, his laborious therapy, and final success in the classic symbol of personality integration, the pearl. By coincidence, he retracted his censorship decree the same year, admitting that "we are not wholly brain, . . . not wholly heart; there are other organs of our make-up which must perform their office in their own way."[27]

It was also the year of *Years of My Youth*, the magnum opus of his autobiographies, in which he looked squarely, as squarely as a self-portraiturist can, at all three phases of his youth—childhood, early and late adolescence—without the transforming lens of fiction. After he finished *A Boy's Town*, he lamented to S. Weir Mitchell: "Some time I should like to lay it all bare; but I never shall."[28] Although no autobiography avoids distortion, this last presents a daringly "bare" record of his youth. All his imaginative discoveries enter the light of consciousness, with each stage of his development amplified by fresh evidence. The process was painfully difficult. During the ordeal of composition, he complained that his task was "hell," that his "miserable memoirs" made him "really sick,"[29] and that the childhood section gave him nightmares. But his struggle yielded the highest psychic gains. In place of the self-alienation and sadness of the first memoirs is a spirit of happiness, poise, and self-union. The sequence of conflict, suprarepression, and illness falls into place, and a child who is mostly "glad" eclipses the "fool" and bad boy.

Rather than a denial of the boy's individuality, Howells begins the book by affirming it. He dismisses the life of the "generalized boy"— the only one who mattered earlier—as external and "easy to recall" and concentrates on the harder, interior realities of "the specialized boy" (*YOMY* 19). With remarkable penetration, he starts with a discussion of his relationship to his mother. Articulating what he had dramatized in *The Flight of Pony Baker*, he admits a "passionate" love for her: "[S]he was not only the centre of home to me, she was home itself" (*YOMY* 20). However, her unqualified love in return was even harder for him to win than for Pony. Rather than an only son, he was one of four who competed for her attention, and her standards and temper surpassed Mrs. Baker's. She whipped him for an unauthorized swim and taught him that words had the same moral consequences as deeds.

In recalling one of his verbal blunders, Howells exposes the nerve of his Oedipal complex. He remembers saying he wished his father were dead. After this admission he openly tells of his father's permissiveness, which allowed him to read "literary filth" (*YOMY* 24), and documents his resulting superprudery and symptoms. He recoiled at the sight of a nude painting and persecuted a compromised servant girl, while terrors of imminent death ravaged him day and night.

Yet these hard confessions have a therapeutic effect. Howells returns to his father, as one must for the resolution of an Oedipal complex, with renewed appreciation and love. He hails his father's, not his mother's, reaction to his *lapsus linguae*. The tolerance with which he treated the episode leads Howells to a tribute to his leniency. In place of the "puritanism" and "austerity" of other men, his father espoused a laudable "doctrine of degrees" (*YOMY* 22). He was the "soul" (*YOMY* 24) of the family, he continues, a gifted, kind, and sensible man whom he sees mirrored in himself.

After similar, tough recognitions about his mother, he also embraces her. He realizes that she reinforced his malaise by making a sick child her "favorite" (*YOMY* 25), then praises her maternal warmth and devotion. At the same time, he accepts his lost child-self with enthusiasm. The judgmental, melancholy mood of *A Boy's Town* disappears, and is replaced by one of acceptance and restored childhood pleasure. In his revised version of the peach blossom–drowning man story, beauty has become paramount. The positive, happy experiences and sensuous pleasures, the rapturous smells, sights, and tastes of his boyhood predominate. Like Pony Baker's world, Hamilton has become "a dream of love and loving," site of "the gladdest of all my years" (*YOMY* 14).

When Howells reaches his utopian year, he distills the insights of *New Leaf Mills* and remembers the sensed enjoyments with increased vividness. Without equivocation, he speaks of his parents' conflict, his phobias and homesickness. Emphasizing the libidinal components of his breakdown away from home, he highlights the laughter of girls and his frightened yearning for his mother. Finally, he confronts the full impact of his mother's negative rewards. The account of the voluptuous homecoming she gave him ends with the judgment: "[M]y defeat was dearer to her than my triumph could have been" (*YOMY* 55).

With these admissions the ecstatic, instinctual realm of his youth regains prestige. Descriptions of the primitive wilderness attain the poetic intensity of free verse and celebrate an almost Wordsworthian oneness with nature. The silence of the woods, he eulogizes, "sang in our ears," and the trees, grass, and sky spoke of "divine promise." Amidst the "perfect beauty," all "fear" dissolved (*YOMY* 51). The horse, the dread id-emblem, changes into a lovable, harmless sorrel named "Baby."

In the adolescent section Howells openly admits his sexual difficulties for the first time. The emotions of puberty, which he discussed indirectly in *My Literary Passions* and "The Pearl," receive candid, direct treatment. After describing the circle of laughing, pretty girls in his father's shop, he says bluntly: "There had come the radiant revelation of girlhood" (*YOMY* 90). Nor does he blink the repression he used to quell his conflict. One by one he itemizes the facts of his "censorious youth" in Cincinnati: his recoil from a sex scandal on the newspaper, his condemnation of girls in a restaurant, his incapacity to face the "squalor of the station house" (*YOMY* 123).

The subsequent nervous collapses now have a more complete and libidinally suggestive explanation. The death terror that informed them involved a hypochondria that had its origins in his earliest childhood. The rabies he feared he had caught from a dog bite and which plagued him with drowning symptoms was a pathologic conflation of those primal images of instinctual evil—the dog and the engulfing river.

This confession, apparently, was the most wrenching of any in *Years of My Youth*. Of his breakdowns, he says, "I cannot bring myself to write it or speak it without some such shutting of the heart as I knew in that dreadful time" (*YOMY* 81). Again, though, the hard purgation is productive. With the benefit of enlightened hindsight, he deplores his "censorious youth" and "devilish ideal of propriety" (*YOMY* 32). He emphasizes the folly of his behavior in Cincinnati and adds that if he had been wiser, he would have kept his job. The quotation about his preference for the "cleanly respectabilities"—so often misconstrued—actually refers to the journalistic value of an exploitative story about a drunken woman. At last, he homes in on the dynamics of his neurosis. After his account of his hydrophobia attacks, he concludes, "I think we denied ourselves too much" (*YOMY* 123, 99).

His review of his young manhood underscores the implied, minor theme of *Literary Friends and Acquaintance*. The societal reinforcement of his negative conscience, which he insinuated there, becomes the focal issue. After admitting his "tawdry" ambitions to be "good society" (*YOMY* 107, 132), he chronicles his "respectable" career in Columbus. To be accepted by that polite world, he notched his prudery tighter: he shunned the theater and courted the girls with "cold, odorless purity" (*YOMY* 136).

What he gains, though, from this exposé of his adult maladjustment is a positive acceptance of his sexuality. He catalogues the beautiful girls he admired and says without hesitation: "I preferred the society of women" (*YOMY* 157). The final pages endorse a nonrepressive ethic that transcends and refutes the bloodless ethic of the age. Using prebellum Columbus as a model of relaxed Eros, he praises the unchaperoned informality and "simpler . . . freer" (*YOMY* 149) sexual morality.

If hydrophobia is the hallmark of Howells's neurotic conflict, *Years of My Youth* contains a cogent image of his cure. Conceding that he had always been secretly attracted to dogs, Howells ends the history of his rabies attacks with a story about a ferocious, ugly bulldog he met at a summer resort. Once, when he went for a drive, the dog leapt into the carriage with him and nestled at his feet. Not to dispel the mood of "reciprocal tenderness" (*YOMY* 82), he kept his leg motionless throughout the trip. Remembering the dog-boy analogy in *The Flight of Pony Baker* and the mythic sense of the dog as guardian of the underworld, this detente seems to encapsulate the psychic integration and peace that finally rewards his long struggle for self-knowledge.

The essay, "Eighty Years and After," written the year before his death, is a radiant affirmation of his achieved wholeness. Norman O. Brown writes that the ultimate test of the fulfilled life is an acceptance of death. When we are free from neurosis and "ripe," with no "unlived lines of our bodies,"[30] we die fearlessly. Calm resignation, therefore, is the keynote of this final reminiscence. No longer afraid of death, he expresses a cautious optimism about the afterlife and lists the advantages of old age. The later years are the "golden age of man," "a blessed time,"[31] in which the rewards of self-integration flower and fructify. In addition to an acquired "perspective of [himself],"[32] he claims an inner youthfulness, a recovery of the lost feelings of childhood. His dreams gain an exalted status. In an echo of the phrase "unconscious cerebration,"[33] which William James used to describe subliminal "discoveries," Howells gives the unconscious mind a major role in his waking, creative life: "I have spent," he admits, "a large part of my life in the unconscious cerebration of sleep."[34] He reopens Freud's *via regia.* His father, too, receives a still warmer appreciation. Awarding him his highest accolades, he calls his father "the most loveable of all octogenarians"[35] and finds his Swedenborgianism—so prudishly misconstrued in the seventies and eighties—a "wise and kind doctrine."[36]

It is in his paean to sexual love, however, that his psychic equilibrium shines most brightly. Here the circle imagery of the pearl combines with the archetypic emblem of perfected erotic love for a culminating expression of personal and sexual harmony. In maturity, he declares "the marriage ring [is] . . . a circle half rounded in eternity."[37] Nor was it a static synthesis. Like the sexual ideal envisioned by Havelock Ellis, Howells's circle "irradiat[es]"[38] from self to wife to family to eternity in expanding spirals of creative love.

His autobiographies, then, from *A Boy's Town* to his last essay form a striking drama of self-therapy. Bit by bit, he chiselled his way down to the primary "injury" behind his neurotic conflict, purged the repressed fixation, and absorbed the rejected, feared half of his psyche. As Freud could have predicted, an Oedipal complex seemed to be the crux of the problem. In Howells's case, the attachment was both unusually passionate and difficult. Besides sibling competition, he apparently had a mother whose extrarespectable standards and temper put an undue burden on the boy. When she rebelled against the instinctual world in his thirteenth year and his father failed her, his dilemma grew critical. The instincts, already dangerous through his Oedipal yearnings, had to be triply repressed just at the time his sexuality was beginning to bud. The excessive conscience of the child became the tense, overrestrictive superego of the adolescent. His symptoms and nervous collapses were the result of sexual energies suppressed to breaking point. Images of sensuality—inverting malignly—burst forth in death-threatening ways, exacting payment for forbidden desires. That his mother rewarded him for his breakdowns and the social environment rewarded him for his suprarepressions further tightened his stranglehold.

According to Freudian theory, release is only possible through a conscious coming to terms with the repressed conflict. The resistance against this process, as Howells's struggles during each memoir attest, is massive and the work severe. But after his labors were over and his complex discharged, he said, "some of the worst things I would not have missed" (*YOMY* 170). By confronting the unacceptable, tabooed side of his psyche, he was able to surmount the irrational "fool" and assimilate the sensuous, pleasure-loving child. The "simple delights" that eluded him at the beginning of his self-exploratory venture, he recovered and celebrated poetically in his mid-seventies:

> Foolish old heart, as glad of wind and sun
> And of the lift of yonder unclouded blue,
> As if the world's delight had just begun!
> Do not you know such joy is not for you?
>
> I know, I know! And yet I know that joy
> Like that which maddens in me from the day,
> While yet I breathe must find me still a boy:
> Off, mocking Fear, and let the young heart play.[39]

Not only do the autobiographies provide a panel by panel mural of psychic growth ,they also enrich and illuminate the novels. They supply a cipher key to his erotic vocabulary. The motifs of entrapment, nightmare, vertigo, "fool," and savagery (dogs, horses, alcohol, and primitives) were deeply embedded in his emotional history. When his imaginative efforts to transcend and integrate them failed and death triumphed, the failure struck at the most intimate chords of his psyche. The achievement of a harmonious sexuality in his fiction must have been equally personal. The success of his self-styled psychotherapy infused his erotic theme with the natural beauty, liberty, passionate womanhood, and domestic joy that had been the pleasure-core of his earliest identity. Autobiography and fiction, then, fed and animated each other in a mutually sustaining partnership, both working toward the same goal of unification.

Of course, every study of personality ultimately bows before mystery. The truth of the self is always inaccessible, elusive, and impossible to net up whole. Modern depth psychology, however, offers a provocative explanation of a life that changed markedly in the middle and later years, that moved from a "valley of shadows" to peace and coherence. The memoirs of those years, like the erotic novels, provide an extended casebook of that healing process. Journeying backwards into his infantile experiences in three separate stages, he was able to break the iron ring of psychological determinism. In Freudian terms, he was able to release his libido from the maternal grip which had divided him against himself, to reidentify with his father, and eventually to integrate his psyche.

In one of his essays Howells speculates that "perhaps we shall return to ourselves more and more."[40] As he predicted, he drew closer and closer to his essential self with each descent into his past, incorporating the "lower," sensuous child-self into his mature identity. According to Herbert Marcuse's definition, he accomplished the classic circle route to maturity: "[T]he consummation of being is not the ascending curve, but the closing of the circle, the *return* from alienation."[41] The circle also epitomizes the fulfillment of sexual love in literature, from Donne's ring to Eliot's matrimonial circle dance—the same fulfillment that enters Howells's novels after *The Flight of Pony Baker*. The two were inextricably interlocked. "A writer must live," Howells insisted, "before he can know what proportion of truth is worth telling."[42] "Live," he had. He had taken the ultimate adventure into the dark night of the psyche and back again in order to affirm life in all of its totality, a life made whole by a creative union of sense and spirit, unconscious and conscious, boy and man.

The Son of Royal Langbrith: The birth of sexual comedy | *Ten*

In 1904, just after *The Son of Royal Langbrith* appeared, Howells told S. Weir Mitchell that the novel had been on his mind for fifteen years. He had all the characters "pretty distinctly outlined,"[1] he said, and by 1894, had sketched the basic plot in his notebook. "Son who prevents his mother's second marriage from devotion to his father's memory whom he never saw. Man dies who wanted her. . . . 'But it is all right,'"[2] he concluded. It was almost a decade later before he could implement his plans and arrange his story so that it came out "all right" in the end. To grapple with this most tragic, most profoundly psychological of his erotic themes, to treat the Oedipal subject matter, he had to face his own Oedipal complex, confront his darker impulses, and prevail. No solution was possible for Eros in his fiction until he had found his own. With the semifictionalized method of *The Flight of Pony Baker* he had been able to sound the repressed, subconscious depths of his psyche and approach self-accord and mastery. He was ready, at last, to write his bleakest sexual tragedy, and bring it to a successful, comic conclusion.

In *The Son of Royal Langbrith*, he coalesced all his insights into destructive Eros and accomplished a dazzling triumph over it. He summoned up the demonic truths of *The Shadow of a Dream*—the book which paralleled the inception of his "grimmish"[3] tale—and overcame them with an erotic synthesis at once classic and progressive, pragmatic and ideal. The accomplishment was large. As Howells said later, "[T]ragedy seemed . . . too easy."[4] Instead, he worked through a circuit of radical evil to a tough-minded and radiant erotic affirmation. The themes of his love stories clarify and cohere, and the subtlest psychosexual perceptions coexist with a new mythopoeic resonance. At sixty-six, Howells broke the long impasse in his fiction. Now he could present a vital order for libidinal chaos, an epithalamium for the sexual tangle.

Among his early choices for a title was *The Legacy of Royal Langbrith*; and indeed, most of the book is taken up with Royal's satanic legacy and its metastasis into the next generation. The old textile baron embodies his accumulated knowledge of sexual evil. He personifies the negative "truth of the secret" (*FC* 241) that had surfaced in *The Shadow of a Dream* and invests it with still darker powers. Sadism, egotism, bigamy, jealousy, perversion reach a culminating expression in Royal's infernal machinations, while the imagery which accompanied destructive sexuality in the past solidifies around him. Wherever his shadow falls, death, darkness, nightmare, asphyxiation, and chaos follow. He becomes a living illustration of the mythic belief in the pestilential force of sexual crime and at the same time, an ultimate extension of Howells's complicity theme. His sins blight the community long after his death—with his innocent son as his agent.

The curse of his legacy, however, is finally vanquished in the novel, and a joyous, harmonious sexuality rung in. Hope Hawberk, the avatar of erotic health, seduces the son-hero into a love strong enough and balanced enough to defeat his father's blight and so transmutes tragedy into comedy. Suffocation yields to open possibilities, death to rebirth, dreams to reality, chaos to order, and darkness to a festival of light. The ascetic, over-repressed spirit with which Halleck or Nevil combatted passion ("moral" though it was) recedes. A firm sexual ethic takes its place. Howells had found the other, positive half of the "truth of the secret" (*FC* 241), a way to reconcile spirit and flesh, principle and passion, in a balanced, relaxed harmony. His locus of value was a nineteenth-century household like Pony Baker's, his heroine a gay, village girl like the "mother"; but his ethic had become trans-Victorian and timeless, universal and mature.

In being educated into this ethic, James Langbrith becomes the first protagonist of an erotic novel to complete his initiation ordeal successfully. A new clarity shows in his maturity drama. His mother fixation and struggle to free himself from her epitomizes the essence of the primitive *rite de passage*.[5] As in the mythic trial, he endures a "night sea journey" and is led out of it to *prudentia*, selflessness, and otherward love by his beautiful guardian, Hope Hawberk. He completes the transformation from April fool to Christmas fool—the god who undergoes ritual death and rebirth.

When Henry Blake Fuller read the first installment of the book, he told Howells that it reminded him of a fresco by Giotto.[6] With the resolution of the sexual quest in *The Son of Royal Langbrith*, a mural-like boldness replaces the "cabinet-picture manner"[7] of the earlier novels. The brushwork is broader, the scale larger, and the design more architectonic. Sexual implications remain as subtle as ever, but there is a dramatic compression and simplification of themes that gives the story a Giottoesque power. Instead of the finely drawn characterizations of *April Hopes*, the protagonists have the mythic stature of actors in a parable. Royal Langbrith is a "Devil" (*SRL* 5, 8, 86, 216, 246); Hope, a *midons* who "chants" and "tilts" (*SRL* 115, 120, 124, 360); and Justin Anther, an antagonist of Eros, is like the classical god Anteros. The erotic imagery, likewise, grows more archetypal. Anther's horse and house incarnate his libido, while Marcia Gaylord's jealous gasps become, in opium-sodden Mr. Hawberk, visions of being buried alive by a green dwarf. Action, too, acquires an almost mythic pattern. James's education into manhood moves with the seasons, from April to Christmas, and his love scenes seem to be danced. No more dramatic work exists among Howells's love novels. Like Ibsen's *Ghosts*, to which it was likened at the time, the story proceeds economically, scenically, and suspensefully to James's anagnorisis and then builds to a climactic end. Episodes such as Anther's and Amelia's opening tryst not only flare with erotic tension but contrast ironically with James's and Hope's. Moreover, the elders' love scene bears the added pressure of sexual bafflement, investing dialogue with confusion and psychic mystery in place of the ideological explicitness of *The Shadow of a Dream*.

While the overall treatment is painterly and dramatic, the sexual notation is extremely finespun—hinting at the deepest psychosexual truths. James's gluttony and his mother's blushes both relay their erotic inclinations (like Bartley's and Marcia's); but this time, the desires are incestuous. Through James's daydreams and involuntary actions, the irrational levels of sexuality come under scrutiny and account for Howells's most "advanced" insights. As he insisted in a letter to his editor, *The Son of Royal Langbrith* was a "novel of some psychological importance."[8]

The major part of the book recounts the extension of Royal Langbrith's infernal empire into the Saxmills community after his death. With his crimes, sexual and fiscal, he has set off a chain reaction of disease and sin that threatens to spread forever into the future. The wife he has battered cannot tell her son the truth, and he in turn perpetuates and fosters his father's reign of evil. The chain of sexual tragedy appears permanently locked.

Always looming over the action is the presence of the dead Royal—

the quintessence of destructive sexuality. His portrait on the wall, with its expression of "feline ferocity" (*SRL* 43), presides menacingly over each significant scene. He apotheosizes the subhuman lusts in passion, and in a realization of Faulkner's nightmare insights, becomes an "incubus" (*SRL* 70)—one of the sexual demons of the night. As "devil," he enacts literally what Faulkner only intuited. He commits real bigamy, real sadistic violence, and ignites a jealousy so pathologic that a man's mind is destroyed. If Eros, in its darker manifestations, seeks to transcend death (as Faulkner wanted), then Royal fulfills that egomaniacal wish. His wife remains trapped in bondage to his memory, and his son is both a slave to his image and a victim of immature perversions. When the curtain rises on the drama, the stage is strewn with Royal's wreckage. Amelia is the classic battered wife—will-broken and eviscerated—tied to her son in a sick dependency and to a lover who is frustrated by her compulsions to the point of desperation. James's fiancée, meanwhile, lives in the "shadow" (*SRL* 50) of Royal's curse on her father.

The first bleak scene establishes the full virulence of Royal's legacy. Inverting every love convention, Amelia and Anther spar through an interview that brings out all the major motifs of the curse. Their encounter is a radical inversion of the sexual trysts in Howells's fiction. Amelia is a middle-aged "orphan" (*SRL* 6) in mourning;[9] Dr. Anther, a "stooped" (*SRL* 7) old drudge like his horse. Instead of nearer, they move further apart during their talk. They begin at opposite ends of the room, join in the center for an abortive confrontation, then withdraw from each other like trapped animals in search of "escape" (*SRL* 14).

As Anther tries unsuccessfully to persuade her to marry him, the effects of Royal's "diabolical" (*SRL* 212) influence accrue. Negation and silence reign over the first half of their conversation until the fear behind Amelia's gasped "no[s]" (*SRL* 5) finally erupts. To her outburst of frightened tears, Anther exclaims, "[H]e [her son/Royal] terrorizes you" (*SRL* 6). Confusion is the prevailing note; and, amidst the "whirl of question" (*SRL* 10) Anther directs at Amelia, he lets his hat sink detumescently to the floor. But the "dark corner" (*SRL* 11) in the Langbrith household—the same spell of darkness Faulkner cast—proves too potent, and Dr. Anther retreats, defeated, to his broken-winded horse.

In addition to forecasting the course of their romance, their opening scene identifies the hopeless dilemma before them and measures the depth of its increased seriousness since *The Shadow of a Dream*. Without question they dispense with the scruple that stymied Hermia and Nevil and address themselves to a deeper, graver problem. Whether they loved each other before Royal died is of no consequence compared to the complex quandary they face. The issue is not so much that James opposes his mother's remarriage through a mistaken father ideal but that they have both been paralyzed by mysterious psychological mutilations. This is what Anther means when he curses Amelia's collaboration in her son's tyranny and when he talks of the "diabolical perfection" (*SRL* 212) of the scheme. Royal has been able to inject his poison into the subconscious core of personality, beyond the control of will or wish.

When James appears on the scene, therefore, his damaged psyche is such that he cannot help going about his father's business. After Royal's early death (perhaps induced by debauchery)[10] and Amelia's brutalization, James has remained locked in the narcissistic, Oedipal stage of childhood. Blindly he tries to enact his infantile fantasies in the adult world but in the process, carries on the legacy of fear, silence, confusion, impotence, defeat, and darkness his father bequeathed. He comes back to Saxmills just after his mother's futile rendezvous with Anther and eerily begins to duplicate Royal's sins. Under the pretense of an elevated gentility,[11] he tyrannizes his mother the way his father did, and shows the first signs of a sexually sadistic streak. "Just imagine I was your master and you couldn't help yourself" (*SRL* 20), James tells his mother, who "gasps" (*SRL* 19, 27, 54) through each of her audiences with her son. At a party later, he squeezes Hope's wrists so hard he leaves "red marks" (*SRL* 48), and, ignoring her protests, brings her to tears. His aristocratic ambitions, also, carry on and enhance the Langbrith tradition of public deception.

The plaque he plans to erect in the town symbolizes the attempt to perpetuate his father's dark heritage and his childish condition. As such, the medallion, with its sentimental and circular image of Royal Langbrith, provides a key satanic icon for the book and is the source of new suffering from its genesis. The immediate effect of James's proposal for the memorial is to tighten his father's grip on his mother. She moves further from marriage to Anther toward increased fear and perversity. After an initial failure to block her son's scheme, she slips—drugged by his flattery—into unhinged support for it. During a second gloomy tryst with Anther, she becomes so panicked she shuts the door on Royal's portrait and answers Anther's pleas for marriage with manic refusals and a plea for his help on the medallion project. Dimly recognizing her Jocasta motives, she confesses that she thinks she is acting somehow for her "own sake" (*SRL* 68).

The result of her pathologic lapse is to exile Anther more hopelessly to his sexual wasteland. Beaten anew, he returns to his boarding house—a monument of sterility, death, and erotic deprivation. "Four funereal firs" surround the "frigid" (*SRL* 76) facade; and Anther's office inside, with its "hard" (*SRL* 72) chairs and enormous skeleton in the center, resembles an anchorite's cell.[12] Precisely the reverse of Amelia's womb-like household, Mrs. Burwell's establishment is a lugubrious, repellant mausoleum where "cold" (*SRL* 73) coffee and steak await Anther after his exhausting rounds.

The first patient to appear there is another Langbrith victim, who has deteriorated further since James's visit. Lorenzo Hawberk, the partner Royal ruined by manipulating his wife's jealousy, has fallen deeper into the clutches of his opium habit. Predictably, the associated afflictions all involve suffocation, silence, and death. Speechless with fear when he is sober, he suffers nightmare visions of a green dwarf who buries him alive in a bone pit when he is intoxicated. As his daughter's tearful interview with Anther testifies, Hawberk is not the only one hurt by his setback. With characteristic pith, the doctor assesses Royal's malignant grip on the Hawberk family: "[H]e [Royal] holds the man in bondage now much more securely than he could have held him living" (*SRL* 65).

In the process of carrying out his dedication dream, James also ropes the community with him into moral error. Judge Garley submits to the "grip of the dead hand" (*SRL* 170) in an evasive speech, and the Rev. Dr. Enderby assures the dark secret's sovereignty through his religious scruples. Even the exemplary Hope Hawberk and Dr. Anther temporarily lose their ethical balance. Hope cannot resist oversatirizing the bloated James, while a progressively "fagged" (*SRL* 158) Anther lapses into a lie and then an endorsement of the project.

The ceremony itself marks the satanic crest of Royal's power. Despite the collapse of the curtain—presaging the exposure of James's true ambitions—Langbrith's evil legacy reaches an operatic crescendo. The entire town of Saxmills, even the drug-dazed Hawberk, joins to eulogize the old mill lord; and, at his peak moment, James becomes transformed into his father's image. Dizzied by the fulfillment of his infantile, time-stopping dreams, James discovers his mother's marriage plans and turns into every bit the "devil" Royal was. With a child's

blind rage, he tyrannically orders Anther out of the house and repudi-
ates his mother. Amelia, in turn, disintegrates, agrees not to marry,
and embarks on a course of regression that continues unchecked until
the end of the book. Defeated and tremulous, she finally surrenders
herself to her Jocasta impulses so completely she asks Anther to prevent Hawberk's recovery and thus James's enlightenment. In the last
frames she has become a woman wholly gutted of life—silent and con-
tractile—enjoying her "shadowy superiority" (*SRL* 269) like a zombie.
Anther is also "beaten in the struggle" (*SRL* 207). Thwarted in his
erotic hopes, he retreats to "duty" (*SRL* 207) and a monkish renunciation that borders on Tolstoy's sex nausea: "[H]e began to feel a sort of
profanation in the idea of making her a wife . . . Anther wondered
whether he had ever really felt a passion for her" (*SRL* 227).

To be sure, he and Hawberk do achieve a qualified victory over
Royal in the end. From a "whirl of question," Anther emerges with
rare insights into the sexual mystery; from Royal's fiery furnace, he
forges a high, generous morality. At last, he "understands" the perverse collusions between Amelia and her son and husband, and, from
that widened sexual knowledge, rises to a selfless forgiveness and love
of all three. Hawberk, meanwhile, beats his drug addiction and masters Royal's diabolic powers with new-found willed gaiety.

Their triumphs, however, are mental and spiritual only and necessarily deny the body. Theirs is the strategy of repression other Howellsian heroes had used against sexual evil in the past, raised to its
highest ethical power. Yet Howells did not stop at these perfected
"head" solutions in *The Son of Royal Langbrith*. Like the mood of sex-
weariness in the nineties, Anther and Hawberk literally die out of the
plot. In their place, a positive erotic ethic comes forward that defies
demonic sexuality. Under Hope Hawberk's sensuous tutelage, the
blight lifts and the endless cycle of sin and suffering ceases. At the
fatal moment when James's fantasy caves in, Hope leads him out of
bondage to his father's curse to a mature and morally responsible love.

Hope is not only the inspiration of the new sexual order but the
crowning achievement of the book. If, as her name suggests,[13] she is a
chivalrous champion of true Eros, she bears no kinship to her knightly
Victorian sister, Joan of Arc. Unlike Twain's lily maid, Hope is nothing if not sexual; and, what is rarer in a sexy nineteenth-century heroine, she is also good. Contained in her poised personality is an erotic
synthesis that has been the goal of amorist thought since antiquity.
She keeps passion and reason, beauty and virtue, pleasure and duty

fused in a fluid, dancing equilibrium. "Tilting" and "chanting" through the drama, she drives out chthonic evil and delivers Saxmills at last to erotic harmony.

With her "passionate[ly] irregular mouth" (*SRL* 98), brunette coloring, "deep throaty voice" (*SRL* 32), "intoxicating" (*SRL* 49) charm, and demonstrativeness, Hope is a composite of the high-pulsed heroines in Howells's fiction. More, she has Julia Anderson's easygoing sensuousness and a new assertiveness in love: twice *she* kisses James first. Yet, with all her ardor, Hope is disciplined, decent, and level-headed. She controls her "panting" (*SRL* 39) in James's presence, and he finds her "grace of mind" (*SRL* 43) and common-sense the most "fascinating" (*SRL* 59) things about her. Summing up her fine integration, Anther says that she is "beautiful . . . as well as good" (*SRL* 67), that it is her "duty to be gay" (*SRL* 146).

Through her gaiety, she demonstrates how a positive Eros will overcome demonic sexuality. With a fine sense of comedy, cleansed of asperity and informed by love, she teaches the secret of tragic optimism. She remains "glad side by side with the darkest anguish" (*SRL* 257) and holds the two in ironic tension, by willfully transmuting suffering into "something fantastic" (*SRL* 268). A muscular cheerfulness can purge and contain tragedy, she promises. It is this inner balance of opposites that gives her resilience against the afflictions that assail her and allows her to rebound so usefully after each setback. Mrs. Enderby encapsulates her personality when she calls her a "black iris . . . sloping in the wind" (*SRL* 116). She is like a flower of hope[14] stained by tragic knowledge whose flexible poise and endurance achieve a small miracle of beauty.

After James's infantile dream disintegrates, he turns to Hope, who initiates him by stages into erotic maturity. In a scene that combines passion and reason, sensuality and sense, she seduces him away from childish fixations to an otherward, associated love capable of defeating sexual evil. Their reunion, which begins with the "mutual transport" (*SRL* 254) of an embrace, gradually reveals major changes in James's character. Replacing his old self-insistence and sadism is a humble surrender to Hope's guidance. "You are my Hope" (*SRL* 257), he exclaims as he delivers himself to her caresses and subtle instruction. With his head on her breast, she restores the lost pleasures of childhood in a redemptive heterosexual form and gradually coaxes him out of his time- and life-denying narcissism. She makes good her opening boast that "it's [Royal's legacy] all past and gone" (*SRL* 256), by banishing the remnants of his father's curse. At her gay prodding, he admits that he had been "blindly selfish" (*SRL* 259), and agrees to renounce his regressive fantasies in favor of a future directed, earthbound pragmatism.

A ritual purgation follows at the Enderbys and, with the blessings of the church, they lead the book to a triumphant epithalamium. Aptly, like the famous wedding of *In Memoriam*, their marriage takes place at Christmas, the traditional festival of light and rebirth. With their blended love and tough optimism, they rout the forces of sexual darkness and brilliantly reverse all the tragic imagery. Rooted in the knowledge of Royal's infamy, settled in his house, they convert suffocation into possibility, nightmare into normal reality, pain into "peace" (*SRL* 271), death into generativity. Simultaneously, the medallion, reflecting both this transformation and James's growth, recedes into a limbo of public neglect and anonymity.

Nor is Hope's and James's happiness too rigidly ideal; theirs is a "poise in imperfection"[15] adaptive to the irresolutions, confusions, and surprises of life. James's maturity, for instance, never becomes an accomplished fact in the novel. It continues evolving fitfully through the epilogue. Though he supplants his mother with Hope, he must be warned against overatonements; though he has learned sensual, relaxed love, he must be teased out of prudery. Even Hope slips into sentimentality and must right herself. Their equilibrium, then, is not static but dynamic, tensile enough to insure happiness against the very forces that paradoxically created it. As Dr. Enderby appraises the final value and victory over radical evil: "But Hope and James are not unhappy. They are radiantly happy and more wisely happy for tasting the sorrow which has not passed down to their generation" (*SRL* 277).

Perhaps to throw emphasis on this magnificently "comic" ending, Howells changed the title from *The Legacy of Royal Langbrith* to *The Son of Royal Langbrith* several months before the novel went to press. Concentrated in the new title, with its resonating ironies,[16] is the history of James's maturation, which parallels and elucidates the book's erotic triumph. From being a reflection of his falsely idealized father, he becomes a true son—a sire of future generations—with an identity freed and grounded by the knowledge of hereditary sin. He is the first hero of the erotic novels to complete such a passage, and his drama recapitulates theirs with archetypal force. His ordeal is literally a struggle out of childish attachments into adult, object-centered love. Ferris's fears,

Bartley's greed, Dan's vanity, Faulkner's and Don Ippolito's perversions all contract into a single case of infantile sexuality that can be transcended only through a traumatic break with the mother followed by painful reeducation. In his account of this maturity rite, Howells's psychological penetration reaches a pitch of acuity. James's inchoate drives, the push-pull of regression and growth, the whole method of his cure, reflect depth psychology insights to be discovered in the next decade.

When he first appears in Saxmills, James is the classic April fool. Like the legendary fool, he is an innocent,[17] a repository of irrational, chaotic impulses, who is the dupe of circumstance. Believing himself to be a nobly born village lord, he is, in fact, an emotional infant in the image of a villainous father. The improvements he thinks he is bringing to the town are actually expressions of a wish to keep his childish condition permanent. A "dreamer" (*SRL* 23), afloat in the fantasy world of childhood, he yearns to immortalize a sexual state still mired in the incestuous, narcissistic, sadistic stages of development.

With his mother he lives in an Oedipal utopia very much like Pierre's in Melville's *Pierre or the Ambiguities*. Enclosed in a hothouse of maternal solicitude, he rules his mother with "sovereign command," plies her with superfluous caresses (*SRL* 15, 16, 20, 37), and gluts himself in an oral paradise. "I believe when I wake up in the other world," he tells her after an orgy of breakfast cakes, "you will be there to offer me something nice to eat" (*SRL* 52). Away from her he "romance[s]" (*SRL* 62) her, and became homesick his first year at Harvard. If every boy wants "Mother to admire *him* as the greatest hero of all,"[18] James seems to have realized that impossible dream from the book's start.

Closely tied to his Oedipal fixation is the self-worship that inspires the deification of his father. In his father cult he not only manages to bind his mother to himself, he also creates a magnified, supernal version of his own ego ideal. With the same childish narcissism, he nourishes visions of "seigneurial supremacy" (*SRL* 151) in the town and betrays his "Vanity-Love"[19] for Hope through his inflated ambitions to champion her. His relationship with his sidekick, Falk, may also contain a homoerotic element, as his dreamy nonsequitur to him hints: "I wonder . . . why I like you so much" (*SRL* 25). And the red imprint he leaves on Hope's wrist in the conservatory scene is the mark both of his father's and a juvenile sadism in his sexuality. The bookplate he designs for himself, with a boat blown from behind by a cherub, is an apt emblem of this immature erotic adjustment. He, too, is being propelled, in his impossible passage to adulthood, by a puerile libido, a prepubescent cupid.

From the onset of his scheme to raise a monument to his father, and thus to his infantile condition, James sinks into a regressive course of development that no one—not even Hope—can retard. With the narcissist's passion to arrest time,[20] he no sooner conceives the idea of honoring his father than he begins to abandon himself to his childish egotism and Oedipal complex. At a party as stiff and pretentious as his ambition to freeze the past, he brandishes his plan before the guests and promptly contracts a dislike for his secret rival, Dr. Anther. He ignores the comic groundfire from Hope and Falk, and, flaunting his mother love, grows progressively antagonistic to the doctor. After assuring Hope that "there are very few things . . . that [his] mother can't do better than anyone else" (SRL 38), he reviles Anther to his mother the next day for not supporting the memorial. His reverie on the train back to Harvard exposes this backward drift of his libido. From Hope, his mind wanders to his mother, then to his glorification of "his forgotten father" (SRL 62), and finally to renewed indignation at Anther.

During the preparation of the medallion, James's slippage continues apace, despite the positive influence of Hope and his growing love for her. In response to her sane mockery, he temporarily abandons his project but soon returns to it with redoubled ardor. As he sees the plaque unveiled, his immature emotions reach a pitch of excitement and clarity. He swells with a "content little short of ecstasy" in front of a portrait (aptly, a sentimental neoclassic) that is an exact, idealized image of himself. His narcissism revealed, James does not heed his friend's sarcasm, but soars to altitudes of self-worship. "My father . . . [is] a religion with me" (SRL 136), he croons to Falk, who bluntly calls him an "ass" (SRL 140). Nor can James's salutary praise of Hope amidst his paroxysm save him; his dreams of "seigneurial supremacy" grow unabated until the day of the dedication.

At the ceremony itself, James's regressive passions reach a crescendo. In apparent fulfillment of his boy's dream of unlimited and incestuous omnipotence, he exults afterwards to his mother: "It's been perfect, mother, beyond my dreams, it's been beautiful, ideal." With the medallion he believes he has set a seal on time. Before his illusion bursts, however, and his first maturity test confronts him, he makes one cautious advance toward manhood. Concurrent with his childish triumph is a competing affection for Hope which "press[es] even the facts of

[the] happy day out of his consciousness" (*SRL* 174), and leads to his engagement. Obeisantly placing his head on her knee, he submits himself to her "common sense" and asks her to keep him "from playing the fool" (*SRL* 178). Yet the moment he leaves her, he falls on his face through the ironic belief that he has been duped.

When his mother punctures his megalomaniacal fantasy with the news of her engagement to Anther, he makes a total fool of himself by thinking he has been gulled by a rival. Like the original Oedipus, he means to "hurt Anther to death" (*SRL* 192) and orders him from the house in a temper tantrum. If his response to the medallion revealed the narcissistic base of his father worship, his reaction to this crisis reveals its Oedipal springs. As he reels under the blow, he has clearer and clearer intuitions of the mother love behind his paternal "religion." Dizzyingly, with an almost physical sense of "vertigo" (*SRL* 193), he circles around the "puzzle" (*SRL* 192) of his father's role in his misery, until he finally fumbles toward the truth: "His heart closed about the thought of his father with an indignant tenderness, which somehow could not leave his mother out. She had always been part of that thought" (*SRL* 193). At a regressive nadir—haunted by nightmare battles with Anther—James turns first, significantly, in the direction of his homoerotic proclivities and looks for Falk.

When he finds Hope instead, he encounters and fails the maturity test she gives him. In the "shadow" of the moon,[21] he admits, under her scrutiny, that he is "insane" (*SRL* 195) but cannot help yielding to his lunacy. Although she tries to make him view the situation in the "right light," although she shows him he is "boyish" (*SRL* 196), he persists in benighted puerilities. He cannot banish the idea that Anther has made him a "fool" (*SRL* 195), questions how Hope could forget *him*, and refuses her parting requests, even on pain of her loss. Complaining that she asks "too much" (*SRL* 198) of him, he vows never to apologize to his mother or condone her marriage and only agrees on a compromise with "sullen finality" (*SRL* 198). That compromise, which he delivers "stonily" (*SRL* 199), is a reluctant promise to attend the wedding which effectively accomplishes what it intended: Mrs. Langbrith breaks her engagement.

James's *Wanderjahre* in Paris does nothing to reverse his retrogression, as the stiff French plays he studies and the arrogant letters he writes to his uncle testify. His trip back, though, proves to be the "night sea journey"[22] that turns the tide of his development. On the way home, he meets his uncle, who, like a diabolical Tiresias, ruthlessly unseals his eyes. The reverse image of his mother's oral, organic paradise, his dyspeptic uncle hurls the truth at him with rancid breath, legs that "saw" into his, and a "spiky forefinger" (*SRL* 245) that stabs his knee vindictively. In place of the "fool" James imagined he was, he learns what sort of fool he truly is. At the end of the climactic exposé, his uncle thunders: "[T]here wasn't a last one of them jackasses [Royal's victims] . . . that wasn't as big a fool as you." Left with the chilling prophecy that he has a "nice job cut out for [him]" (*SRL* 247), James begins the archetypal struggle through subterranean darkness toward maturity.

Under the impact of the shock, he is pitched, like Basil, into a confrontation with the demonic[23]—the traditional initiation ordeal. The reality of his father's evil engulfs him "like a demonical obsession" (*SRL* 248), and preconsciously he discovers that he had always known the truth. He stands in the "shadow" (*SRL* 249) of the dimly lit depot when he gets home and moves into deeper and deeper darkness as his night "passage" advances. Exercising his first "forbearance" (*SRL* 250) with his mother, he listens to her revelation and, in a fit of tears, faces himself and his tyranny. As though the "fountains of being [had] broken up" (*SRL* 253), he drops into a dazed, all-night vigil. After a penitent reconciliation with the dead Anther, he accepts his mother's kiss (rather than vice versa), refuses the light she offers, and sits before his father's portrait in pitch-blackness until dawn. Psychologically this corresponds to the introspective descent and "inclusion of the negative"[24] that precedes self-regeneration. James's rejection of food afterwards, too, parallels the ritual fast—the break with childish, mother-bound orality—required by initiation rites.[25]

When James meets Hope, then, that morning for his second maturity test, he is ready for her instruction. His head cleared of fantasy, his heart of self, he entrusts himself to her for further psychic cleansing. As if roused from a dream, he exclaims that he is "awake for the first time in [his] life . . . sane at last" (*SRL* 255), and, with a new selflessness, "sees" Hope in all her uniqueness. Surrendering to her guidance, he presses his head on her breast and suddenly becomes aware of her identity: "How strange you are, Hope" (*SRL* 250), he marvels. In the interview which follows, Hope completes the exorcism of James's childish complexes. She dispels his lingering narcissism, which makes him want to denounce himself publicly, with the comment that he is "crazy" (*SRL* 258), and deflates his fantasies of atonement with a lesson in moral pragmatism. Finally, her reminder of his duty to her effectively snaps the last cord of his self and mother love. "Daunted by what had not occurred to him before" (*SRL* 259), he plights himself to her and to a reality that is other-directed, unheroic, and complex.

After he purges his guilt at Dr. Enderby's, he takes up the burden and business of manhood. Like the Christmas fool, who is beheaded and rises again, James comes back from his psychic dismemberment, his "dark night of the soul," to a glorious Christmas rebirth. He survives his demonic passage and gains wholeness in place of incoherence. He wins marriage in place of Oedipal suffocation, creative love in place of sterile egoism. He achieves the classic reconciliation with his father through a reclamation of his house, and conquers his wish to stop time by investing in the future with a child. The metamorphosis of his playwriting career neatly dramatizes this transformation. From a would-be writer of stiff French plays (reflecting his rigid puerilities), he becomes the benefactor of his illegitimate half-sister's comic opera ambitions. He enters the real world in time, with its imperfect moral adjustments and its constant demands for responsibility, growth, and tolerance. Hope's tender laughter at his squeamish hesitations is a promise of his continuing development and wisdom in response to those demands.

The definition of marriage, then, which is offered ironically and tragically at the beginning of the book, becomes true and comic by the end. The mockery Royal and Amelia made of a union of the "divine" and "bestial," "immortal" and "perishable" (*SRL* 10), James and Hope make a reality. Through their wedding and James's integration, they attain the archetypal fusion of sense and reason that "marriage" has always symbolized. Theirs is doubly a psychological and a moral triumph. For they not only meet and defeat external radical evil, they also—James dramatically—battle internal demonic powers and win. The imagery surrounding both manifestations of Eros the Destroyer is the same. Confusion, entrapment, death, darkness, and nightmare afflict James in his maturation agony as much as they menace Royal's victims in their ordeals. Similarly, the erotic victory, with its psychic and ethical consummations, ushers in a reign of clarity, freedom, rebirth, and the light of common day.

Hope is the guardian of this concord, maintaining a sexual balance that is strong and translucent and proof against the future James feared. Defying every norm of her time, she brings together passion and virtue, excitement and security in an equilibrium midway between libidinal extremes. She strikes an erotic harmony that is universal: the ideal sought throughout history. At the same time, she looks forward to the neo-Marxists' rationality of gratification[26] with her relaxed, non-repressive, "good" sexuality.

Not surprisingly, *The Son of Royal Langbrith* became the most Swedenborgian of Howells's novels. Even the imagery has a stronger Swedenborgian resonance than usual. Houses, like Anther's, mirror men's libidos in Swedenborg's heaven; flowers, like Hope's, their love; and the seasons, their state of sexual grace. Hawberk's opium nightmare, accordingly, opens onto a prospect that is almost an exact replica of the monster-filled caves in hell.

But it is the incorporation of Swedenborg's erotic beliefs in the novel that is most striking. Royal, the personification of sexual evil, resembles nothing so much as a devil in the *Conjugial Love* inferno. There, the damned, each with a noble title, revel in what was to Swedenborg the epitome of libidinal sin: polygamy, cruelty, and self-love. Out of these depths, too, spring the same chaos and confusion that besiege Royal's victims, the same insanity that accompanies James's sexual maladjustment. More significant is Swedenborg's positive erotic thought in *The Son of Royal Langbrith*. One of the rare "body mystics" in the West, Swedenborg celebrated the union of spirit and flesh in marriages that were models of moderation, joy, and relaxation. Hope's virtuous lustiness he called "the wonderful communication of the inmost bosom with the genital region";[27] her playfulness was his "inward gaiety of love";[28] and her tolerant pragmatism was like his. And just as Hope seduces James into erotic health, so Swedenborg's women are the sexual adepts who patiently instruct men into the mysteries of an associated, voluptuous, and ethical love.

When the novel appeared, one reviewer noted that the "lasting value of the work [would] be found in its self-revelation of the author,"[29] and Howells went further and admitted that "everything [had] happened,"[30] in the book. His Langbrith drama contains, like no other work before, an intimate, compressed account of his psychic history and path to health. All that he learned in *The Flight of Pony Baker* he distilled into the character of James, who suffers the same Oedipal complex and symptoms, and proceeds through a *rite de passage* which metaphorically mirrors his autobiographical pilgrimage of the nineties. James's "passionate" (*YOMY* 133) love for his mother and arrested attachment to her duplicates Pony's, and his homesickness at Harvard duplicates that of the young Will in Xenia, Ohio. So, too, the feasts

James enjoys at his mother's table when he comes home recreate the gastronomic receptions Howells's mother used to reward his dependencies. Besides the Oedipal similarities, James's character incarnates the boy-self of the autobiographies. Sadistic, snobbish, and so narcissistic he thinks he is the "center of all life on earth" (*BT* 6), the child of the memoirs even has the nickname Falk gives James—the "dreamer" (*NLM*).

James's maturity ordeal also obliquely recounts Howells's "night sea journey" at the end of the decade. Like James, he regressed, via his autobiographies, back to the unorganized, primitive bases of his psyche, where he encountered a "black heart's truth"[31] about himself. The "demon" James faces in his father's portrait dramatizes what Howells discovered. In Royal's personality is an image of his shadow, negative self. He represents the sum total of instinctual evil, which Howells feared in himself and which recoiled on him during his breakdowns. He is the "devil" (*BT* 12) who haunted his childhood, the essence of "feline ferocity"—the cat killing the martin—which first inspired him with "horror" (*BT* 18), the penultimate "savage" of his nightmares. The legacy Royal disseminates corresponds to the phobias Howells suffered when his nerves gave way. The asphyxiation, entrapment, death, darkness, and vertigo Royal causes were the special terrors that pursued him throughout his teens. James's immersion in this black, tabooed side of himself during his all-night vigil and incorporation of it, is a truncated, symbolic version of the self-descent and integration Howells, too, accomplished at the turn of the century.

After his dark passage, Howells also followed a path like James's. He turned toward Hope and the sexual ideals she embodies. Rejecting the dominant Victorian morality,[32] he recurred to the "simpler and freer" (*YOMY* 133) values of his village youth. Vitally concerned with women's sexual happiness, he urged them away from the corseted, cold stereotypes of the age to an earlier sensuality, gaiety, and "charming liberty"[33] like Hope's. The guidance she gives James was the sort Howells came to recommend; women were men's natural guides in the pleasurable "art of living"[34] and, with proper erotic education, might reform and redeem marriage.

The withdrawal of his sex-weariness in favor of this new affirmative spirit has its fictional counterpart in Anther's death. The doctor's ascetic, repressed, and flesh-resolved mood, so near that of the nineties, dies out of the book and gives place to marriage, what Howells called the "divinest of human institutions"[35] in 1905. More, the Swedenborgianism that informs this marital vision supremely testifies to his reconciliation, like James's, with his father. Providing the classic proof of Oedipal transcendence, Howells returned to his father and his lenient Swedenborgian philosophy. The wide, easy tolerance, against which he rebelled in his adolescence, had become his own by the end of *The Son of Royal Langbrith*, where he moves toward forgiveness of libidinal evil.[36] As a final blessing on James's marriage, Dr. Anther pardons Royal and his legacy.

It was during the serialization of the novel that Gertrude Atherton launched her famous attack on Howells. He and his whole school of realists were "timid," she charged, without "originality," and hopelessly "prudish"—even "anemic."[37] While writers of sterner stuff tackled larger, more virile themes, Howells cravenly confined himself to the Sunday school world of the bourgeois and the pursuit of "Littleism."[38] She could not have timed her assault more inappropriately.

Far from "timid," the book is remarkably brave. Howells faced his accrued knowledge of sexual evil in himself and life in one searing image of destructiveness. Nothing in the libido's terrible power is scanted. No hero of modern fiction does more or worse than Royal: he philanders, beats his wife, robs her soul and Hawberk's, and heaps perversions on his son. Neither did Howells shirk the lasting effects of Royal's virulence. The novel shows how it advanced and multiplied after his death and syringed its toxin deep within the subconscious fiber of his victims. And, although a few are saved, Howells squarely acknowledges Royal's permanent, irreversible mutilations. Dr. Anther and Hawberk die, after all, unfulfilled; and Amelia remains a broken, shell-shocked husk of a woman. To go further, as Howells did, and seize an affirmation out of these truths, represented what Jung called an act of "heroic courage."[39]

The erotic solution itself was the very opposite of Miss Atherton's allegations. A complete departure from the orthodox morality, Howells's ethic was startlingly original: redblooded, nonprudish, unsentimentally informed by tragedy. The synthesis was classic, transvaluing the Victorian values in a way unique among Howells's contemporaries.

The Son of Royal Langbrith is a summing up, an elucidation of the sexual exploration that had begun in Don Ippolito's dark alley thirty years before. Howells gathered in all the erotic themes of his career and forced them to a point of clarity. From Ferris's vague fears of becoming a fool, he took a real "fool" through an encounter with the epitome of that fear to a maturity at once psychic, civic, and mythic. Adding yet another dimension of significance, the journey to maturity was in some ways Howells's own.

Rather than "Littleism," then, Henry Blake Fuller's sense of a "big thing burgeoning"[40] in the book comes nearer the truth. In a novel as powerfully crafted, as psychologically prescient as any he had written, Howells set before himself the challenge of a libidinal evil so radical it invaded and polluted the next generation. Sexuality takes its ultimate advance into the community and time. His response was to create a heroine on a scale equal to the challenge. The fruition of his long love-hate affair with American women, Hope Hawberk is tremendous enough, passionate and balanced and wise enough, to win the day. The iron lock of destructive Eros breaks and yields to an expanding circle of married love, radiating eternally from self, to society, into the future.

When he finished *The Son of Royal Langbrith*, Howells wrote S. Weir Mitchell about an idea for another book. "It involves some tremendous things,"[1] he said, and two years later told his brother that he thought it would be his "last great novel."[2] The novel was *The Leatherwood God* (1916), his final masterpiece, which he confessed fulfilled plans made "twenty or thirty years earlier."[3] Religious mania is the ostensible subject, but the deeper one is sexual passion and represents the culmination of the theme Howells began in 1875 with *A Foregone Conclusion*. In Joseph Dylks, the God pretender who ravages Leatherwood Creek, he distilled all of his accumulated knowledge of libidinal evil. Dylks's defeat, likewise, recapitulates the victory he achieved over destructive Eros in *The Son of Royal Langbrith* and carries his sexual affirmation to higher levels.

The Leatherwood God is indeed a novel of "tremendous things." In the most explicit language he had ever dared, Howells registers his darkest observations about passion. At bottom, sexuality craves nothing less than omnipotence and immortality, and contains negative capacities strong enough to disrupt an entire community. The convergence of Eros and Thanatos, implicit in the other novels, now becomes overt in Dylks's messianic reign of "death and destruction" (*LG* 100). Still more alarming is the titanic power of Dylks's appeal, which continues past his death and lies concealed (as it does in sentimentality) in man's highest sublimation—his religion.

Equally "tremendous" is the positive sexual synthesis that succeeds Dylks's overthrow. The harmony of the last chapters, with men and women, head and heart, public and private interests joined in a relaxed, sensuous equilibrium, mirrors an erotic ideal as old as Plato and advanced as the neo-Marxists. The book carries large implications, too, for America's cultural history and Howells's own. Far from the stale tea Berenson called all novels written after sixty,[4] *The Leatherwood*

God is one of Howells's strongest: the summa and ultimate elucidation of the problem of love in his work.

To expose the primal truths of sexuality, he moved to a primitive, frontier world and the language of folklore and myth. With a pared-down realism, the action advances ritualistically, from chaos to order, and the characters have the stylistic mannerisms of figures in an allegory. Joseph Dylks, for instance, snorts and storms through the story like a wild stallion—an emblem of the anarchic id. A "devil" (*LG* 27, 55, 61, 62), a "power of darkness" (*LG* 60), he encapsulates everything Howells had learned about destructive Eros and spreads the same legacy of death, darkness, fear, suffocation, nightmare, and temporal distortion as Royal Langbrith. Against his demonic sway, the good protagonists in the drama are both helpless, and damaged themselves. Squire Braile, the old lawyer and Logos of the piece, cannot reason the villagers away from their delirium and grows progressively misanthropic as Dylks's cult advances. His complement, Nancy Billings, the perfection of Eros, suffers so keenly from her ex-husband's villainy that she turns from grace to vengeance.

But with the classic circularity of lust,[5] Dylks goes down before id forces like his own and incurs the very penalties he has inflicted on others. His ordeal repeats the maturity struggles of previous heroes, and his failure reiterates and clarifies theirs. At the same time, Nancy and Squire Braile rise to greater maturity and usher in a final order that marks the summit of Howells's positive erotic thought. The secular miracle of a nonrepressive sexual estate replaces Dylks's false religious "miracles." His promises reverse and a world of light, freedom, rebirth, and peace, bounded by mortality, comes into being. Within this world, the threat of chthonic evil remains. Dylks's cult persists, the Redfields replicate his wrong, and the travelling scholar at the end invites a return of Dylks's power by his blindness to the sexual realities that had spawned Leatherwood's false messiah. But, in the presence of these dangers, an erotic faith prevails, an affirmation of the flesh and of life and love that is at once the toughest and happiest of Howells's career.

Just as Mondrian's first "realistic" trees are refined over his career into a grid of geometric lines, Howells's sexual theme becomes sparer and more condensed in *The Leatherwood God*. His erotic artistry gathers a heightened, parable-like explicitness. Using primitive, agricultural post-frontier Ohio as a background, Howells gives passion its most elemental expression. The subtle seasonal symbolism of earlier novels

moves to the forefront of *The Leatherwood God*, in which the plot literally reenacts a harvest festival. The old sexual imagery becomes more
fundamental. The stove heat which evoked Marcia's and Bartley's lust
is now a stifling August. The fire in Marcia's cheeks turns to bonfires
in the night, and Mrs. Farrell's sham black magic becomes the real
thing. Food, Howells's standard register of the libido, indicates the
primal erotic dualities: salacity on the one hand and sensual blessedness on the other. The intricacies of body language simplify into a series of kinetic leitmotifs. Like repeated figures in a dance, Squire
Braile tilts back on his porch, Nancy makes her domestic rounds, and
Dylks towers over his prostrate followers.

By the same token, there is a new frankness of sexual notation. No
Howells character flaunts his appetites more flagrantly than Dylks, as
he struts up and down in his conical fur hat, snorts his mating cry, and
brandishes a long-necked gourd. The effect he produces is bluntly
rendered. In one of the oldest metaphors, Nancy calls Dylks a "plow"
(*LG* 61) that went over her, and Sally Reverdy describes his impact on
the camp meeting in orgasmic terms: "Plenty of 'em keeled over where
they sot, and a lot bounced up and down like it was an earthquake and
pretty near all the women screamed" (*LG* 14). Through the Reverdys'
commentary, Howells draws on the American bawdy tradition of the
Southwest humor for the first time, giving the book a "Rabelaisian"[6]
quality. Braile's depiction of Dylks, for instance, as a horse who "tried
to play man" (*LG* 12) echoes a racy Sut Lovingood yarn of almost the
identical name.[7]

In addition to the explicit sexuality in the novel is a strand of lyric
sensuality that appeared only sporadically in Howells's previous fiction. Basil's sensory epiphany at Hermia's house in *The Shadow of a
Dream* now extends through the entire book: all the faculties of the
flesh are intensified in the rapturous backwoods intimacy with nature.
To reach the truths of the subconscious, Howells had consistently recurred to dreams; but here the novel itself assumes a dream-like, ex-
pressionistic quality. Allusions now draw upon a source as basic to
Howells's experience as the Bible. It is the consummation of his sexual
thought given perfect luminous form; it is—if such a thing could be—
an agnostic miracle play of Eros, realistically conceived.

The first half of the book, as in myth, depicts the invasion of chaos
and the old night into the peaceful settlement of Leatherwood Creek.
Judge Taneyhill, from whom Howells took the story, calls Joseph
Dylks the "Destroyer,"[8] and indeed, he is the human incarnation of

Eros the Destroyer. The essence of Howells's accrued knowledge of erotic evil, Dylks proceeds to rain down on the community the curses inflicted by his demonic predecessors. He is Taneyhill's religious imposter with satyr's hoofs. Taller, younger, and shapelier than his historical prototype,[9] he not only snorts like a horse, he becomes the icon of one in Howells's rendition. As an archetypal symbol of the id, he prances, gallops, flings his black mane of hair seductively, and is linked with a host of other animal associations: over the course of his conquest, he successively earns the names of skunk, snake, coon, goat, and turkey-cock.

He is Howells's most blatantly sexual character. He wears the costume of an opera bouffe rapist, has eyes like "black fire" (*LG* 8), a voice with "witchery" (*LG* 21) in it, and the appetite of a beast. When he preaches, he swells up phallically, "straight as a ramrod" (*LG* 14). What he does to the community reinforces his sexual identity. With a literal application of Mrs. Farrell's magic, he spellbinds his followers into submission, driving the women into frenzies that mime the moment of climax.[10] Neither is there any question of his underworld origin. Royal Langbrith's associations with the devil solidify in Dylks, who becomes a genuine Satan, surrounded by images of night and witchcraft wherever he appears. An aura of supernatural spookiness haunts his habitations, and he works his mischief consistently under a cloak of darkness. As Nancy says, he is a "thief in the night" (*LG* 60) and he steals over the community like a legendary incubus.

Trailing a history of promiscuity behind him,[11] he descends on Leatherwood Creek and begins to inflict scourges like those of all the other erotic villains—but with terrible intensity. Every sexual evil, from Bartley Hubbard's sadism and Marcia's self-loss to Faulkner's egomania, emanates from him as he unleases an epidemic of death, darkness, fear, suffocation, confusion and nightmare on the inhabitants. In true Trickster fashion, he promises them the very reverse, thus placing the capstone on Howells's "fool" theme. His fraud upon the villagers demonstrates conclusively what it means to be sexually fooled. Giving another ironic turn of the screw, his adherents multiply in exact proportion to his increasing revelation of his real sexual designs.

Dylks's first appearance in Leatherwood establishes the full force of his *érotisme* and adumbrates the trouble he will wreak. On a hot, sultry night, amidst blazing bonfires, he suddenly bursts upon a camp meeting with a wild, brutish snort and a "cry of 'Salvation!'" (*LG* 21), reducing the women to shrieks of excitement. The sexual nature of his appeal is unmistakable. Together the Reverdys describe a response to Dylks just short of orgiastic: people "bounce up and down," want to "die" (the Elizabethan pun intended) (*LG* 8), and submit to him like birds to a "snake" (*LG* 15).

Dark omens surround his initial scenes. Portentously, a bat, symbolic of death,[12] heralds his second sermon, which he ends with a song that predicts the damnation he will deliver in place of his promised salvation.[13] Reinforcing Dylks's demonic affiliations, Squire Braile scents the "smell of brimstone" (*LG* 15) on him. There are intimations, as well, of the kinds of afflictions he will impose. Abel Reverdy describes the sight of him as a nightmare vision whose shout goes "through [him] like a [*sic*] axe" (*LG* 8), and remains locked in the prophet's "hold" (*LG* 9) despite Braile's mockery.

Dylks's persecution of the Gillespie family both foreshadows what he will do to the community and confirms his ambitions to power. With Jane Gillespie "under [his] spell" (*LG* 18), he squares off with her father beside the forest and parades his dark sexuality before him. As he struts and "swell[s]" (*LG* 26) in the night, David Gillespie indicts him for the id force that he is: "[Y]ou turkey cock, you—stallion! . . . you can't prance *me* down, or snort me down" (*LG* 27). But Dylks does manage to trample the Gillespies. An incarnation of the ego-maniacal underside of passion,[14] he proclaims that he is God, and inflicts self-loss (Jane's), bigamy (Nancy's), and sadism (David's) in his Langbrithian oppression of the family. Duplicating Royal, he deprives his legal wife, Nancy, of her vitality and true husband, and casts her into the "shadows" (*LG* 30). Her house, after her brother has sadistically supervised her marital separation, becomes "dark and still" as though someone had died, and time, as in Saxmills, ceases to move forward. Under the crush of suffering, the day "seems a thousand years" (*LG* 38) to her. Amidst all this wreckage, Dylks boasts triumphantly to David of his paralyzing grip on them: "But I'm not afraid; I've got you safe, and I've got your sister safe" (*LG* 26).

In the next few weeks, Dylks extends the same hold over the rest of Leatherwood Creek. For the light he promises them, he brings darkness; for the salvation, damnation, and for the New Jerusalem, hell itself. Rather than the dream of cohesion and harmony he extends to his flock, he diabolically (etymologically *dia* + *bollein*, "to tear apart") rends the community apart. His first converts, in predictable Howellsian fashion, are not the rustics of the settlement but its most respectable members, who dub themselves apostles and envision halos, miracles, and a light capable of "burst[ing] their darkness and silence" (*LG* 41). With their support, Dylks catches on like "fire in dry grass" (*LG* 49). Progressively inflating his claims and betraying his true carnality, he tightens his grip on the Gillespies and begins to dismantle Leatherwood Creek. Jane Gillespie becomes so "rapt" (*LG* 46), literally raped, by Dylks's growing swagger, that her father has to drag her away from his feet like a sleepwalker. David, meanwhile, suffers nightmares and a "living fire" (*LG* 61) of pain, while Nancy loses her will to live.

The larger community around them fares no better with the advance of the cult. Just as Jane psychically disintegrates, the whole populace falls apart in the face of a religious crusade that grows more and more flagrantly erotogenic. In justification of his life of "fried chicken" and "fine linen" (*LG* 57), Dylks cites St. Paul's example[15] and swears he will bring the New Jerusalem to his followers on earth. His adherents, attracted to these spiritually veiled sensual lures, grovel and flop before him as though "they had been drinking" (*LG* 61). Sally Reverdy becomes suddenly beset with fears. Violence and hostility rack the settlement. Husbands beat their wives (as Royal did), families and neighbors fight, the pillars of the old temple fall, and a time of "hate and dissension" (*LG* 42) sets in.

The Hingston Mill "miracle" brings this discord to a head and coalesces the themes of Dylks's career. In the dark, stifling mill, haunted by a "grewsome [*sic*] strangeness" (*LG* 86), the community assembles to watch Dylks miraculously change cloth into seamless raiment. The sexual undercurrents of his faith now become plain. As they wait in tense anticipation, the local mavericks, the "Hounds," goad the women for a "dance before the Lord" (*LG* 83) and for kisses until at last violence erupts. There is jealous challenge and counterchallenge; and, when Dylks refuses to come out, the dam breaks. A Dionysian frenzy explodes in which the bolt of cloth, like a ritual lamb, is torn to shreds in a "tumult of destruction" (*LG* 92). Deep into the night the mob rages—the realization of Eros the Destroyer's worst propensities.

During Dylks's unholy jihad, two positive characters defy him without success. They represent the two sides of Howells's erotic synthesis: humanized reason and informed passion. Squire Braile, the happily married old judge, is the book's paragon of reason and Dylks's precise foil. Like the hawk he resembles, he is a symbol of light and eventual victory over concupiscence.[16] All his major scenes occur in

the morning on his porch, where he surveys Leatherwood, "tilted"—
suggesting chivalry and balance—against his double log cabin. The
house itself, which he calls the "Temple of Justice" (*LG* 11) is a meta-
phorical extension of himself. Airtight, clean, and solid, it forms a circle of order in the surrounding wilderness and contains a statue of
Samuel at the center, the lawgiver who defended Yahweh against the
fertility cults of the Canaanite Baals. Significantly, he keeps a caged
raccoon in the attic. However, despite his hawk-eyed[17] resistance to
Dylks and his apostasies, Braile can neither stop him nor remain un-
affected. His "kindly mockery" (*LG* 76), which regulates the community, turns bitter and intolerant. Misanthropically he calls everyone a
"fool" (*LG* 16, 22, 55, 57), and at the lowest point of the revival, blazes
out at Sally Reverdy. He also evades the deeper, irrational complexities of Dylks's cult—to Nancy's harm. When she confesses that she is
losing her strength against Dylks and wants to take her husband back,
Braile grows rattled, and, trembling to his feet, walks stiffly away.

Howells called Nancy the "chief figure in the drama,"[18] and she is
his penultimate erotic heroine. To fulfill his long quest for a positive
feminine sexuality, she brings Hope Hawberk to a rich, passionate
maturity. Presiding over the story like a fertility deity, she is middle-
aged, a mother, and schooled in tragic sexuality through her "hell[ish]"
(*LG* 31) marriage to Dylks. As such, she combines light and dark in
her personality—the "white[ness] . . . of the saints" (*LG* 116) and the
swarthiness of sirens—and always appears in chiaroscuro. Her first
entrance across a shade-checkered pasture captures both the essence of
her character and forecasts her fate, as she repeatedly slips on rotting
logs and rights herself. With an even more magnificent balance than
Hope's, she harmonizes passion and reason, desire and discipline.
Twice she asks Laban to kiss her,[19] voluptuously she coddles her baby
and absorbs the spring day. Yet she renounces her husband and restrains her impulses when she must. She perfects Julia Anderson's
easygoingness with her relaxed morality; she realizes Hope's implied
strength with her pioneer pluck and bravery. "I can get along," she
boasts when she is stranded, "I'm not a man!" (*LG* 35).

But she, too, fails to thwart Dylks or escape his snares unharmed.
Although she denounces him fiercely, she suffers the worst from his
takeover and loses her inner poise in the process. At her darkest hour,
when her soul seems "dead" (*LG* 61) with grief, she veers toward vin-
dictiveness in repudiating Dylks. Training all his charms on her and
flourishing a "long-necked gourd" (*LG* 67) before him, he tries to lure

her back and she flares out at him. She crushes his phallic gourd un-
derfoot, wishes him his "reckoning" (*LG* 68), and banishes him with a
full admission of his power over her: "I won't make you my God now,
though you're as handsome as ever you was; handsomer, if that's any
comfort to you . . . I've outlived you, you and your will" (*LG* 69). Afterwards, her anguish increases and she buckles under the strain. The
second time she separates from Laban, who greets her in "fright"
(*LG* 72), she succumbs to nightmares, and a bitterness so intense she
spurns God.

Chaos and old night, however, are not destined to prevail over
Leatherwood Creek. With the self-propagating force of evil, Dylks's
lust circles back on him, and he is besieged by his mirror image. The
riotous "Hounds," led by the "rangy young horse" (*LG* 183) Jim Redfield, hunt him down and turn *him* into the fool. Everything he has
inflicted—discord, nightmare, entrapment, fear, fire, and darkness—
returns to him, until he dies, like the "old man" (his nickname) in the
ritual harvest festival.[20] Cornered by the "Hounds" in an orgiastic raccoon chase, he endures the same humiliation and self-loss his followers experienced. They trap him, tear his clothes the way he has
torn the community, and symbolically castrate him through the lock
of hair and skin they rip from his scalp.[21] That night, during his house
arrest, he "fall[s] forward" (*LG* 100) on the Temple bench in the very
posture of his devotees. The mob treat him with the violence he has
brought to their homes, and the next day Braile makes him a laughingstock before the crowd.

But it is his "week in tall timber" (*LG* 157) when Dylks truly suffers
what he has imposed on others. It also serves as the consummate maturity ordeal of Howells's fiction, which Dylks manages to fail most
completely. Exiled to his right habitat, a ghost- and snake-infested
swamp in the forest, he descends into the dark heart of the irrational.
On a wild spit of land where the "Hounds" have treed him, he sus-
tains a *rite de passage* as terrible as his rule in Leatherwood. Night envelops him, the stars go "black" (*LG* 109), his scalp flames, and, weep-
ing with an abandon that equals Nancy's, he sinks into a nightmarish
delirium. The "woof" (*LG* 110) of his being breaks. Afterwards,
though, he does not awake to a higher maturity; he regresses into
deeper childishness. Like a "cry-baby" (*LG* 111), he crawls back to
Nancy and begs her, with infantile ploys and tears, for mother love.
To her admonitions, he replies that he has grown too afraid to reform.
With Squire Braile later, his regression continues. Dylks cowers be-

fore him, sobs uncontrollably, and, at Braile's cross-examination, admits that he has become insane. In ironic reversal of his touted grip on the community, he cries out at one point: "[T]hey had me fast, faster than I had them" (*LG* 117).

His final exit marks the nadir of his career and encapsulates it. When he arrives for his send-off, he is at his lowest ebb. "Bowed and humble" (*LG* 126), he wears a black fool's cap in place of his phallic beaver and is subjected to a hail of jeers and laughter. His farewell sermon, similarly, in which he reconverts himself and his audience, elucidates his cult. Its innate carnality becomes explicit and his fraud an outright flimflam. Dropping spiritual pretensions entirely, he promises his remaining followers a New Jerusalem that is a gaudy pleasure dome and concludes explicitly: "I can make millions of gold and silver coins" (*LG* 130).[22] Their enthusiasm matches his in sensual frankness. With "sighs and groans of ecstasy" (*LG* 129), they fling themselves on the ground at his feet and cry, "[T]ake us all with you in the flesh!" (*LG* 130). When he does in fact do this, leading his flock on a wild goose chase to impoverishment instead of the promised riches and New Jerusalem, his exposure is complete. His own deterioration proceeds apace to death. Deranged and terrified, he drowns himself in a creek, crying and losing his beaver hat as he goes. He has returned to the dark subconscious underworld from which he sprang. He has accomplished the fatal union of Eros with Thanatos.

While he fails his maturity ordeal, Nancy and Squire Braile move to higher levels of development, becoming the perfected custodians of a new erotic order in Leatherwood Creek. Nancy surmounts her vengeance and grows to a more complex moral understanding. When Dylks returns a second time on his knees, she compassionately bathes his wound and retracts her previous wish for his death. She exchanges mercy for hate, forgiveness for retaliation, still acknowledging that he is "the wickedest man in the world" (*LG* 134). The vituperative certainties of the past dissolve into a larger ethical awareness. In response to Jane Gillespie's threat of how she would punish Dylks if she were a man, Nancy replies: "I'm glad I ain't a man, for I wouldn't know what to do" (*LG* 135).

By the same token, Squire Braile's humor mellows and he gains a grasp of the dark intricacies and compulsions of the irrational. At the mock trial, he temperately balances his ridicule of Dylks with ridicule of the community, and his teasing acquires a fresh sympathy. He takes Dylks into his home after his exile, and with alternating mockery, hospitality, and empathy, listens to his explanation. From Dylks he learns what he tells the scholar in the epilogue: that we have "tucked away in us . . . the longing to know if we will live again" (*LG* 157). His deeper comprehension of the sexual mysteries in these irrational wishes emerges next in his shrewd analysis of the Redfield marriage. Ultimately—as his strengthened bond with the Reverdys testifies—he perceives that we are all "fools," deserving the widest compassion.

Under these two rubrics—reason tempered with blood and sentiment with judgment—a positive Eros emerges. With yet another reversal, Dylks's false promises are redefined and fulfilled. The real earthly miracle of a nonrepressive sexuality occurs. The light of common day replaces Dylks's "divine" light. Mortality eclipses immortality, and Leatherwood Creek turns into the New Jerusalem of the love poets. Opposites meld, the sexes equalize, and public and private interests join in a relaxed affirmation of life. Eros sensualizes the whole environment and a true mode of freedom supervenes. The "miracle," however, is not impervious to genuine threats and imperfections. Beneath Leatherwood's placid surface, like the "wilde Bore"[23] under the Garden of Adonis, fester tremendous disruptive potentialities. It is a thoroughly pragmatic erotic utopia—open to risk, chance, and the flux of time, yet bravely affirmative.

Nancy ushers in this accomplished sexual ideal, aptly, with a hymn of thanksgiving. She sings, sealing the chinks in her cabin, at the nerve center of Howells's erotic ethic, the home. Not unlike Dickens's *Bleak House*,[24] it operates as a cosmic defense against chaos, a circle of order from which all preservative virtues radiate. Thus the significance of the carefully detailed household rituals in the book and the emphasis on Squire Braile's solid, well-built double log cabin. Within these homes, men and women enjoy a very un-Victorian equality. Nancy and Mrs. Braile are their husbands' partners in work, possess their own identities, and, if anything, have the stronger voice in the marriages. The coffee they dispense throughout the story becomes the sacrament of this domestic "miracle." Elevating its aphrodisiacal associations to a new level of meaning, they lend their coffee a eucharistic significance akin to Elizabeth Bishop's "Miracle for Breakfast."[25]

In keeping, too, with the amorist quest for a society between the extremes of restraint and license, the restored Leatherwood Creek is a model of sexual moderation. With a permissiveness unknown in turn-of-the-century America, Nancy's son roams the country at will, teenagers go unchaperoned and kiss casually "in their games or in their walks through the woods" (*LG* 89). The procession of couples to the Hingston Mill "miracle" conveys something of the wonder of such an erotic ethos: "In all there was an air of release, and the young people . . . walked in couples . . . as if the miracle before them were the wonder of coming home through the woods with their arms around each other" (*LG* 79).

At its highest, Eros flows out of the personal, heterosexual matrix, fertilizing the universe. So an intensified sensuousness suffuses the Leatherwood world, accompanied by a spirit of loving cooperation among the inhabitants. Instead of Marcia's and Bartley's genital furor, the libido expands into a tranquil enjoyment of all the senses. Bartley's and the Dylksites' intoxicated debauches metamorphose into Nancy's reunion with her son at the end, in which she reels "drunk with slumber" into his arms and prepares him a sumptuous breakfast of bacon, cornpone, and coffee with "good cream" (*LG* 144). Besides a relish of culinary pleasures—especially those at Mrs. Braile's table—there is a sensed intimacy with nature little short of rhapsodic. The "dense rich smell" (*LG* 5) of ripening corn, the music of night birds, the vision of undulating farmland, the feel of bare feet "that felt winged and ached to fly" (*LG* 80) transform Leatherwood into a luxurious sensorium.

Dylks's departure restores the community to the egalitarian paradise that existed before his siege. According to the neighborhood's "sacred laws of hospitality" (*LG* 17), Braile harbors the visiting scholar of the epilogue and shows him a society interknit by mutual help and care. The Reverdys support the Brailes in their old age as the Brailes earlier supported them. The Hingstons absorb the orphaned Joey into their family and business; and the society reverts to the communal harmony David hailed: "[W]e were all brethren and dwelt together in unity. . . . We loved one another in the Scripture sense" (*LG* 62).

Dylks's mirage of liberation has dissolved into the only real erotic freedom for mankind: a "coming to rest in the transparent knowledge and gratification of being."[26] When Dylks leaves, Braile says rightly, "I haven't breathed so free in a coon's age" (*LG* 138). Yet, paradoxically, Leatherwood achieves freedom because it accepts the ultimate limitation, death. Time is set right; Nancy, Laban, and her child die; and Squire Braile jokes to the visitor that he may not live until morning. Through this assent to death, however, an affirmation of life occurs that makes the epilogue a hymn to generativity. The season is spring, the roads stream with water, Joey marries, and turkey chicks succeed the satanic turkey-cock.

Although Eros triumphs and masters the demonic, its victory can never be secure. The same evils that Dylks exploited still simmer beneath the carefully sustained harmony in Leatherwood Creek. What is left of the "Little Flock" (*LG* 154) continues "as strong in the faith as ever" (*LG* 155), and Jim and Jane Redfield, with their marital difficulties, represent the negative, dissimilatory powers of sexuality. The next "stranger" (*LG* 154) to enter the community introduces a more subtle threat to the erotic peace, giving the ending a final ironic twist. A Boston scholar of religious phenomena, T. J. Mandeville—named after the historic commentator who falsified his travels—misses the meaning of Dylks's history and thus risks its repetition. He ignores Braile's explanation of the emotional bases of the cult, refuses to equate Dylks with other prophets, and grows bored when the conversation touches sexual bedrock. To Braile's comment about Jane's maternal instinct—the index of her libido and another displaced erotic quest for immortality—Mandeville simply does not seem "greatly interested" (*LG* 158). Despite all the dangers which menace Leatherwood's poise, however, the tonic note remains hopeful. Against all the odds—and the power of evil is nowhere less underestimated than in *The Leatherwood God*—the novel casts its lot with a positive sexuality. It makes a leap of erotic faith.

Concealed within this triumphant sexual fable is another success story: Howells's own. Covertly, the novel provides a dramatization of an achievement as large as Leatherwood's erotic ethic, his own self-integration. The two, of course, go hand in hand; but compressed into the text is a telling account of his personal, creative growth. Perhaps the simultaneous work on *Years of My Youth* helps explain the rich autobiographical underlay. There, in his last memoir, he makes his fullest exposure of his early neurosis, in the same way that he confronts the heart of his inner darkness through Dylks and his scourge. Both cases represent the classic encounter with the unconscious necessary for psychic wholeness. Like his characters, Howells subjects himself to a maturity ordeal. The final harmony of Leatherwood Creek and that of his later prose attests to the brilliance of his "passage." Observers at the end of his life were amazed at Howells's serene vitality.[27] *The Leatherwood God* provides a subtle allegory of his path to that heightened consciousness and its erotic synthesis, a mirror of his own.

The tragic half of the book charts the terrain of his night journey.

Dylks is a portrait of Howells's negative boy-self; and Dylks's career both touches the major themes of Howells's neurosis and suggests a source. An archetypic emblem of the "lower" mind, Dylks personifies the bad child of Howells's autobiographies. He epitomizes the shadow self that traditionally must be faced, mastered, and integrated in a maturity drama. Coincidentally, perhaps, he even has the same nickname, "The Old Man" (*BT* 238). More than that, his savagery, egomania, "carnal greed" (*LG* 108), ferocity, dandyism, and laziness exactly duplicate the *Boy's Town* boy's vices. What the child dreamed of being—a villain on the stage—Dylks realizes to the *n*th power. Surrounding him are the very evils that haunted Howells's childhood. The mantle of fear Dylks spreads over the community was the prevailing mood of his youth; and his particular phobias were Dylks's specialities. Death, darkness, suffocation, ghosts, and nightmares (the name he actually gave his horse) (*MYLC* 38), plagued Howells as much as the inhabitants of Leatherwood Creek.

Dylks's dark night of the soul reveals still deeper reaches of Howells's psyche. If an Oedipal complex lay beneath Howells's terrors, then Dylks dramatizes it during his wilderness ordeal. In his infantile regression, he reenacts a prototypic scene of Howells's "neurosis."[28] He crawls back to Nancy, just as Howells returned to his mother after each of his psychic breakdowns. According to psychoanalytic theory, once these primal truths have been excavated, the dark side of the mind admitted, a new self-accord takes place. The negative is conquered and productively reassimiliated. After Dylks's death, therefore, Joey can tell his mother that he pitied and finally "liked" (*LG* 150) him. The appellation "Good Old Man" ceases to be altogether facetious: Howells had made his peace with his demon.

The affirmative end of the novel demonstrates the inner harmony which followed this "dark descending." As the fissure between conscious and unconscious, man and child, healed,[29] he struck a balance with sexuality no less exquisite than Leatherwood's. "The moral of the whole drama of existence," he said in a 1911 essay on passion, "[is to] determine where we stand in regard to it."[30] In his old age, privy at last to the "secret of love," he gained a "vantage-ground"[31] and an erotic faith that was glowingly, wisely optimistic. He moved away from the suprarepressive mores of his age and its equally unbalanced reaction, to the "middle course"[32] of the love philosophers. Reversing his earlier dicta, he applauded the frank treatment of sexuality in fiction[33] and looked to the "simpler and freer" (*YOMY* 149) manners of his Ohio youth for erotic inspiration. The same year he wrote *The Leatherwood God* he praised his past as a time when the relation of the sexes was "pure" and love "the greatest and most beautiful thing in the world."[34] What he celebrated imaginatively in Leatherwood—the sexual equality, erotic leniency, and equipoise—he consciously and rationally defended in his final prose. Home, the linchpin of his ethic, he valued more and more with age, calling marriage the "divinest of human institutions,"[35] and the family "the supreme expression of humanity."[36]

The diffusion of Eros into the environment, which accompanies his fictional synthesis, also seems to have marked his own life. With an expansion of the libido like the polymorphous sexuality Simone de Beauvoir discovers in old age,[37] Howells brought an enhanced sensuousness to his later writings. Sights, sounds, the scent and taste of "new corn grated" (*MYLC* 24), the feel of dancing nude in the rain (*FPB* 117), take on an almost hallucinogenic brilliance. By neo-Marxist standard, he had performed the supreme task: he had recovered "the lost body of childhood."[38] His further extension of Eros into a philosophy of cooperation and the "unification of mankind"[39] fulfills their demand for a "libidinal rationality"[40] as well.

Vitality overflowing into a joy in the next generation is the keynote of his last years. With the exuberance of the epilogue, he buoyantly championed life and the will to live in "Eighty Years and After," and plighted himself to the future through a passionate love for his grandsons. His last letter to one of them proves the corollary truth that the fully rounded self does not fear death. The black night sky which had earlier saddened him in one of Billy's paintings now delights him in little Joey's. "I never saw anything so glorious,"[41] he exclaimed. Accepting his own mortality as squarely as Nancy's and Braile's, he submitted hopefully to death and saw love constituted by it.[42] By *The Leatherwood God*, his reconciliation with his father was assured, to the extent that he borrowed the story from him and wrote the year it was published: "I find father's figure and bearing in mine, and his face looking at me from the glass."[43] So, too, the optimistic, idealistic mood is his father's, qualified and grounded by his own realism.

Another instance of his atonement with his father is the book's Swedenborgianism—again characteristically despiritualized. From the beginning, Howells's work had been permeated with Swedenborg's sexual thought, but here it comes into luminous focus. So accurately does the novel reflect Swedenborg's beliefs that Leatherwood's drama could be a Swedenborgian erotic parable, without the transcendence. The faith which baffled Howells throughout his middle age became "something to grip"[44] before he died. He reassimilated "the wise and kind doctrine"[45] his father taught him and used it to illuminate his last erotic novel.

Swedenborg's negative sexual ideas crystallize in Dylks's reign of terror. Dylks is a composite of *Conjugial Love* devils. With flashing eyes like theirs, he wears the same false halo, conical hat, and black apparel and believes that he too is "God of Heaven [and] . . . omnipotent."[46] He shares their insanity and breathes fire through the community as they do. An animal like Swedenborg's symbol of lust, he exudes the filth and infusoria of the sexually damned. When he turns up on Squire Braile's porch covered with dirt, the judge sentences him to the lecher's inferno, a mephitic raccoon's nest. On a larger scale, the "Hounds" exile him to the precise equivalent of the *Conjugial Love* land of the lost, the "dreadful forest,"[47] where wild beasts wallow lasciviously amid stagnant pools in complete darkness. Dylks's curse on them, similarly, is just what scortatory love promises: chaos, strife, and a gold, bejeweled haven, filled with real "filth and rubbish"[48] inside.

The positive order that replaces Dylks follows Swedenborg even closer. The union of flesh and spirit, reason and passion, is central to his credo—one of the few in the West to envision an erotic paradise. In the heaven he describes so voluptuously, the sexes join equally (with a slight edge for the women) and enjoy a sexuality balanced by love and intensified by virtue. The tenor is cooperative and relaxed. Public and private spheres interlock in mutual helpfulness, and all work with a Fourieristic pleasure like Nancy's. On the theory that repression befouls, Swedenborg's climate is temperate, permitting occasional lapses, divorces, and remarriages, and diffusing the sensuousness of Leatherwood Creek. The blessed bask in "the delight of the five senses."[49] As with Howells's final ethic, home is the fulcrum of this sexual elysium. For Swedenborg, marriage is the seminary of human existence where happily paired couples dwell in what Braile calls his own house, a "Temple," a "Temple of Wisdom."[50] Out of such unions well a vitality, a fertilizing force that matches the spirit of the epilogue. Marriage love, according to Swedenborg, "expands the inmost things of the mind, and . . . the body,"[51] filling the earth with gaiety, coherence, and fecundity. Significantly, spring reigns eternal in his paradise, the season on which the novel closes. However, with the repudiation of Dylks's New Jerusalem—a simulacrum of Sweden-borg's—Howells rejects the hope of sexual transcendence. He extracts the essence of *Conjugial Love*'s erotic wisdom but suggests (with Denis de Rougemont) that to extend Eros beyond the bounds of time and space is to breed perversions of love, to invite the satanic.

If Howells pried out the heart of passion in his last novel, he also exposed the heart of American sexuality. Cults, Robert Lifton observed in a recent article,[52] contain a buried clue to a nation's psyche, and Dylks's cult reveals a deeply embedded one. In the dream of marriage and domestic peace we publicly espouse, we conceal the desire for its opposite: anarchic, unbounded sexual expression. As Dylks's triumph illustrates, a propensity for uncontrolled erotic freedom, disorder, and sexual division hides beneath our pious sublimations. And in the Leatherwood debacle, Howells corroborates Leslie Fiedler's view that America's true allegiance is to death.

At the same time, he took America's ideal of a sexual synthesis seriously and attempted to reconcile the contradictions in his affirmative ethos. Through Dylks's diabolical con game, he sought to tragically educate the naive American lust for escape and convert it into a higher, more real freedom. Within the bounds of community and marriage, he designed a sexuality that attains genuine liberty—the expansion of spirit and sense in an open, harmonious society. Crevecoeur's prediction that Americans would "finish the great circle"[53] reaches fulfillment. The supreme erotic integration, archetypically symbolized by the circle, becomes a reality. With cyclic perfection, the plot descends into chaos, conquers it, and rises up to an epithalamion in which opposites coalesce and order prevails. Parabolically, Howells cleansed and rehabilitated the perfectionist tradition in America. He reduces to level ground their transcendental attempts to fuse freedom and family. He showed, via Dylks (so like Howells's uncle-in-law, John Humphrey Noyes), how their spirituality actually promoted carnality and disorder. He gave them instead, a tough, flexible synthesis balanced adventurously against actual evil.

In a 1907 essay, Howells imagined himself as an old author at a loss with his sexual theme, who suddenly gets an inspiration. He would write a novel about sex from the "vantage-ground of age," from the standpoint of the "sage," looking back upon it philosophically. "I must be in the whole secret,"[54] he decided. With such a perspective, he surveyed his erotic investigations of a lifetime in *The Leatherwood God* and brought them into final coherence. It is the most architectonic of Howells's books, as solidly, symmetrically constructed as Squire Braile's double log cabin. Dylks, the concentration of all libidinal evil, shadows half the tale in infamy and chaos; the second half perfectly overturns the first, with a precise exchange of imagery. As Dylks's star descends and his initiation fails, the new order ascends toward the radiance of erotic virtue and maturity. The result of Howells's long search for an affirmative sexuality, the positive end of the drama has a structural harmony exactly commensurate with the wild disharmony that preceded it. Nancy, the flower of Howells's heroines, supports the passional side of the equilibrium; Squire Braile supports the rational; and every antinomy fuses in a classic erotic balance.

In addition to the secret of a love ethic, Howells uncovered some stupendous secrets about sex in *The Leatherwood God*. He found, as he hoped in 1907 and Ferris hoped in *A Foregone Conclusion*, the "whole" truth—the limit of man's knowledge. Rooting out the essence of the relationship between Eros and Thanatos, he discovered that love and mortality are inseparable, that denial only unleashes the destructive forces of the death instinct. His earlier novels had shown the fatal effects of sexual repression. Here he completes the observation, proving how Thanatos seizes control when any life process is suppressed. Eros, he realized with the Greeks, is an egg laid by the time spirit. If it is to live, there must be a proper acceptance of nature and all her laws.

About himself, he also exhumed the ultimate "secret." Within his psyche he recognized his own lust for immortality and omnipotence, his potential for radical evil. He faced the black stallion of Plato's *Phaedrus* in all its bestiality and violence. By the same token, he dug up the dark truth of American sexuality. Behind the gilt facade of home and family, he revealed the submerged craving for the illimitable and frenzied. He saw the infantile "blood chaos"[55] in our body politic and demonstrated its lethal consequences.

In these sexual revelations, Howells seems astonishingly modern. His solution to the sexual dilemma, too, anticipates twentieth-century theories. His is the new humanism Thomas Mann proposed, which takes full account of the irrational; his, the libidinal order neo-Marxists envision, which reconciles mind and body in a nonrepressive commonwealth.

Like the memoir that followed it, though, the novel did not come easily to Howells. He put it down at least three times between 1912 and 1914 and complained to his sister that the "dreadfulness and the mystery"[56] of the story distressed him terribly. Both the tragic confrontation and resolution demanded a courage not usually associated with writers in their seventies. The novel is a testament to his strength and daring. Boldly he pulled together the theme of a lifetime and produced a tremendous *éclaircissement*. Love is a thorny problem in the best of times; his was an age of chasmic dissociations, and his reconciliation was audaciously ambitious and *avant-garde*.

Nor had he said everything about sex. Before he died, he planned another novel around the movie industry, where the "wilde Bore" was destined to enjoy its most unconfined revel in America. For the aged writer, Simone de Beauvoir says, "[T]he happiest fate . . . is to have begun with projects . . . so immense that they remain open until his death."[57] If *The Leatherwood God* contains a record of his inner history, then the ending symbolizes the close of his life. From a traumatic encounter with blackness, he came into a limpid peace and fullness of being that remained genuinely endangered by a new Dylks, and that was flexible enough to imagine still greater ameliorations to safeguard the supremacy of sexual love on earth.

Notes

Prologue

1. Edward Marshall, "A Great American Writer," 1894, in *Interviews with William Dean Howells*, ed. Ulrich Halfman (Arlington, Tex.: American Literary Realism, 1973), p. 39.

2. Henry James, letter to W. D. Howells, January 2, 1888, *The Letters of Henry James*, ed. Percy Lubbock, I (New York: Charles Scribner's Sons, 1920), p. 134.

3. Henry James, letter to W. D. Howells, January 8, 1904, *The Letters*, II, 9.

4. W. D. Howells, "Novel-Writing and Novel-Reading: An Impersonal Explanation," ed. William M. Gibson (1899; rpt. New York: The New York Public Library, 1958), p. 11.

5. G. E. Demille, "The Infallible Dean," in *The War of the Critics over William Dean Howells*, ed. Edwin H. Cady and David L. Frazier (Evanston, Ill.: Row, Peterson and Company, 1962), p. 149.

6. Sinclair Lewis, "The American Fear of Literature," in *The War*, p. 153.

7. Ambrose Bierce, "Sharp Criticism of Mr. Howells," in *Critics on William Dean Howells: Readings in Literary Criticism*, ed. Paul A. Escholz (Coral Gables, Fla.: University of Miami Press, 1975), p. 5.

8. Lionel Trilling, "William Dean Howells and the Roots of Modern Taste," in *The Opposing Self* (New York: Viking Press, 1955), p. 217.

9. Edward Wagenknecht, *William Dean Howells: The Friendly Eye* (New York: Oxford University Press, 1969), p. 224.

10. W. D. Howells, letter to S. L. Clemens, February 14, 1904, *Life in Letters of William Dean Howells*, ed. Mildred Howells, II (Garden City, N.Y.: Doubleday, Doran & Company, Inc., 1928), 423.

11. George Spangler, "*The Shadow of a Dream*: Howells' Homosexual Tragedy," *American Quarterly*, 23 (Spring 1971), 110–119, and Gary A. Hunt, "The Reality that can't be quite Definitely Spoken: Sexuality in *Their Wedding Journey*," *Studies in the Novel*, 9 (1977).

12. Bjornstjerne Bjornson, letter to W. D. Howells, March 13, 1889, *Life in Letters*, I, 423.

13. W. D. Howells, "The Writer and the Rest of the World," 1894, in *Interviews*, p. 39, and W. D. Howells, "A Niece's Advice to her Uncle," *Imaginary Interviews* (New York: Harper & Brothers Publishers, 1910), p. 180.

14. "With William Dean Howells," 1893, *Interviews*, p. 31, and W. D. Howells, quoted in Edwin H. Cady, *The Road to Realism* (Syracuse: Syracuse University Press, 1956), p. 204.

15. Ernst Kris, *Psychoanalytic Explorations in Art* (New York: International Universities Press, Inc., 1952), pp. 253–254 and 251.

16. D. H. Lawrence, "A Propos of Lady Chatterley's Lover," in *Literature and Censorship*, ed. Harry T. Moore (London: William Heinemann Ltd., 1955). "We shall never free the phallic reality," Lawrence wrote, "from the 'uplift' taint till we give it its own phallic language and use the obscene words," p. 267.

17. Howells, "Novel-Writing and Novel-Reading," p. 19.

18. W. D. Howells, letter to William White Howells, February 14, 1909, *Life in Letters*, II, 261.

Chapter one

1. Everett Carter, *Howells and the Age of Realism* (Hamden, Conn.: Archon Books, 1966), p. 140.

2. Edward Wagenknecht, *Willian Dean Howells: The Friendly Eye* (New York: Oxford University Press, 1969), p. 224.

3. W. D. Howells, "A Niece's Literary Advice to Her Uncle," in *Imaginary Interviews* (New York: Harper & Brothers Publishers, 1910), p. 177.

4. Henry James, letter to W. D. Howells, January 8, 1904, *The Letters of Henry James*, ed. Percy Lubbock, II (New York: Charles Scribner's Sons, 1920), 9.

5. To appreciate the unorthodoxy and the tolerance of William Cooper Howells's sexual ideas, it should be noted how shocking Owen's proposals were to his contemporaries. "Charges of libertinism [and] free love-ism" were regularly directed at him by the respectable majority, and in 1860 Horace Greeley of the *Tribune* launched a full-scale attack. Indiana (site of New Harmony) was a "paradise of free lovers," he fulminated, and accused Owen of "'lax morality.'" Sidney Ditzion, *Marriage Morals and Sex in America* (New York: W. W. Norton & Company Inc., 1978), pp. 108–110. Milton Rugoff summarizes Owen's sexual philosophy as the belief that "repression is unhealthy and does not produce an inner purity," *Prudery and Passion* (New York: G. P. Putnam's Sons, 1971), p. 162.

6. W. D. Howells, "I Talk of Dreams," in *Impressions and Experiences* (New York: Harper & Brothers Publishers, 1896), p. 124.

7. W. D. Howells, "A Hoosier's Opinion of Walt Whitman," in *W. D. Howells as Critic*, ed. Edwin H. Cady (London: Routledge & Kegan Paul, 1973), p. 14.

8. W. D. Howells, "Some Lessons from the School of Morals," in *Suburban Sketches* (Boston: James R. Osgood and Company, 1872), p. 231.

9. Letter to Charles Eliot Norton, April 26, 1878, *Life in Letters of William Dean Howells*, I: 254.

10. See Karen Horney, *The Neurotic Personality in Our Time* (New York: W. W. Norton & Company, Inc., 1937), p. 290.

11. Sir William Acton, quoted in Steven Marcus, *The Other Victorians: A Study of Sexuality and Pornography in Mid-Nineteenth-Century England* (New York: Basic Books, Inc., Publishers, 1964), p. 18.

12. William A. Alcott, *The Young Man's Guide*, quoted in Ronald G. Walters, ed., *Primers for Prudery: Sexual Advice to Victorian America* (Englewood Cliffs, N.J.: Prentice-Hall, Inc., 1974), p. 36.

13. George N. Dangerfield, "The Symptoms, Pathology, Causes and Treatment of Spermatorrhoea," *Lancet*, 1 (1843), 211, quoted in John S. Haller, Jr., and Robin M. Haller, *The Physician and Sexuality in Victorian America* (New York: W. W. Norton & Company, Inc., 1974), p. 213.

14. Henry Ward Beecher, *Twelve Lectures to Young Men*, in *Primers for Prudery*, p. 69.

15. See Ernst Kris, *Psychoanalytic Explorations in Art* (New York: International Uni-

versities Press, Inc., 1952), for the seminal work on the curative role of creativity in neurosis.

16. Herbert Marcuse, *Eros and Civilization: A Philosophic Inquiry into Freud* (New York: Random House, 1962), pp. 129 and 107.

17. W. D. Howells, "Eighty Years and After," *Harper's Monthly*, 140 (December, 1919), 23.

18. Henry James, "Howells's *Foregone Conclusion,*" in *The War of the Critics*, p. 10.

19. Howells, letter to Charles Eliot Norton, December 11, 1892, *Life in Letters*, II, 29.

20. Spenser, *The Fairie Queene* III, VI, xlviii.

21. Plato, "Phaedrus," in *The Works of Plato*, ed. Irwin Edman (New York: Random House, Inc., 1928), p. 329.

22. W. D. Howells, "Novel-Writing and Novel-Reading: An Impersonal Explanation," ed. William M. Gibson (1899; rpt. New York: The New York Public Library, 1958), p. 8.

23. Richard Chase, *The American Novel and Its Tradition* (Garden City, N.Y.: Doubleday & Company, Inc., 1957), p. 177.

24. M. L. Franz, "The Process of Individuation," in *Man and His Symbols*, ed. Carl G. Jung (New York: Dell Publishing Co., Inc., 1964), p. 174.

25. W. de Wagstaffe, "The Personality of Mr. Howells," 1908, in *Interviews with William Dean Howells*, ed. Ulrich Halfman (Arlington, Tex.: American Literary Realism, 1973), quoting Howells, p. 362.

26. John Updike, *The Centaur* (Greenwich, Conn.: Fawcett Publications, Inc., 1963), p. 212.

Chapter two

1. Edwin Cady, *The Road to Realism: The Early Years 1837–1885 of William Dean Howells* (Syracuse: Syracuse University Press, 1956), quoting Howells, p. 187.

2. Henry James, "Howells's 'Foregone Conclusion,'" in *The War of the Critics*, p. 13.

3. A. Orr, "International Novelists and Mr. Howells," *The War of the Critics*, p. 17.

4. James, "Howells's 'Foregone Conclusion,'" p. 10.

5. "Howells's 'Foregone Conclusion,'" review in *The Nation*, 497 (January 7, 1875), 12.

6. Richard Freeborn, *Turgenev: The Novelists' Novelist* (London: Oxford University Press, 1960), p. 191.

7. See Kenneth Eble, "Howells's Kisses," in *Howells: A Century of Criticism*, ed. Kenneth E. Eble (Dallas, Tex.: Southern Methodist University Press, 1962), pp. 173–181, and Carter, *Howells and the Age of Realism*, pp. 140–151.

8. See James, "Howells's 'Foregone Conclusion,'" who concluded his review with the observation that "the story is Don Ippolito's," p. 15.

9. For a summary of the Victorian penalties for incontinence, see John S. Haller, Jr., and Robin M. Haller, *The Physician and Sexuality in Victorian America*, pp. 191–234, and Steven Marcus, *The Other Victorians*, pp. 17–33.

10. Dogs were special anathemas to Howells during his adolescent breakdowns and also, significantly symbols of lust in Emanuel Swedenborg, his family prophet. See *The Delights of Wisdom pertaining to Conjugial Love: After which follow the Pleasures of Insanity pertaining to Scortatory Love*, trans. Samuel M. Warren (Boston: Houghton Mifflin Company, 1907), p. 109.

11. See Anna Freud's classic description of adolescent sexuality in *The Ego and the*

Mechanisms of Defense, trans. Cecil Baines (New York: International Universities Press, 1946), pp. 166–189. She explains: "Alternating with instinctual excesses and irruptions from the id with other apparently contradictory attitudes, there is sometimes in adolescence an antagonism towards the instincts which far surpasses in intensity anything in the way of repression which we are accustomed to see . . ." (p. 167). "[W]e find almost invariably a swing-over from asceticism to instinctual excess, the adolescent suddenly indulging in everything which he had previously held to be prohibited and disregarding any sort of external restrictions" (p. 170).

12. James, "Howells's 'Foregone Conclusion,'" p. 14.

13. "Howells's 'Foregone Conclusion,'" *The Nation*, p. 12.

14. Studies of nymphomania in the nineteenth century stressed the excitable, explosive dispositions of the women. Dr. Charles Meigs cautioned against "highly exalted" temperaments, while Dr. Joseph Howe warned specifically of "blondes" who were "nervous [and] easily excited," *Primers for Prudery*, pp. 72–74. Turgenev also used a hot temper strategically to convey sexual passion. Irina's flammability in *Smoke* is an index to her erotomania, which unseats the hero, Litimov, and destroys his well-planned life.

15. W. D. Howells, *Venetian Life* (New York: Hurd and Houghton, 1867), p. 368.

16. See the discussion of the meaning of the fool in J. E. Cirlot, *A Dictionary of Symbols*, trans. Jack Sage (New York: Philosophical Library, 1962), pp. 105–106.

17. I am using Norman O. Brown's term for the religious tradition that stresses the recovery of the body, sensuality, and luxury in its spiritual aspirations. See *Life Against Death: The Psychoanalytic Meaning of History* (Middletown, Conn.: Wesleyan University Press, 1959), p. 310.

18. Letter to William Cooper Howells, February 27, 1872, *Life in Letters*, I, 167.

19. See Freud's explanation of the unconscious aspect of a genuine neurosis, *A General Introduction to Psychoanalysis*, trans. Joan Riviere (1924; rpt. New York: Simon & Schuster, Inc., 1952), pp. 376–378. Norman O. Brown also puts it succinctly: "The neurotic mechanism involves repression and a shutting of the eye of consciousness, and a resultant psychic automatism. Art does not withdraw the eye of consciousness," *Life Against Death*, p. 65.

20. James, "Howells's 'Foregone Conclusion,'" p. 11.

Chapter three

1. "Mark Twain: An Inquiry," *W. D. Howells as Critic*, p. 341.

2. Letter to John Hay, December 18, 1875, *Life in Letters*, I, 215.

3. For a review of Howells's method of composition, see his interviews in *Interviews*, pp. 31, 58, 82. In his 1908 talk with W. D. Wagstaffe, he summarizes the unstructured semi-conscious technique he used: "A novel is born very much on the same plan as any other event in the artistic, the ethical, or the active world. You intend a certain course of action and something grows from the germ of your intention. My method of work is a sort of psychic puzzle to myself. Each day's work seems to be the result of a new motive," p. 82. Edwin Cady's discussion is also valuable, *The Road to Realism*, pp. 203–206.

4. William Dean Howells, letter to Edmund Clarence Stedman, December 8, 1874, *Life in Letters*, I, 197.

5. William Dean Howells, "Recent Italian Comedy," *North American Review*, 99 (October, 1864), 367–368.

6. "Scene" refers to James' term for the dramatic presentation of a scene without reflective comment or summary, while "picture" refers to the description of a scene by way of résumé.

7. "With William Dean Howells," 1893, *Interviews*, p. 31.

8. William Dean Howells, "Life and Letters," *Harper's Weekly*, 39 (August 17, 1895), 773.

9. Charles Darwin, *The Descent of Man and Selection in Relation to Sex* (1871; rpt. Detroit: Gale Research Co., 1974), p. 579: "If all our women were to become as beautiful as Venus de Medici, we should for a time be charmed; but we should soon wish for variety."

10. See Carl G. Jung's discussion of the horse as "priapic animal," *Symbols of Transformation*, Bollingen Series, XX (Princeton: Princeton University Press, 1956), 274–278.

11. See Eric Partridge, *Shakespeare's Bawdy: A Literary and Psychological Essay and a Comprehensive Glossary* (London: Routledge & Kegan Paul, 1968), p. 106.

12. See G. J. Barker-Benfield, "Men Earn—Women Spend," *The Horrors of the Half-Known Life: Male Attitudes toward Women and Sexuality in Nineteenth-Century America* (New York: Harper & Row, Publishers, 1976), pp. 189–196.

13. The sexual historian, G. Rattray Taylor, illustrates this point well. To demonstrate the thesis that libidinal lawlessness as well as libidinal overcontrol ends in sterility and impotence, he cites the Dionysian festivals which culminated in self-castration. *Sex in History*, Harper Torchbooks (New York: Harper & Row, Publishers, 1980), pp. 232–236.

14. Norman O. Brown, *Life Against Death*, p. 216.

15. William Dean Howells, letter to Charles Dudley Warner, September 4, 1875, *Life in Letters*, I, 210.

Chapter four

1. Alexander Black, "William Dean Howells," 1925, in *Interviews with William Dean Howells*, quoting Howells, p. 117.

2. Letter to James R. Osgood, February 18, 1881, Clifton Waller Barrett Library, University of Virginia.

3. Ibid.

4. Letter to Brander Matthews, July 22, 1911, *Life in Letters*, II, 301: "Yesterday I read a great part of *A Modern Instance*, and perceived that I had drawn Bartley Hubbard, the false scoundrel, from myself."

5. Cady, *The Road to Realism*, p. 211.

6. Ibid., quoting Howells, p. 157.

7. Howells wrote Clemens in July of 1875 about Elinor: "Her health has been wretched all summer," *Life in Letters*, I, 209.

8. Ibid., p. 217.

9. Letter to Hjalmar Hjorth Boyeson, June 14, 1880, Clifton Waller Barrett Library, University of Virginia.

10. Two short stories, "The Sign of the Savage" and "A Fearful Responsibility," pursued the subject of Mrs. Farrell's promiscuity to extramarital desire, and his novels turned steadily toward the darker manifestations of passion with new seriousness. "I am now striking all the witty things out of my work," he told W. H. Bishop (letter, March 21, 1880, *Life in Letters*, I, 282) and tried a tragedy of sexual abandonment (later *A Woman's Reason*) that he had to discard. The three novels in between *Private Theatricals* and *A Modern Instance* all touch more profoundly on truths Mrs. Farrell exhumed: sadomasochism (*Undiscovered Country* and *Dr. Breen's Practice*), jealousy (*Undiscovered Country*), and personality disintegration (*The Lady of the Aroostook*).

11. Letter to C. E. Norton, April 16, 1878, *Life in Letters*, I, 254.

12. Among some of them were Harvey Kellogg's *Plain Facts about Sexual Life*, 1877;

Henry Ward Beecher's fanatical *Twelve Lectures*, 1879; John Cowan's *The Science of a New Life*, 1880; and George M. Beard's *American Nervousness*, 1881. Selections from the first three can be found in *Primers for Prudery*.

13. Goldwin Smith, "Pessimism," *Atlantic Monthly*, 45 (February 1880), 210–211.

14. See Angus Wilson, *Emile Zola: An Introductory Study* (New York: William Morrow & Company, 1952) for a superb discussion of Zola's sexual "horror and despair" combined with his bloodless "rejection of physical sexuality," pp. 49 and 9. Howells recognized this in a later essay and chastised him for his "austere puritanism." "Emile Zola," in *W. D. Howells as Critic*, p. 389.

15. Henry James wrote Howells continually about Zola and naturalism during the late seventies and said in 1879: "[C]ontinue to Americanize and to realize: that is your mission . . . you will become the Zola of the USA" (July 22, 1879, Harvard Collection), quoted in Kenneth S. Lynn, *William Dean Howells: An American Life* (New York: Harcourt Brace Jovanovich, Inc., 1970), p. 244. The *Atlantic Monthly*, as well, was a forum for debate on Zola when Howells was editor. See especially "The Contributors' Club," *Atlantic Monthly*, 39 (May 1877), 610–612 and T. S. Perry, "Zola's Last Novel," *Atlantic Monthly*, 45 (May 1880), 693–699.

16. Letter to John Hay, March 18, 1882, *Life in Letters*, I, 311.

17. W. D. Howells, *My Literary Passions* (New York: Harper & Brothers Publishers, 1891), p. 180.

18. Pendennis, "Mr. Howells Talks about Fiction and Fiction-Writers," 1905, *Interviews*, p. 78.

19. Grace D. Pattan, letter, *New York Tribune*, December 4, 1882, p. 10.

20. Letter to Hay, March 18, 1882, *Life in Letters*, I, 311.

21. Letter to Osgood, February 18, 1881, Clifton Waller Barrett Library, University of Virginia.

22. Steven Marcus, *The Other Victorians*, quoting William Acton, p. 18.

23. See *A Boy's Town* for Howells's lyric response to the birds that filled the woods around Hamilton. One particularly halcyon day when he went hunting with his brother he listened ecstatically to the "faint twitter of doves' wings" (p. 156).

24. A South Sea Islander was a common nineteenth-century euphemism for a sexual truant and "savage." See H. R. Hays, *From Ape to Angel: An Informal History of Social Anthropology* (New York: Capricorn Books, 1958), pp. 42–43.

25. See chapter fifteen, "The Spermatic Economy and Proto-Sublimation," in G. J. Barker-Benfield, *The Horrors of the Half-Known Life*, pp. 175–188. This central metaphor of the nineteenth century was also Zola's favorite, and Howells may well have been influenced by him.

26. Letter to William Cooper Howells, November 15, 1881, *Life in Letters*, I, 303.

27. See Howells's review of Mary Wollstonecraft's letters to Imlay, *Atlantic Monthly*, 44 (July 1879), 124–125; "Carlo Goldini," *Atlantic Monthly*, 40 (November 1877), 601–613; and letters to C. E. Norton, April 16, 1878; to Arthur G. Sedgwick, December 27, 1880; and to John Hay, March 18, 1882, in *Life in Letters*, I, 254, 291, 310–311.

28. January 20, 1882, *Selected Mark Twain-Howells Letters, 1872–1910*, ed. Frederick Anderson, William M. Gibson, Henry Nash Smith (New York: Atheneum, 1968), p. 183.

29. January 31, 1882, *Life in Letters*, I, 307.

30. Herbert Marcuse, *Eros and Civilization*, p. 34.

31. Howells, letter to R. W. Gilder, March 1882, Houghton Library, Harvard University.

32. "Howells on the Novel," 1899, in *Interviews*, p. 67.

33. Shakespeare, *As You Like It*, II, vii, 156.

34. A. Schade van Westrum, "Mr. Howells on Love and Literature," 1904, *Interviews*, quoting Howells, p. 72.

35. Emanuel Swedenborg, *Conjugial Love*, p. 314.

36. Ibid., p. 431.

37. For an example of his rigid, puritanical interpretation of Swedenborg, see Henry James, Sr., "Is Marriage Holy?," *Atlantic Monthly*, 25 (March 1870), 360–368. Edwin Cady discusses the relationship between Howells and the elder James in *The Road to Realism*, p. 150. If it is true that James acted as a surrogate father for Howells in Boston, supplanting William Cooper's Swedenborgianism, *A Modern Instance* anticipates the return he would make to his own more lenient father in the next decade.

38. See Clifton Johnson, "Sense and Sentiment," 1895, in *Interviews*, p. 48. He quotes Howells: "The Swiss have a divorce law that seems to me almost perfect . . . what we need is not only the same law about divorce, but a similar law about marriage."

39. Oscar W. Firkins, *William Dean Howells: A Study* (1924; rpt. New York: Russell & Russell, Inc., 1963), p. 107.

40. A. Schade van Westrum, *Interviews*, quoting Howells, p. 72.

41. February 21, 1884, *The Letters of Henry James*, I, 103.

42. To Clemens, March 15, 1882, *Life in Letters*, I, 310.

43. March 18, 1882, *Life in Letters*, I, 311.

44. Stephen Crane, "Fears Realists Must Wait," 1894, in *Interviews*, quoting Howells, p. 45.

Chapter five

1. Letter to Richard W. Gilder, July 31, 1884, *Selected Letters of W. D. Howells*, ed. Robert C. Leitz III et al., III (Boston: Twayne Publishers, 1980), 103.

2. "Novel-Writing as a Science," in *The War of the Critics over William Dean Howells*, ed. Edwin H. Cady and David L. Frazier (Evanston, Ill.: Row, Peterson and Company, 1962), p. 36.

3. William R. Thayer, "The New Story-Tellers and the Doom of Realism," in *The War*, p. 70.

4. The most notable are: Oscar Firkins, *William Dean Howells: A Study* (1924; rpt. New York: Russell & Russell, Inc., 1963), p. 112; George Arms, "Introduction," *The Rise of Silas Lapham* (New York: Rinehart & Co., Inc., 1949), pp. viii–ix; Harry Hartwick, *The Foreground of American Fiction* (New York: American Book Company, 1934), pp. 324–325; Warner Berthoff, *The Ferment of Realism* (New York: The Free Press, 1965), p. 53; H. E. Scudder, review of *The Rise of Silas Lapham*, in *The War*, p. 34; Edward Wagenknecht, *William Dean Howells: The Friendly Eye* (New York: Oxford University Press, 1969), p. 63.

5. See particularly: Donald Pizer, "The Ethical Unity of *The Rise of Silas Lapham*," *American Literature*, 32 (November 1960), 322–327; G. Thomas Tanselle, "The Architecture of *The Rise of Silas Lapham*," *American Literature*, 37 (January 1966), 430–457.

6. See Everett Carter, *Howells and the Age of Realism* (Hamden, Conn.: Archon Books, 1966), p. 165; "Introduction," *The Rise of Silas Lapham* (New York: Harper and Row Publishers, 1958), p. xi; and Tanselle, "The Architecture," p. 440, n. 15.

7. Hamlin Garland, "Sanity in Fiction," in *The War*, p. 94.

8. Everett Carter, *Howells*, p. 165.

9. "Savings Bank" Diary 1883–1897, Houghton Library, Harvard University.

10. The dictionary Howells consulted was Worcester's (Joseph Emerson Worcester, *A Comprehensive Dictionary of the English Language* (Boston: Swan, Brewer, and

Tileston, 1860), which particularly emphasized Silenus's debauched character, p. 681.

11. Howells first used Florida Vervain's red hair as a symbol of hot-bloodedness in *A Foregone Conclusion*, and repeated it again in *A Modern Instance* with Bartley Hubbard and in *The Landlord at Lion's Head* with Jeff Durgin.

12. Classically the tree is a "symbol of the inexhaustible life force" (cf. the yggdrasil), whose roots signify the "primal forces." J. E. Cirlot, *A Dictionary of Symbols*, trans. Jack Sage (New York: Philosophical Library, 1962), pp. 329 and 331. C. G. Jung goes further and discusses "the hole in the earth" as the archetypal maternal matrix. *Symbols of Transformation*, trans. R. F. C. Hull, Bollingen Series XX (Princeton: Princeton University Press, 1956), p. 158. Also compare Emile Zola's use of earth as a sexual symbol in *La Terre*.

13. For discussion of the horse as an archetypal emblem of the id, see Cirlot, *A Dictionary*, pp. 144–145; Jung, *Symbols*, pp. 275–280; and Eric Partridge, *Shakespeare's Bawdy: A Literary and Psychological Essay and Comprehensive Glossary* (London: Routledge & Kegan Paul, 1968), p. 130. Although this use of horses becomes more pronounced in Howells's later fiction, he featured them extensively in his early novels, particularly *A Foregone Conclusion* (in which the oversexed priest is named Don Ippolito—little horse), and *Mrs. Farrell* (in which the timid hero is morbidly afraid of the horses his lover whips with pleasure).

14. See Cirlot, *A Dictionary*, p. 146; Sigmund Freud, *The Interpretation of Dreams*, trans. James Strachey (New York: Avon Books, 1965), p. 117; and C. G. Jung, "Jung on Freud," ed. Aniela Jaffe, *Atlantic Monthly*, 210 (November 1962), 52–54. Howells came closest to articulating this symbolic use of houses in *A Woman's Reason* (Boston: Houghton Mifflin Company, 1883). Mr. Harkness, explaining the significance of his house to his daughter says: "It gets to be your body and usurps all your reality" p. 35.

15. The standard explanation is in Otto Fenichel, *The Psychoanalytic Theory of Neurosis* (New York: W. W. Norton & Company Inc., 1945), pp. 66–68 and 278–284.

16. Susanne K. Langer, *Feeling and Form*, quoted in *The Comic in Theory and Practice*, ed. John J. Enck et al. (New York: Appleton-Century-Crofts, Inc., 1960), pp. 85–86.

17. "Howells' *The Rise of Silas Lapham*," *The Explicator*, 22 (November 1963), no. 16.

18. Goethe's *Faust*, trans. Walter Kaufmann (Garden City, N.Y.: Doubleday & Company, Inc., 1962), 1. 1338.

19. See *A Boy's Town* (New York: Harper & Brothers Publishers, 1890), p. 23. Howells tells how he gave to the poor, against his parents' approval: "There were circumstances of indignity or patronage attending the gift which were recognized in my boy's home and which helped afterwards to make him doubtful of all giving, except the humblest, and restive with a world in which there need be any giving at all."

20. In fact, his whole relationship with the sordid Millons—usually considered unjustifiable and superfluous—may be another tie to the "love story," dramatizing the latent corruption in sentimentality.

21. The "fool" historically represents the incoherent, irrational unconscious, see Cirlot, *A Dictionary*, pp. 105–106.

22. Cirlot, *A Dictionary*, pp. 100–101; Jung, *Symbols*, pp. 279–280.

23. See n. 23, chap. 7. Throughout his fiction, Howells invests trains with libidinal significance. Not surprisingly, the "horror" of two runaway trains figures prominently in Howells's nightmares. "I Talk of Dreams," in *Impressions and Experiences* (New York: Harper & Brothers publishers, 1896), pp. 106 and 120.

24. Howells, synopsis of *The Rise of Silas Lapham*, Huntington Library, California, or quoted in Everett Carter, "Introduction," *The Rise of Silas Lapham*, p. xiv.

25. Demonic is used throughout *Silas Lapham* in the root sense as Rollo May defines it: "The daimonic is any natural function which has the power to take over the whole

person . . . the unflattering, cruel, and hideous aspects of [oneself] . . . the denied part of you." *Love and Will* (New York: Dell Publishing Co., Inc., 1969), pp. 120, 121, 127.

26. *Heroines of Fiction* (New York: Harper & Brothers Publishers, 1901), pp. 11, 67.

27. A husky voice has been considered a measure of passionality in women throughout literature, which John Atkins ascribes to the fact that "after intercourse many women's voices drop a tone or two." *Sex in Literature* (New York: Grove Press, Inc., 1980), p. 209. Howells gave several women these low, cozy voices: Florida Vervain in *A Foregone Conclusion*, Julia Anderson in *April Hopes*, Madison Woodburn in *A Hazard of New Fortunes*, and Hope Hawberk in *The Son of Royal Langbrith*.

28. For a discussion of this, see Anna Freud's discussion of adolescence, "The Ego and Id at Puberty," in *The Ego and the Mechanisms of Defense* (New York: International Universities Press, 1966), pp. 137–151.

29. Silas and Penelope admit their mutual blame in their respective troubles when they attend the theater together:

"Pen, I presume you know I'm in trouble?
"We all seem to be there," said the girl.
"Yes, but there's a difference between being there by your own fault and being there by somebody else's.'
"I don't call it his fault," she said.
"I call it mine," said the Colonel. (p. 286).

And later, Penelope condemns her own superlative vision of reparation in language identical to her father's. Silas says that he "jumped at the chance" (p. 260) to over-repay Rogers; Penelope, that she "jumped at . . . the chance" (p. 304) to overatone to Irene.

30. Venice, where Howells was a consul from 1861–1865, was a formative influence in his prudery, exposing him to a sensuous culture and teaching him a cosmopolitan breadth of tolerance.

31. Since Donald Pizer has shown ("The Ethical Unity") that Lapham followed the "economy of pain" formula in his business with the Englishmen, this has become a commonplace in criticism of *The Rise of Silas Lapham*.

32. "Savings Bank" Diary.

33. Henry Steele Commager's observation in the Limited Editions Club edition, 1961, that the novel "discloses unmistakable autobiographical elements, material and psychological" (p. vi) has been echoed by almost every critic. The most noteworthy are Mildred Howells, "Introduction," Centenary Edition (Boston: Houghton Mifflin Company, 1937), pp. v–vi; Edwin Cady, *The Road to Realism* (Syracuse: Syracuse University Press, 1956), pp. 222–245; and Kermit Vanderbilt, "Howells among the Brahmins, Why 'the Bottom Dropped Out' during *The Rise of Silas Lapham*," *The New England Quarterly*, 35 (September 1962), 291–317.

34. Letter to Henry James, August 22, 1884, *Selected Letters*, p. 109.

35. Marrion Wilcox, "Works of William Dean Howells," *Harper's Weekly*, July 4, 1896, p. 656.

36. See especially, Kermit Vanderbilt, "Howells among the Brahmins."

37. For the seminal article that established Howells's neuroticism, see Edwin Harrison Cady, "The Neuroticism of William Dean Howells," *PMLA*, 61 (March 1946), 229–238.

38. See *Psychoanalytic Explorations in Art* (New York: International Universities Press, 1965), pp. 253–254, for the original theory of "regression in the service of the ego."

39. Howells told a curious reader: "I took the name of Lapham from a family I

knew in the Southeastern Ohio town where my boyhood was passed," *New York Times*, April 20, 1885, p. 3.

40. Howells best describes these symptoms, chief of which was an imaginary case of rabies (hydrophobia) that caused drowning sensations, in *My Literary Passions* (1895; rpt. New York: Greenwood Press, Publishers, 1969), pp. 55–92 and 144–182, and *Years of My Youth and Three Essays*, ed. David J. Nordloh (1916; rpt. Bloomington, Ind.: University Press, 1975), pp. 51–55, 69, 78–82, 120–124.

41. This is Kermit Vanderbilt's suggestion, "Howells among the Brahmins," p. 311.

42. Edwin Cady explains the root, Ohio meaning of this phrase in which the canal bottom suddenly develops a break, causing flood and desolation, in *The Road to Realism*, p. 243.

43. "Realism: The Moral Issue," 1887, in *W. D. Howells as Critic*, ed. Edwin H. Cady (London: Routledge & Kegan Paul, 1973), p. 102.

44. The predominant view is that of Everett Carter, who says in his introduction to *The Rise of Silas Lapham* (New York: Harper & Row Publishers, 1958) that "liberal optimism" is the prevailing mood, p. xii.

45. Rev. of *The Rise of Silas Lapham*, *The Nation*, October 22, 1885, p. 345; Rev. of *The Rise of Silas Lapham*, *The New York Times*, September 27, 1885, p. 5; Rev. of *The Rise of Silas Lapham*, *Life*, April 23, 1885, p. 228; "Novel-Writing as a Science," p. 36.

46. Helen Thomas Follett and Wilson Follett, "Contemporary Novelists: William Dean Howells," in *The War*, p. 119.

47. Booth Tarkington, "Introduction," Centenary Edition, *The Rise of Silas Lapham* (Boston: Houghton Mifflin Company, 1937), p. xiv.

Chapter six

1. Letter to James R. Osgood, February 18, 1881, Clifton Waller Barrett Library, University of Virginia.

2. William Dean Howells, Gould Interview, May 17, 1909, quoted by Edwin H. Cady, *The Realist at War: The Mature Years of 1885–1920 of William Dean Howells* (Syracuse: Syracuse University Press, 1958), p. 58.

3. Letter to Osgood.

4. See *Documents of Literary Realism*, ed. George J. Becker (Princeton: Princeton University Press, 1963). In Becker's introduction he observes that the realists upheld the "physiological man [as] the fundamental being," and that realism in general "refers us back to a physical, existing reality," pp. 26 and 34.

5. Edwin Cady points out that it was during these years that the "curve of departure" from his father began to "bend back." Howells may have shifted away from his surrogate father, the puritanical Swedenborgian, Henry James, Sr., to his more tolerant, real one as he began to build his nonrepressive sexual ethic. See *The Realist at War*, p. 65.

6. William Dean Howells, "Lyof N. Tolstoy," 1980, in *W. D. Howells as Critic*, p. 461.

7. Howells once wondered whether Tolstoy had ever read Swedenborg, their emphases on selflessness, tolerance, and inner goodness are so similar. "Editor's Easy Chair," *Harper's Monthly*, 127 (October 1913), 798.

8. William Dean Howells, "Editor's Study," *Harper's Monthly*, 81 (October 1890), 802.

9. A. Schade van Westrum, "Mr. Howells on Love and Literature," 1904, in *Interviews with William Dean Howells*, quoting Howells, p. 352.

10. Henry James, letter to William Dean Howells, January 2, 1888, *The Letters of Henry James*, p. 134.

11. Letter to Joseph A. Howells, December 9, 1906, *Life in Letters*, II, 231.

12. On the one hand, Howells said that Tolstoy had the greatest influence on him "both as an artist and as a moralist" (W. J. Gent, "Mr. Howells' Socialism," 1898, in *Interviews*, quoting Howells, p. 52), and that he "meant everything to [him]—his philosophy as well as his art" (Joyce Kilmer, "War Stops Literature, Says W. D. Howells," 1914, in *Interviews*, quoting Howells, p. 114). On the other, he demurred: "Artistically, he has shown me a greatness he can never teach me" (*MLP* 188), and "as a writer I have not been influenced by him . . . my work has no trace of his influence." (Van Wyck Brooks, "Mr. Howells at Work at Seventy-two," 1909, in *Interviews*, quoting Howells, p. 90).

13. William Dean Howells, letter to T. S. Perry, October 30, 1885, *Life in Letters*, I, 372–373. About Anna Karenina he wrote: "The subtlety of the observation in it is astounding, simply."

14. Negroes were symbolic of oversexuality and promiscuity in Howells's day. See *Primers for Prudery*, p. 10.

15. This is a phrase Ralph E. Matlaw uses in his introduction to *Tolstoy: A Collection of Critical Essays* (Englewood Cliffs, N.J.: Prentice-Hall, Inc., 1967), p. 10, to describe Tolstoy's method of rendering the interior life of his characters.

16. The "open" ending of Alice's and Dan's love story is perhaps the best testimony to that enthusiasm. The April 1886 "Editor's Study" in 72 *Harper's* which contains Howells's famous realistic decree, "the novel ends well that ends faithfully," is a direct reference to Tolstoy's organic "open" endings. The same article goes on to extoll his ability to grasp the essential rhythms of life: "As you read on you say, not 'This is like life,' but 'This is life.' It has not only the complexion, the very hue, of life, but its movement, its advances, its strange pauses, its seeming reversions to former conditions, and its perpetual change," p. 809.

17. William Dean Howells, "'Negative Realism': Stevenson, Balzac," 1886, in *W. D. Howells as Critic*, p. 81.

18. Henry Mills Alden, "Editor's Study," *Harper's Monthly*, 102 (December 1900), 159–160, describes the occasion in which he asked Howells, during the serialization of the novel, to rewrite "one particular passage [where] the author had allowed his young lovers unusual freedom of emotional expression," p. 159.

19. "Golden Calf," *New Catholic Encyclopedia*, 1967, specifically associates the golden calf with a phallic cult: "Since the bull was an apt fertility symbol, it was inevitably connected with pagan cult practices. The golden calves of Bethal and Dan became marks of Israel's apostasy."

20. In his criticism at the time, Howells reserved special censure for Dan's overzealous courtship of feminine approval, calling it "a fibreless soft-heartedness that cannot bear to have pretty women disappointed," "Editor's Study," *Harper's Monthly*, 72 (April 1886), 811.

21. Throughout I have used this Howells's coinage, which he used interchangeably with neo-romantic to mean "seeking romantic emotional effects in the cynical absence of romantic belief," *W. D. Howells as Critic*, p. 5.

22. Eric Partridge, "Cotton-top," *A Dictionary of Slang and Unconventional English* (New York: The Macmillan Company, 1961), p. 183.

23. This is Robert Browning's "Gold Hair: A Story of Pornic."

24. "Fascination" is a favorite Howellsian euphemism for sexual excitement throughout his work. By using it strategically in his love scenes, he was able to elicit some of the original sense of the word, "fascinum," Latin for the male sex organ.

25. The actual quote is "You are a treacherous man!" and involves a villainous betrayal instead of Dan's immature evasiveness. Just before Howells began *April Hopes*, he indicted *Romola* in the "Editor's Study" as an example of dangerous feminine quixotism in literature. "Editor's Study," *Harper's Monthly*, 73 (August 1886), 477.

26. In China boys are given sprigs of forsythia when they graduate. Gertrude Jobes, "forsythia," *Dictionary of Mythology Folklore and Symbols* (New York: The Scarecrow Press, Inc., 1961), p. 596.

27. Ibid., p. 811. Significantly, Hygeia's emblems are the sexual snake and urn.

28. See James's essay by that title in *Pragmatism and Other Essays*, intro. Joseph L. Blau (1896; rpt. New York: Washington Square Press, 1963), pp. 236–250.

29. Henry James, *The Notebooks*, ed. F. O. Matthiessen and Kenneth B. Murdock (New York: Oxford University Press, 1947), p. 129. About "the growing divorce between the American woman (with her comparative leisure, culture, grace, social instincts, artistic ambitions) and the male American immersed in the ferocity of business," James declared: "This divorce is rapidly becoming a gulf—an abyss of inequality, the like of which has never before been seen under the sun."

30. Letter to Hamlin Garland, March 18, 1888, *Life in Letters*, I, 410.

31. Emanuel Swedenborg, *Conjugial Love*, p. 423.

32. Ibid., p. 504.

33. Review of *April Hopes*, by William Dean Howells, in *The Academy*, 32 (November 1887), 350.

34. Review of *April Hopes*, by William Dean Howells, in *The Nation*, 46 (February 16, 1888), 142.

35. Review of *April Hopes*, by William Dean Howells, in *The Tribune*, January 1, 1888, p. 10.

36. Letter to Edmund Clarence Stedman, February 4, 1888, *Life in Letters*, I, 409.

37. D. H. Lawrence, "Pornography and Obscenity," in *Sex, Literature and Censorship*, ed. Harry T. Moore (New York: The Viking Press, 1953), p. 71.

38. A recurrent theme in his "realism war" was the lasciviousness of sentimental fiction. The sly titillations of chivalric romance were "poisonous," its mists, "unwholesome vapors," he declared sixty years before Lawrence. ("Realism: the Moral Issue," 1887, in *W. D. Howells as Critic*, p. 99). Also see "Effectism," 1889, pp. 162–171, and "Civilization, Barbarism, Romance and Reality," 1887, pp. 112–120.

39. Samuel Clemens, "Various Literary People," 1908, in *Mark Twain in Eruption*, ed. Bernard De Voto (1922; rpt. New York: Harper & Row, 1968), p. 316: Since "the laws of Nature, that is to say the laws of God, plainly made every human being a law unto himself, we must steadfastly refuse to obey those laws, and we must steadfastly stand by the conventions . . . [which are] better for us than the laws of God, which would soon plunge us into confusion and anarchy."

40. Letter to Edmund Clarence Stedman, February 4, 1888, *Life in Letters*, I, 409.

Chapter seven

1. Letter to Samuel Clemens, February 11, 1884, *Life in Letters*, I, 359.

2. I am using "demonic" here to indicate libidinous energy in its raw, primitive form, with its dual capacities for destruction and creativity. Rollo May in *Love and Will* (New York: Dell Publishing Co., Inc., 1969) defines "demonic" this way: "The daimonic is *any natural function which has the power to take over the whole person*. Sex and eros . . . are examples. The daimonic can be either creative or destructive and is normally both," p. 21. This is also how Plato uses "demon" in the Symposium when he quotes Diotima's definition of love as a "great spirit," *The Works of Plato*, p. 369.

3. On numerous occasions Howells referred to this book as romantic. See letter to Hjalmer H. Boyesen, December 30, 1889, *Selected Letters of William Dean Howells*. Also see Howells's talk with Hamlin Garland about *The Shadow of a Dream* in Hamlin Garland, "Meetings with Howells," *The Bookman* 45 (March 1917), 5: "It *is* rather romantic," he said of the projected book, "and I may never write it."

4. Howells wrote Pyle about Nevil's and Hermia's romance, which ends so fatally: "At first I meant to have him marry Hermia, but he convinced me, as he wormed it out, that this was not possible," letter to Howard Pyle, April 17, 1890, *Life in Letters*, II, 11.

5. Letter to James Osgood, February 18, 1881, Clifton Waller Barrett Library, University of Virginia. This refers to the mood he told Osgood he wished to avoid in *A Modern Instance*, and which he was unable, as here, to avert.

6. Letter to Edward Everett Hale, April 5, 1889, *Life in Letters*, I, 424.

7. For his praises of Zola and Ibsen, see "Editor's Study," *Harper's Monthly*, 75 (March 1888), 640–644 and "Editor's Study," *Harper's Monthly*, 78 (May 1889), 982–987.

8. William Dean Howells, "Editor's Study," *Harper's Monthly*, 77 (November 1888), 967. Speaking of Henley, he said that it was the poet's business to face the "painful facts of life."

9. William Dean Howells, "Sex in Literature," June 1889, in *W. D. Howells as Critic*, p. 155.

10. James Russell Lowell wrote Howells in a letter of acknowledgement: "You have written nothing more daintily subtle . . . ," letter to William Dean Howells, June 19, 1890, Houghton Library, Harvard University.

11. "Fool," here is used in the same sense as in the other chapters, as a repository of the unorganized, unconscious powers of the psyche. See J. E. Cirlot, *A Dictionary of Symbols*, p. 106.

12. See especially Dr. Harvey Kellogg's list from *Plain Facts about Sexual Life* (1877) in *Primers for Prudery*, pp. 37–38.

13. For the equation between smoking and sexual delinquency in Howells's day, see Dr. Frederick Hollick, *The Male Generative Organs in Health and Disease from Infancy to Old Age* (New York: n.d.) in *Primers for Prudery*, p. 60 and Bertrand Russell's account of a doctor's advice to him in *Marriage and Morals* (New York: Bantam Books, 1929), p. 31. Morbid dreams as a symptom of incontinence was also well publicized in the purity literature. See John S. Haller, Jr., and Robin M. Haller, *The Physician and Sexuality in Victorian America*, p. 212, and Stephen Marcus, *The Other Victorians*, p. 20.

14. See George Spangler, "*The Shadow of a Dream*: Howells Homosexual Tragedy," *American Quarterly*, 23 (Spring 1971), 110–119.

15. Gertrude Jobes, *Dictionary of Mythology*, pp. 465–466. Sir James, the first Black Douglas and hero of Scott's novel, *Castle Dangerous*, was so terrible that English parents used to frighten their children with stories of him.

16. A composite picture of the ruin caused by sexual intemperance can be found in *The Physician and Sexuality*, pp. 212–214; *The Other Victorians*, p. 24; and G. J. Barker-Benfield, *The Horrors of the Half-Known Life*, p. 170. Especially interesting is the association of heart disease with sexual corruption in *The Other Victorians*, pp. 26–28, and in *The Physician and Sexuality*, pp. 212–213.

17. Compare Faulkner's listing posture with Dan's inner imbalance and Bartley's vertigo when *they* stray into sexual excess and sin.

18. William Dean Howells, "Life and Letters," *Harper's Weekly*, 41 (March 13, 1897), 270.

19. Jobes, *Dictionary of Mythology*, p. 239. Traditionally, the leaves will reveal the truth to a lover if he crackles them between his fingers. At the same time, box is the funeral shrub of ancient Greece.

20. Ibid., p. 761.

21. Ibid., p. 1685.

22. Rollo May discusses this at some length in *Love and Will*, pp. 128–130. "When the daimonic is repressed," he explains, "it tends to *erupt* in some form—its extreme forms being assassination . . . murders . . . and other horrors," p. 128. In sum, he concludes: *"Not to recognize the daimonic itself turns out to be daimonic; it makes us accomplices on the side of the destructive possession.*

"The denial of the daimonic is, in effect, a self-castration in love and a self-nullification in will. And the denial leads to the perverted forms of aggression . . . in which the repressed comes back to haunt us," pp. 129–130.

23. See especially the erotic use of trains in *A Foregone Conclusion*, *A Modern Instance*, *The Rise of Silas Lapham*, and the farces, "The Parlor Car" and "The Sleeping Car." Compare these with Emile Zola's *La Bete Humaine*.

24. Wayne C. Booth, *The Rhetoric of Fiction* (Chicago: The University of Chicago Press, 1961), p. 274.

25. George N. Bennett in *The Realism of William Dean Howells* summarizes the possible sources for the book's title and the critical debate surrounding it, p. 80.

26. There is an excellent discussion of this aspect of the maturity rite by Joseph L. Henderson, "Ancient Myths and Modern Man" in *Man and His Symbols*, pp. 97–128.

27. According to Eric Fromm, *The Forgotten Language: An Introduction to the Understanding of Dreams, Fairy Tales, and Myths* (New York: Holt, Rinehart, and Winston, 1951), the difference between normal and neurotic dreams is that the latter returns the dreamer to an infantile stage and causes anxiety instead of "hallucinatory gratification," p. 161. Perhaps Basil's nightmares, in view of his inner conflict, belong to this category.

28. Norman O. Brown, *Life Against Death*, p. 60.

29. When Dan Mavering has fallen in love with Julia Anderson and doesn't know it, he dreams self-delusively of their being "good friends and comrades" throughout life (*AH* 327–328).

30. Letter to Richard H. Newton, January 27, 1889, *Selected Letters*, III, 244.

31. Howard Pyle, letter to William Dean Howells, July 15, 1891, Houghton Library, Harvard University.

32. Two letters to his father, October 4 and October 11, 1891, complain of vertigo attacks, one so severe that he "could not work," October 4, Houghton Library, Harvard University.

33. William Dean Howells, "True, I Talk of Dreams," *Harper's Monthly*, 90 (May 1895), 842–843.

34. "Heredity" sums up this mood and is worth quoting in full:

> "That swollen paunch you are doomed to bear
> Your gluttonous grandsire used to wear;
> That tongue, at once so light and dull,
> Wagged in your grandam's empty skull;
> That leering of the sensual eye
> Your father, when he came to die,
> Left yours alone; and that cheap flirt,
> Your mother, gave you from the dirt
> The simper which she used upon
> So many men ere he was won.

Your vanity and greed and lust
Are each your portion from the dust
Of those who died, and from the tomb
Made you what you must needs become,
I do not hold you aught to blame
For sin at second hand, and shame:
Evil could but from evil spring;
And yet, away, you charnel thing!"

Stops of Various Quills (New York: Harper & Brothers Publishers, 1895).

35. The locus classicus of his self-accusatory letters is the one to Edward Everett Hale, May 6, 1890: "I am all the time stumbling to my feet from the dirt of such falls through vanity and evil will, and hate, that I can hardly believe in that self that seems to write books which help people," *Life in Letters*, II, 4. His yearning for the quiescence and forgetfulness of death is also striking in the letters of the early nineties. See these particularly: to Aurelia Howells, January 5, 1890; to Charles Eliot Norton, February 28, 1892; and to Charles Eliot Norton, October 16, 1892, the first in *Selected Letters*, III, 269–270, and the last two in Volume IV.

36. Letter to Charles Eliot Norton, December 11, 1892, *Life in Letters*, II, 29.

37. See particularly the essays: "Degeneration," April 13, 1895, pp. 217–224; "The Ibsen Influence," April 27, 1875, pp. 225–230; "New York Low Life in Fiction," July 26, 1896, pp. 256–262; and "My Favorite Novelist and his Best Book" April 1897, pp. 268–280, all in *W. D. Howells as Critic*. His turn of the century essay, "Novel-Writing and Novel-Reading: An Impersonal Explanation," retracts his earlier defense of reticence and advises the new novelist not to "reject anything . . . or shun any aspect of life," p. 21.

38. Letter to Howard Pyle, May 17, 1891, in Charles D. Abbott, *Howard Pyle: A Chronicle* (New York: Harper & Brothers Publishers, 1892), p. 188; Letter to Henry James, August 21, 1894, in *Selected Letters*, IV and letter to Aurelia, July 8, 1900, *Life in Letters*, II, 130–131.

39. Letter to Howard Pyle, April 17, 1890, *Life in Letters*, II, 11.

40. Letter to Samuel Clemens, February 11, 1884, *Life in Letters*, I, 360.

Chapter eight

1. William Dean Howells, "The Man of Letters as a Man of Business," in *Literature and Life* (New York: Harper & Brothers Publishers, 1902), p. 29.

2. To Samuel Clemens, February 14, 1904, *Life in Letters of William Dean Howells*, II, 186.

Chapter nine

1. Howard Pyle, letter to William Dean Howells, July 15, 1891, Houghton Library, Harvard University.

2. James defines this state of extreme melancholia as a "passive joylessness and dreariness, discouragement, dejection, lack of taste and zest and spring," in *The Varieties of Religious Experience: A Study in Human Nature* (1902; rpt. New York: Random House, 1929), p. 142.

3. Letter to William Cooper Howells, February 22, 1891, Houghton Library, Harvard University.

4. Letter to Joseph A. Howells, November 5, 1892, in *Selected Letters of William*

Dean Howells, ed. Thomas Wortham, Christoph K. Lohman, and David J. Nordloh, IV (Boston: Twayne Publishers, 1981).

5. Letter to Hamlin Garland, October 28, 1894, in *Selected Letters*, IV.

6. Letter to Mrs. Henry M. Alden, February 4, 1890, Houghton Mifflin Library, Harvard University.

7. Howells wrote his father about the way he wrote the autobiographies: "The selection is rather puzzling, but I let myself *go*, somewhat, and trust to what comes first." February 19, 1893, in *Selected Letters*, IV.

8. Letter to John Mead Howells, January 12, 1914, *Life in Letters*, II, 331.

9. M. L. von Franz, "The Process of Individuation," in *Man and His Symbols*, p. 174.

10. S. Weir Mitchell, letter to William Dean Howells, n.d., University of Pennsylvania Library.

11. "I Talk of Dreams" in *Impressions and Experiences*, pp. 116 and 106.

12. See n. 10, chap. 2. Dogs, the agents of evil lust in Swedenborg, were one of Howells's special phobias. See, too, letter to Gertrude Van R. Wickham, August 25, 1886, *Selected Letters*, III, 162: "I have no dog," he wrote in answer to a query, "and I'm very much afraid of other people's."

13. Ibid., pp. 111 and 102.

14. See J. E. Cirlot, *A Dictionary*, p. 223.

15. "I Talk," p. 223.

16. G. Rattray Taylor in *Sex in History* uses Apollo as the ideal of erotic balance, since he personifies measure and restraint and is also empowered by the sibyl's irrational knowledge: "Apollo did not deny the unconscious," he concludes, "and the Delphic sibyl, who spoke from the unconscious in a state of trance was under his aegis. Apollo and Dionysos are not opponents but partners," p. 237.

17. William Dean Howells, "Novel-Writing and Novel-Reading," p. 8.

18. See "What Should Girls Read?" *Harper's Bazaar*, 36 (November 1902), 956–960 and "Editor's Easy Chair," *Harper's Monthly*, 132 (May 1916), 958–961.

19. "Henrick Ibsen," 1906, in *W. D. Howells as Critic*, ed. Edwin H. Cady (London: Routledge & Kegan Paul, 1973), p. 441, letter to Samuel Clemens, May 1, 1903, *Life in Letters*, II, 175, and "Lyof N. Tolstoy," 1908, *W. D. Howells as Critic*, p. 460.

20. See letter to Thomas Bailey Aldrich, July 3, 1902; letter to Samuel Clemens, February 14, 1904; to Aurelia Howells, July 8, 1900, all in *Life in Letters*, II, 158, 373, and 130.

21. "The Rise of Psychologism," in *W. D. Howells as Critic*, p. 424.

22. Howells's father, like Owen Powell's, exorcised his terrors by reminding him, as Powell does here, that the date for his "death" had already passed.

23. "The Pearl," *Harper's Monthly*, 139 (August 1916), 412.

24. Ibid., p. 412.

25. Sigmund Freud, *A General Introduction to Psychoanalysis*, p. 165.

26. "The Pearl," p. 413.

27. "Editor's Easy Chair," *Harper's Monthly*, 132 (May 1916), 961.

28. Letter to S. Weir Mitchell, April 2, 1891, University of Pennsylvania Library.

29. Letter to Henry James, June 29, 1915, *Life in Letters*, II, 350.

30. Norman O. Brown, *Life Against Death*, p. 108.

31. "Eighty Years and After," *Harper's Monthly*, 140 (November 1919), 23.

32. Ibid., 21.

33. William James, *Varieties*, p. 203.

34. "Eighty Years," p. 28.

35. Ibid., p. 27.

36. Ibid., p. 21.

37. Ibid., p. 23.

38. Havelock Ellis, *Studies in the Psychology of Sex*, II (New York: Random House, 1937), 570: "Love is not a little circle that is complete in itself. It is the nature of love to irradiate."

39. "On a Bright Day," *Harper's Monthly*, 137 (November 1913), 835.

40. "Storage," in *Literature and Life* (New York: Harper & Brothers Publishers, 1902), p. 305.

41. Herbert Marcuse, *Eros and Civilization*, p. 107.

42. "William Dean Howells a Literary Optimist," 1908, in *Interviews*, p. 85.

Chapter ten

1. Letter to S. Weir Mitchell, December 11, 1904, University of Pennsylvania Library.

2. Notebook, 1894, Houghton Library, Harvard University.

3. Letter to Charles Eliot Norton, April 6, 1903, *Life in Letters*, II, 171.

4. "Howells's Unpublished Prefaces," ed. George Arms, *New England Quarterly*, 42 (December 1944), 584.

5. See Sigmund Freud, *A General Introduction to Psychoanalysis*, p. 344: "The meaning of the savage rites of puberty which represent rebirth is the loosening of the boy's incestuous attachment to the mother."

6. Letter to William Dean Howells, January 11, 1904, Houghton Library, Harvard University.

7. Henry James, "Howells's *Foregone Conclusion*," in *The War of the Critics over William Dean Howells*.

8. Letter to Frederick A. Duneka, February 4, 1904, Brown Unversity Library.

9. She also, coincidentally, wears Jocasta's color in her mourning, "subdued to the paler shades of purple" (p. 6). See H. A. Guerber, "Myths of Greece and Rome," in *Oedipus: Myth and Drama*, ed. Martin Kallich, Andrew MacLeish, and Gertrude Schoenbohm (New York: The Odyssey Press, 1968), p. 351. He claims that Jocasta is "like Iole, a personification of the violet-tinted clouds of dawn."

10. According to Victorian medical and purity literature, death was the penalty for sexual delinquency. See Steven Marcus, *The Other Victorians*, pp. 26–33; Ronald G. Walters, ed., *Primers for Prudery*, pp. 32–64; John S. Haller, Jr., and Robin M. Haller, *The Physician and Sexuality in Victorian America*, pp. 212–213. Howells used this belief metaphorically before in *A Modern Instance* and *The Shadow of a Dream*.

11. Cf. *April Hopes* and *The Shadow of a Dream*. In these books Howells explicitly linked the genteel cult of chivalry with salacity and negative Eros.

12. To take their minds off of sexual temptation, Buddhist monks commonly put a skeleton in their cells.

13. Hauberk is a medieval coat of armor. George N. Bennett, in *The Realism of William Dean Howells*, believes Howells intended the name for the "tragi-comic chivalric figure" of Mr. Hawberk, but perhaps he intended it for Hope as well, since it is she who "tilts" and "chants" through the book, p. 208n.

14. Besides being akin to "Eros," the iris is also "symbolic of . . . hope," Gertrude Jobes, *Dictionary of Mythology*, p. 839.

15. Denis de Rougemont, *Love in the Western World*, trans. Montgomery Belgion (New York: Harper & Row, Publishers, 1956), p. 302.

16. See Edwin H. Cady's excellent discussion of this in *The Realist at War*, pp. 240–241.

17. See discussion under "fool," in *Dictionary of Mythology*, pp. 591–592, and J. E. Cirlot, *A Dictionary of Symbols*, pp. 105–106.

18. Bruno Bettelheim, *The Uses of Enchantment; The Meaning and Importance of Fairy Tales* (New York: Vintage Books, 1975), p. 111.

19. Stendahl, *Love*, trans. Gilbert and Suzanne Sale (1829; rpt. London: Penguin Books, 1957), p. 43.

20. See E. Mark Stern, "Narcissism and the Defiance of Time," in *The Narcissistic Condition: A Fact of Our Lives and Times*, ed. Marie Coleman Nelson (New York: Human Sciences Press, 1977), p. 181.

21. The moon is always an index of dangerous and/or false emotions in Howells's love scenes. See, for instance, Bartley's and Marcia's opening scene, Mrs. Farrell's seduction of Gilbert, Don Ippolito's moonlight love confession, Penelope Lapham's assault on Tom Corey, and Alice Pasmer's reverie beneath the moon.

22. See Jung's discussion in *Symbols of Transformation*, pp. 350–351. Also J. E. Cirlot, *A Dictionary of Symbols*, p. 218.

23. I am using "demonic" in the same way it was used in *The Shadow of a Dream* discussion, as any galvanic natural force with the power to overwhelm and with equal capacities for redemption and damnation. See Rollo May, *Love and Will*, p. 21.

24. Ibid., p. 147.

25. Jung, *Symbols*, p. 335.

26. Herbert Marcuse, *Eros and Civilization*, p. 142.

27. Emanuel Swedenborg, *Conjugial Love*, p. 227.

28. Ibid., p. 350.

29. E. C. Chamberlayne, "Mr. Howells' Philosophy and *The Son of Royal Langbrith*," *Poet Lore*, 16 (Autumn 1905), 144–151, quoted in *William Dean Howells: A Research Bibliography*, ed. Clayton L. Eichelberger (Boston: G. K. Hall & Co., 1976), p. 244.

30. Letter to Joseph Howells, August 25, 1904, Houghton Library, Harvard University.

31. Letter to Samuel Clemens, February 14, 1904, *Life in Letters*, II, 186.

32. For some of Howells's major attacks on his puritanical culture, see "The Ibsen Influence," (1895), pp. 225–230: "New York Low Life in Fiction," (1896), pp. 256–262; "Henrick Ibsen," (1906), pp. 433–445, all in Edwin H. Cady, ed. *W. D. Howells as Critic*. In 1901, he spoke heatedly of the "ugliness and error and soul-sickness which Puritanism produced," *Heroines of Fiction*, II (New York: Harper & Brothers Publishers, 1901), p. 180.

33. "Life and Letters," *Harper's Weekly*, 39 (May 4, 1895), 417.

34. "Editor's Easy Chair," *Harper's Monthly*, 111 (October 1905), 797.

35. "Editor's Easy Chair," *Harper's Monthly*, 110 (February 1905), 479.

36. In the same way, Howells demonstrated a marked leniency toward the sexual misdeeds of another scoundrel. About Bret Harte's marital irregularities, he wrote Twain: "After all, such things had better be left to the judgment day, which I see more and more use for as I live along," letter to Samuel Clemens, December 20, 1903, *Life in Letters*, II, 179.

37. Gertrude Atherton, "Why is American Literature Bourgeois?" in *The War of the Critics*, pp. 100, 102, 104.

38. Ibid., p. 101.

39. Jung, *Symbols*, p. 337.

40. Fuller, letter to Howells, January 11, 1904.

Chapter eleven

1. Letter to S. Weir Mitchell, December 11, 1904, University of Pennsylvania Library.

2. Letter to Joseph A. Howells, February 24, 1907, *Life in Letters*, II, 235.

3. Letter to Aurelia Howells, June 21, 1914, Houghton Library, Harvard University.

4. Of novelists in old age, Bernard Berenson said, "'What a man writes after he is sixty is worth little more than tea continually remade with the same leaves.'" Quoted in Simone de Beauvoir, *The Coming of Age*, trans. Patrick O'Brian (New York: Warner Paperback Library, 1973), p. 593.

5. See Ulysses' speech in Shakespeare *Troilus and Cressida* I, iii, 119–124, and J. P. Broadbent's summation of this motif in erotic literature in *Poetic Love* (London: Chatto and Windus, 1964), p. 150: "Lust forms a circle, hunting the luster as he hunts his deadly prey to both their deaths."

6. Review of *The Leatherwood God*, *North American Review*, 204 (December 1916), 939.

7. See "Sut Lovingood's Daddy, Acting Horse," George Washington Harris, *Sut Lovingood's Yarns*, ed. M. Thomas Inge (New Haven: College & University Press, Publishers, 1955), pp. 33–38.

8. Richard H. Taneyhill, *The Leatherwood God*, ed. George Kummer (1869–1870; rpt. Gainesville, Fla.: Scholars' Facsimiles & Reprints, 1966), p. 12.

9. Compare Taneyhill's account, p. 14, with Abel Reverdy's, p. 8. Taneyhill portrays a shorter (5'8" vs. Reverdy's 6'), older (forty-five to fifty), and stockier Dylks: "little heavy in the shoulders and taper[ing] symmetrically to the feet" vs. "thickset, round the shoulders . . . [and] slimming down towards his legs."

10. See pages 14, 21, 29, 42, 53, 61 for these verbal simulations of orgasm.

11. Not only has he deserted Nancy under mysterious circumstances but, according to her hint, has "known" lots of women over the mountain, p. 147.

12. Gertrude Jobes, *Dictionary of Mythology*, p. 185.

13. See the full text of Isaac Watts' hymn "Plunged in a Gulf of Dark Despair" which relates the takeover of the "Prince of Hell" and his final defeat. The suffering he inflicts in the hymn is remarkably similar to what Dylks causes: darkness, entrapment, grief, and death. *Hymns and Spiritual Songs* (London: 1779), pp. 202–203.

14. Denis de Rougemont believes that egomania resides at the heart of the negative, Western concept of passion: "The passion of love is at bottom narcissism, the lovers' self-magnification . . . Passion requires that the self shall become greater than all things, as solitary and powerful as God," *Love in the Western World*, p. 260.

15. He cites the 1 Cor. 3:2 verse in which Paul tells the Corinthians that they must hear lower material truths until they are ready for the highest spiritual ones. Misquoting the original: "I have fed you with milk and not with meat for hitherto ye were not able to bear it . . . ," Dylks applies it to himself instead: "I can endure strong meat, but I must be fed on milk for awhile" (p. 49).

16. See Gertrude Jobes, *Dictionary*, p. 733.

17. Edwin Cady, in this regard, notes the significance of his name. Braile is literally one of the few characters who can see through Dylks's darkness and read its meaning. *The Realist at War*, p. 266.

18. Letter to Hamlin Garland, March 25, 1916, *Life in Letters*, II, 356.

19. See Kenneth Eble, "Howells Kisses," in *Howells: A Century of Criticism*, pp. 173–181, in which he traces the use of this famous Howellsian metaphor for sexual intercourse through his novels.

20. See Gertrude Jobes's synopsis of the harvest rites in *Dictionary*, p. 729.

21. For another instance of hair loss as a symbol of castration in Howells, see the use he makes of Don Ippolito's tonsure (originally an emblem of this in the Catholic church) in *A Foregone Conclusion*.

22. Money carries strong sexual resonances in Howells's work. See *A Modern Instance* and *The Rise of Silas Lapham*.

23. See Spenser *The Faerie Queene* Book III, canto vi.

24. See J. Hillis Miller's excellent discussion of this in "Bleak House and the Moral Life," in *Dickens' Bleak House: A Casebook*, ed. A. E. Dyson (Nashville: Aurora Publishers Incorporated, 1969), pp. 157–191.

25. After Dylks leaves, Sally Reverdy stops by for one of Mrs. Braile's cups of coffee, which instantly cures her toothache, p. 138.

26. Herbert Marcuse, *Eros and Civilization*, p. 104.

27. See Anon., "William Dean Howells a Literary Optimist," 1908, pp. 363 and 368, and Van Wyck Brooks, "Mr. Howells at Work at Seventy-two," pp. 368–371 in *Interviews with William Dean Howells*.

28. This scene Howells recounted four times: in *My Year in a Log Cabin, My Literary Passions, Years of my Youth and Three Essays*, and semifictionally in *The Flight of Pony Baker*.

29. After a "dreamy fumbling [for his] . . . identity," letter to Thomas Bailey Aldrich, July 3, 1902, *Life in Letters*, II, 158, his attitude to dreams and his boy-self, each of which had been repudiated, began to change. Compare "True I Talk of Dreams" (*Harper's Monthly*, May 1895) with "The Rise of Psychologism" (*Harper's Monthly*, June 1903) and *A Boy's Town* (1890) with *The Flight of Pony Baker* (1902). In 1903, dreams were no longer emanations from the devil, but open "communication . . . between our inner and outer selves" (*W. D. Howells as Critic*, p. 423). Likewise the boy becomes an object of affection rather than disapproval in *The Flight of Pony Baker*.

30. "Editor's Easy Chair," *Harper's Monthly*, 123 (September 1911), 636.

31. "A Niece's Literary Advice to her Uncle," in *Imaginary Interviews*, p. 182.

32. "Editor's Easy Chair," *Harper's Monthly*, 123 (September 1911), p. 637.

33. For the classic texts, see: "Novel-Writing and Novel-Reading: An Impersonal Explanation," "Lyof N. Tolstoy," 1908, in *W. D. Howells as Critic*, pp. 452–468, "The Novels of Robert Herrick," *The North American Review*, 188 (June 1909), 812–820, letter to Hamlin Garland, July 15, 1914, University of Southern California, and Editor's Easy Chair, *Harper's Monthly*, 132 (May 1916), 958–964.

34. Howells, quoted in Joyce Kilmer "'War Stops Literature,' Says W. D. Howells," in *Interviews with William Dean Howells*, p. 394.

35. "Editor's Easy Chair," *Harper's Monthly*, 110 (February 1905), 479.

36. "Editor's Easy Chair," *Harper's Monthly*, 121 (September 1910), 634.

37. Simone de Beauvoir, *The Coming of Age*, pp. 470–471.

38. Norman O. Brown, *Life Against Death*, p. 289.

39. "Editor's Easy Chair," *Harper's Monthly*, 129 (November 1914), 960–961.

40. Herbert Marcuse, *Eros and Civilization*, p. 18.

41. Letter to John Noyes Mead Howells, March 17, 1920, *Life in Letters*, II, 394.

42. "Eighty Years and After," *Harper's Monthly*, 140 (December 1919), 22. Love, he called "the most beautiful thing in life" and added ". . . without it there can be no death."

43. Letter to Aurelia H. Howells, July 4, 1916, *Life in Letters*, II, 361.

44. Letter to J. G. Mitchell, February 9, 1914, *Life in Letters*, II, 361.

45. Howells, "Eighty Years," p. 21.

46. Emanuel Swedenborg, *Conjugial Love*, p. 305.

47. Ibid., p. 109.

48. Ibid., p. 493.

49. Ibid., p. 89.

50. Ibid., p. 76.

51. Ibid., p. 76.

52. Robert Jay Lifton, "The Appeal of the Death Trap," *The New York Times Magazine*, January 7, 1979, pp. 26–31.

53. St. John de Crevecoeur, quoted in Harry T. Moore, "Introduction," *American Dreams, American Nightmares*, ed. David Madden (Carbondale, Ill.: Southern Illinois University Press, 1970), p. xviii.

54. "A Niece's Literary Advice," p. 182.

55. Havelock Ellis, *Studies in the Psychology of Sex*, II, 459.

56. William Dean Howells, letter to Aurelia Howells, June 21, 1914, Houghton Library, Harvard University.

57. Simone de Beauvoir, *The Coming of Age*, p. 601.

Bibliography

This bibliography only includes those works by Howells discussed in *The Circle of Eros*. I have not listed any of the papers from Harvard and other collections. The list of secondary sources is equally incomplete, omitting many quoted works in order to concentrate on the major study aids.

I. Works by W. D. Howells

Novels

April Hopes. Ed. Kermit Vanderbilt, Don L. Cook, James P. Elliott, and David J. Nordloh. 1888; rpt. Bloomington: Indiana University Press, 1974.

A Foregone Conclusion. Boston: James R. Osgood and Company, 1875.

The Leatherwood God. Ed. Eugene Pattison. 1916; rpt. Bloomington: Indiana University Press, 1975.

A Modern Instance. Ed. William H. Gibson. 1882; rpt. Boston: Houghton Mifflin Company, 1957.

Mrs. Farrell. New York: Harper & Brothers Publishers, 1921.

The Rise of Silas Lapham. Ed. Walter J. Meserve et al. 1885; rpt. Bloomington: Indiana University Press, 1971.

The Shadow of a Dream and an Imperative Duty. Ed. Martha Banta, Ronald Gottesman, and David J. Nordloh. 1890 and 1892; rpt. Bloomington: Indiana University Press, 1970.

The Son of Royal Langbrith. Ed. David Burrows. 1904; rpt. Bloomington: Indiana University Press, 1969.

Autobiography

A Boy's Town. New York: Harper & Brothers Publishers, 1890.

"Eighty Years and After." *Harper's Monthly*, 140 (December 1919), 21–28.

The Flight of Pony Baker. New York: Harper & Brothers Publishers, 1902.

"I Talk of Dreams." *Impressions and Experiences*. New York: Harper & Brothers Publishers, 1895.

Literary Friends and Acquaintance: A Personal Retrospect of American Authorship. Ed. David F. Hiatt and Edwin H. Cady. 1900; rpt. Bloomington: Indiana University Press, 1968.

My Literary Passions. New York: Harper & Brothers Publishers, 1891.

My Year in a Log Cabin. New York: Harper & Brothers Publishers, 1893.

New Leaf Mills. New York: Harper & Brothers Publishers, 1913.

"The Pearl." *Harper's Monthly*, 133 (August 1916), 409–413.
Years of My Youth and Three Essays. Ed. David J. Nordloh. 1916; rpt. Bloomington: Indiana University Press, 1975.

Essays

Atlantic Monthly, 44 (July 1879), 124–125.
"Carlo Goldoni." *Atlantic Monthly*, 40 (November 1877), 601–613.
"The Contributors' Club." *Atlantic Monthly*, 95 (June 1880), 859–860.
"Editor's Easy Chair." *Harper's Monthly*, 107 (June 1903), 146–150.
"Editor's Easy Chair." *Harper's Monthly*, 110 (February 1905), 479–483.
"Editor's Easy Chair." *Harper's Monthly*, 111 (October 1905), 794–797.
"Editor's Easy Chair." *Harper's Monthly*, 121 (September 1910), 633–639.
"Editor's Easy Chair." *Harper's Monthly*, 123 (September 1911), 634–637.
"Editor's Easy Chair." *Harper's Monthly*, 126 (April 1913) 796–799.
"Editor's Easy Chair." *Harper's Monthly*, 127 (October 1913), 798.
"Editor's Easy Chair." *Harper's Monthly*, 129 (November 1914), 960–961.
"Editor's Easy Chair." *Harper's Monthly*, 132 (May 1916), 958–961.
"Editor's Study." *Harper's Monthly*, 72 (April 1886), 808–812.
"Editor's Study." *Harper's Monthly*, 73 (August 1886), 475–480.
"Editor's Study." *Harper's Monthly*, 76 (March 1888), 640–644.
"Editor's Study." *Harper's Monthly*, 77 (November 1888), 962–967.
"Editor's Study." *Harper's Monthly*, 78 (May 1889), 982–987.
"Editor's Study." *Harper's Monthly*, 81 (October 1890), 800–804.
"Henrik Ibsen." *North American Review*, 183 (July 1906), 1–14.
"Life and Letters." *Harper's Weekly*, May 4, 1895, pp. 416–417.
"Life and Letters." *Harper's Weekly*, August 17, 1895, p. 773.
"Life and Letters." *Harper's Weekly*, March 13, 1897, p. 270.
"A Niece's Literary Advice to Her Uncle." *Imaginary Interviews*. New York: Harper & Brothers Publishers, 1910.
"The Novels of Robert Herrick." *The North American Review*, 188 (June 1909), 812–820.
"Recent Italian Comedy." *North American Review*, 99 (October 1864), 364–401.
"What Should Girls Read?" *Harper's Bazaar*, 35 (November 1902), 956–960.

Essay collections and other prose

Heroines of Fiction. Vol. II. New York: Harper & Brothers Publishers, 1901.
"Howells's Unpublished Prefaces." Ed. George Arms. *New England Quarterly*, 42 (December 1944), 580–591.
Impressions and Experiences. New York: Harper & Brothers Publishers, 1896.
Literature and Life. New York: Harper & Brothers Publishers, 1902.
"Novel-Writing and Novel-Reading: An Impersonal Explanation." Ed. William M. Gibson. 1899; rpt. New York: The New York Public Library, 1958.
Suburban Sketches. Boston: James R. Osgood and Company, 1872.
Venetian Life. Boston: Houghton Mifflin Company, 1867.
W. D. Howells as Critic. Ed. Edwin H. Cady. London: Routledge & Kegan Paul, 1973.

Poetry

"On a Bright Day." *Harper's Monthly*, 137 (November 1913), 835.
Stops of Various Quills. New York: Harper & Brothers Publishers, 1895.

Interviews and letters

Interviews with William Dean Howells. Ed. Ulrich Halfmann. Arlington, Tex.: American Literary Realism, 1973.
Life in Letters of William Dean Howells. Ed. Mildred Howells. 2 vols. Garden City, N.Y.: Doubleday, Doran & Company, Inc., 1928.
New York Times, April 20, 1885, p. 3.
Selected Letters of W. D. Howells. Ed. Robert C. Leitz et al. Vol. III. Boston: Twayne Publishers, 1980.
Selected Letters of W. D. Howells. Ed. Thomas Wortham et al. Vol. IV. Boston: Twayne Publishers, 1981.
Selected Mark Twain-Howells Letters 1872–1910. Ed. Frederick Anderson, William M. Gibson, and Henry Nash Smith. New York: Atheneum, 1968.

II. Works about Howells

Criticism and reviews: his lifetime

Alden, Henry Mills. "Editor's Study." *Harper's Monthly*, 111 (December 1900), 159–160.
Atherton, Gertrude. "Why Is American Literature Bourgeois?" In *The War of the Critics over William Dean Howells.* Ed. Edwin H. Cady and David L. Frazier. Evanston, Ill." Row, Peterson and Company, 1962.
Black, Alexander. Review of *Mrs. Farrell*, by W. D. Howells. *New York Times*, September 4, 1921, p. 3.
Garland, Hamlin. "Meetings with Howells." *The Bookman*, 45 (March 1917), 1–7.
Harvey, Alexander. *William Dean Howells: A Study of the Achievement of a Literary Artist.* New York: B. W. Huebsch, 1917.
"Howells's '*Foregone Conclusion.*'" Review of *A Foregone Conclusion. The Nation*, January 7, 1875, p. 12.
James, Henry. "Howells's *Foregone Conclusion.*" *The War of the Critics over William Dean Howells.* Ed. Edwin H. Cady and David L. Frazier. Evanston, Ill.: Row, Peterson and Company, 1962.
Pattan, Grace D. Letter. *New York Tribune*, December 4, 1882, p. 10.
Perry, Thomas Sergeant. "William Dean Howells." *Century*, 23 (March 1882), 680–686.
Quinn, Arthur H. "The Thirst for Salvation." Review of *The Leatherwood God*, by W. D. Howells. *The Dial*, December 14, 1916, 534–535.
Rev. of *April Hopes*, by W. D. Howells. *The Academy*, 32 (November 1887), 350.
Rev. of *April Hopes*, by W. D. Howells. *The Nation*, February 16, 1888, p. 142.
Rev. of *April Hopes*, by W. D. Howells. *The Tribune*, January 1, 1888, p. 10.
Rev. of *A Foregone Conclusion*, by W. D. Howells. *The Nation*, January 7, 1875, pp. 12–13.
Rev. of *The Leatherwood God*, by W. D. Howells. *New York Times*, October 29, 1916, pp. 453–460.
Rev. of *The Leatherwood God*, by W. D. Howells. *Times Literary Supplement*, November 16, 1916, p. 548.
Rev. of *A Modern Instance*, by W. D. Howells. *Century*, 24 (October 1882), 106–107.
Rev. of *A Modern Instance*, by W. D. Howells. *Century*, 25 (January 1883), 463–465.
Rev. of *A Modern Instance*, by W. D. Howells. *The Nation*, January 11, 1883, p. 41.

Rev. of *The Rise of Silas Lapham*, *Life*, April 23, 1885, p. 228.
Rev. of *The Rise of Silas Lapham*, *The Nation*, October 22, 1885, p. 345.
Rev. of *The Rise of Silas Lapham*, *The New York Times*, September 27, 1885, p. 5.
Thompson, Maurice. "The Analysts Analyzed," *The Critic*, 6 (July 1886), 19–22.
Wilcox, Marrion. "Works of William Dean Howells," *Harper's Weekly*, July 4, 1896, p. 656.
"Young Men and *A Modern Instance*." Review of *A Modern Instance*, by W. D. Howells. *Century*, 25 (January 1883), 473.

Criticism: Modern

Bennett, George N. *The Realism of William Dean Howells: 1889–1920*. Nashville: Vanderbilt University Press, 1973.
Berthoff, Warner. *The Ferment of Realism: American Literature 1884–1919*. New York: Free Press, 1965.
Brooks, Van Wyck. *Howells: His Life and World*. New York: E. P. Dutton & Co., Inc., 1959.
Budd, Louis J. "W. D. Howells' Defense of the Romance." *PMLA* 67 (March 1952), 32–42.
Cady, Edwin H. *The Light of Common Day*. Bloomington: Indiana University Press, 1971.
———. "The Neuroticism of William Dean Howells." *PMLA*, 61 (March 1946), 229–38.
———. *The Realist at War: The Mature Years 1885–1920 of William Dean Howells*. Syracuse: Syracuse University Press, 1958.
———. *The Road to Realism: The Early Years, 1837–1885, of William Dean Howells*. Syracuse: Syracuse University Press, 1956.
———, ed. *W. D. Howells as Critic*. London: Routledge & Kegan Paul, 1973.
Cady, Edwin H., and David L. Frazier, eds. *The War of the Critics over William Dean Howells*. Evanston, Ill.: Row, Peterson and Company, 1962.
Carrington, George C., Jr. *The Immense Complex Drama: The World and Art of the Howells Novel*. Columbus: Ohio State University Press, 1966.
Carter, Everett. *Howells and the Age of Realism*. Hamden, Conn.: Archon Books, 1966.
Chase, Richard. "The Vacation of the Kelwyns." In *The American Novel and Its Tradition*. Garden City, N.Y.: Doubleday Anchor Books, 1957.
Coana, Richard. "Howells' *The Rise of Silas Lapham*," *The Explicator*, 22 (November 1963), number 16.
Crowley, John W. "Howells' Questionable Shapes: From Psychologism to Psychic Romance." *English Studies Quarterly*, 21 (Summer 1975), 169–178.
Dean, James L. *Howells' Travels Toward Art*. Albuquerque: University of New Mexico, 1970.
Eble, Kenneth E., ed. *Howells: A Century of Criticism*. Dallas: Southern Methodist University Press, 1962.
Firkins, Oscar W. *William Dean Howells: A Study*. 1924; rpt. New York: Russell & Russell, Inc., 1963.
Fryckstedt, Olov W. *In Quest of America: A Study of Howells' Early Development as a Novelist*. Cambridge: Harvard University Press, 1958.
Gargano, James W. "A Modern Instance: The Twin Evils of Society." *Texas Studies in Literature and Languages*, 4 (Autumn 1962), 399–407.
Gibson, William M. *William Dean Howells*. Minneapolis: University of Minnesota Press, 1967.

Hough, Robert L. *The Quiet Rebel: William Dean Howells as Social Commentator.* Lincoln: University of Nebraska Press, 1959.

Kazin, Alfred. "The Opening Struggle for Realism." In *On Native Grounds: An Interpretation of Modern American Prose Literature.* Garden City, N.Y.: Doubleday & Company, 1942, pp. 1–36.

Kirk, Clara M. "Reality and Actuality in the March Family Narratives of W. D. Howells." *PMLA*, 74 (March, 1959), 137–152.

Lewis, Sinclair. "The American Fear of Literature." In *The War of the Critics over William Dean Howells.* Ed. Edwin H. Cady and David L. Frazier. Evanston, Ill.: Row, Peterson and Company, 1962.

Lynn, Kenneth S. *William Dean Howells: An American Life.* New York: Harcourt Brace Jovanovich, Inc., 1970.

McMurray, William J. *The Literary Realism of William Dean Howells.* Intro. Harry T. Moore. Carbondale: Southern Illinois University Press, 1967.

Meserve, Walter J. "Truth, Morality, and Swedenborg in Howells' Theory of Realism." *The New England Quarterly*, 27 (June 1954), 252–257.

Parker, Gail Thain. "William Dean Howells: Realism and Feminism." *Harvard English Studies*, No. 4. Ed. Monroe Engel. Cambridge: Harvard University Press, 1973.

Pizer, Donald. "The Ethical Unity of *The Rise of Silas Lapham*," *American Literature*, 32 (November 1960), 322–327.

Stronks, James. "*A Modern Instance.*" *American Literary Realism 1870–1910*, 1 (Fall 1968), 87–89.

Sweeney, Gerard M. "The Medea Howells Saw." *American Literature*, 42 (March 1970), 83–89.

Tanselle, Thomas G. "The Architecture of *The Rise of Silas Lapham*," *American Literature*, 37 (January 1966), 430–457.

Tarkington, Booth. "Introduction." Centenary Edition. *The Rise of Silas Lapham.* Boston: Houghton Mifflin Company, 1937.

Trilling, Lionel. "William Dean Howells and the Roots of Modern Taste." In *The Opposing Self.* New York: Viking Press, 1955, pp. 76–103.

Tuttleton, James W. "William Dean Howells: Equality as the Basis of Good Society." In *The Novel of Manners in America.* New York: W. W. Norton & Company, Inc., 1972, pp. 86–121.

Vanderbilt, Kermit. *The Achievement of William Dean Howells: A Reinterpretation.* Princeton: Princeton University Press, 1968.

———. "The Conscious Realism of Howells' *April Hopes.*" *American Literary Realism 1870–1910*, 3 (Winter 1970), 53–60.

———. "Marcia Gaylord's Electra Complex: A Footnote to Sex in Howells." *American Literature*, 34 (November 1962), 365–374.

III. General Background

Abbott, Charles D. *Howard Pyle: A Chronicle.* New York: Harper & Brothers Publishers, 1925.

Ahnebrink, Lars. *The Beginnings of Naturalism in American Fiction 1891–1903.* New York: Russell & Russell, 1950.

American Dreams, American Nightmares. Ed. David Madden. Intro. Harry T. Moore. Carbondale: Southern Illinois University Press, 1970.

Atkins, John. *Sex in Literature: The Erotic Impulse in Literature.* New York: Grove Press, Inc., 1970.

Barker-Benfield, G. J. *The Horrors of the Half-Known Life: Male Attitudes Toward Women and Sexuality in Nineteenth-Century America.* New York: Harper & Row, Publishers, 1976.

Basler, Roy P. *Sex, Symbolism and Psychology in Literature.* New Brunswick: Rutgers University Press, 1948.

Beauvoir, Simone de. *The Coming of Age.* Trans. Patrick O'Brian. New York: Warner Paperback Library, 1973.

Becker, George J., ed. *Documents of Literary Realism.* Princeton: Princeton University Press, 1963.

Bettelheim, Bruno. *The Uses of Enchantment: The Meaning and Importance of Fairy Tales.* New York: Vintage Books, 1975.

Booth, Wayne C. *The Rhetoric of Fiction.* Chicago: The University of Chicago Press, 1961.

Boucicault, Dion. *The Colleen Bawn, or The Brides of Garryowen: A Domestic Drama in Three Acts.* In *The Dolmen Boucicault.* Chester Springs, Pa.: Dufour Editions, 1965.

Boyesen, H. N. "Why We Have No Great Novelists." *The Forum,* 2 (January 1887), 614–622.

Broadbent, J. B. *Poetic Love.* London: Chatto and Windus, 1964.

Brown, Norman O. *Life Against Death: The Psychoanalytic Meaning of History.* Middletown, Conn.: Wesleyan University Press, 1959.

Calverton, V. G. *Sex Expression in Literature.* Intro. Harry Elmer Barnes. New York: Boni & Liveright, 1926.

Campbell, Joseph. *The Hero with a Thousand Faces.* New York: Pantheon Books, 1949.

Chase, Richard. *The American Novel and Its Tradition.* Garden City, N.Y.: Doubleday & Company, Inc., 1957.

———. *Quest for Myth.* Baton Rouge: Louisiana State University Press, 1949.

Cirlot, J. E. *A Dictionary of Symbols.* Trans. Jack Sage. New York: Philosophical Library, 1962.

The Comic in Theory and Practice. Ed. John J. Enck et al. New York: Appleton-Century Crofts, Inc., 1960.

Crow, Duncan. *The Victorian Woman.* London: George Allen & Unwin Ltd., 1971.

Darwin, Charles. *The Descent of Man and Selection in Relation to Sex.* 1871; rpt. Detroit: Gale Research Co., 1974.

De Voto, Bernard, ed. *Mark Twain in Eruption: Hitherto Unpublished Pages about Men and Events.* New York: Harper & Row, 1968.

Ditzion, Sidney. *Marriage, Morals and Sex in America.* New York: Bookman Associates, 1953.

Edel, Leon. *Literary Biography: The Alexander Lectures 1955–56.* Toronto: University of Toronto Press, 1957.

———. "Sex and the Novel." *New York Times,* November 1, 1964, sec. 7.

Edman, Irwin, ed. *The Works of Plato.* New York: Random House, Inc., 1928.

Edwards, Herbert. "Zola and the American Critics." *American Literature,* 4 (May 1932), 114–118.

Eliade, Mircea. *Birth and Rebirth: The Religious Meanings of Initiation in Human Culture.* Trans. Willard R. Trask. New York: Harper & Brothers Publishers, 1958.

———. *The Myth of the Eternal Return.* Trans. William R. Trask. New York: Pantheon Books, 1954.

Ellis, Havelock. *Studies in the Psychology of Sex.* 2 vols. New York: Random House, 1905.

Emerson, Ralph Waldo. "Demonology." In *The Complete Writings of Ralph Waldo Emerson*. Vol. II. New York: Wm. H. Wise & Co., 1929, pp. 947–955.

Erikson, Erik H. *Childhood and Society*. New York: W. W. Norton & Company, Inc., 1950.

———. *Identity: Youth and Crisis*. New York: W. W. Norton & Company, Inc., 1968.

———. *Young Man Luther: A Study in Psychoanalysis and History*. New York: W. W. Norton & Company, Inc., 1958.

The Essential Swedenborg: Basic Teachings of Emanuel Swedenborg, Scientist, Philosopher, and Theologian. Ed. and intro. Sig. Synnestvedt. New York: Swedenborg Foundation, 1970.

Euripides. *Medea*. In *Five Plays of Euripides*. Trans. Gilbert Murray. New York: Oxford University Press, 1934, pp. 3–96.

Falk, Robert. *The Victorian Mode in American Fiction, 1865–1885*. East Lansing: Michigan State University Press, 1965.

Fast, Julius. *Body Language*. New York: Pocket Books, 1970.

Fenichel, Otto, M.D. *The Psychoanalytic Theory of Neurosis*. New York: W. W. Norton & Company, Inc., 1945.

Fiedler, Leslie A. *Love and Death in the American Novel*. New York: Stein and Day Publishers, 1960.

Fiske, John. *Myths and Mythmakers*. Boston: Houghton Mifflin & Co., 1872.

Freeborn, Richard. *Turgenev: The Novelists' Novelist*. London: Oxford University Press, 1960.

Freud, Anna. *The Ego and the Mechanisms of Defense*. Trans. Cecil Barnes. New York: International Universities Press, Inc., 1946.

Freud, Sigmund. *Beyond the Pleasure Principle*. Trans. and ed. James Strachey. Intro. Gregory Zilboorg. 1922; rpt. New York: W. W. Norton & Company, Inc., 1961.

———. *Civilization and Its Discontents*. Trans. Joan Riviere. Garden City, N.Y.: Simon & Schuster, Inc., 1952.

———. *The Interpretation of Dreams*. Trans. James Strachey. 1900; rpt. New York: Avon Books, 1965.

———. *Three Essays on the Theory of Sexuality*. Trans. and ed. James Strachey. Intro. Steven Marcus. New York: Basic Books, Inc., Publishers, 1962.

Fromm, Erich. *The Forgotten Language: An Introduction to the Understanding of Dreams, Fairy Tales, and Myths*. New York: Holt, Rinehart and Winston, 1951.

Frye, Northrop. *Anatomy of Criticism: Four Essays*. Princeton: Princeton University Press, 1957.

Gass, William H. *On Being Blue: A Philosophical Inquiry*. Boston: D. R. Godine, 1976.

Glasgow, Ellen. *The Woman Within*. New York: Harcourt, Brace & Company, 1954.

Goldfarb, Russell M. *Sexual Repression and Victorian Literature*. Lewisburg, Pa.: Bucknell University Press, 1970.

Gorer, Geoffrey. "The Erotic Myth of America." *Partisan Review*, 17 (Summer 1950), 589–594.

Grillparzer, Franz. *Medea: A Tragedy in Five Acts*. In *Plays on Classic Themes*. Trans. Samuel Solomon. New York: Random House, 1969.

Guerber, H. A. "Myths of Greece and Rome." In *Oedipus: Myth and Drama*. Ed. Martin Kallich, Andrew MacLeish, and Gertrude Schoenbohm. New York: The Odyssey Press, 1968.

Hadfield, J. A. *Dreams and Nightmares*. Baltimore: Penguin Books, 1969.

Haller, John S., Jr., and Robin M. Haller. *The Physician and Sexuality in Victorian America*. New York: W. W. Norton & Company, Inc., 1974.

Harris, George Washington. *Sut Lovingood's Yarns*. Ed. M. Thomas Inge. New Haven: College & University Press, Publishers, 1966.

Hays, H. R. *From Ape to Angel: An Informal History of Social Anthropology*. New York: Capricorn Books, 1958.

Henderson, Joseph L. "Ancient Myths and Modern Man." In *Man and His Symbols*. Ed. Carl G. Jung. New York: Dell Publishing Company, 1964, pp. 97–156.

Hofstadter, Richard. *Social Darwinism in American Thought*. Boston: Beacon Press, 1944.

Holbrook, David. *Sex and Dehumanization in Art, Thought, and Life in Our Time*. London: Pitman Publishing, 1972.

Horney, Karen. *The Neurotic Personality in Our Time*. New York: W. W. Norton & Company, Inc., 1937.

Houghton, Walter E. "Love." In *The Victorian Frame of Mind, 1830–1870*. New Haven: Yale University Press, 1957, pp. 341–393.

Howells, William Cooper. *Recollections on Life in Ohio from 1813 to 1840*. Ed. Edwin H. Cady. Gainesville, Fla.: Scholars' Facsimiles & Reprints, 1963.

Humphrey, Robert. *Stream of Consciousness in the Modern Novel*. Berkeley: University of California Press, 1954.

Hyman, Stanley Edgar. "Maud Bodkin and Psychological Criticism." In *The Armed Vision: A Study in the Methods of Modern Literary Criticism*. New York: Vintage Books, 1955, pp. 132–161.

Jacobi, Jolande. *Complex, Archetype, Symbol in the Psychology of C. G. Jung*. Trans. Ralph Manheim. New York: Pantheon Books, 1959.

James, Henry, Jr. *The Letters of Henry James*. Ed. Percy Lubbock. 2 vols. New York: Charles Scribner's Sons, 1920.

———. *The Notebooks*. Ed. F. O. Matthiessen and Kenneth B. Murdock. New York: Oxford University Press, 1947.

James, Henry, Sr. "The Increase of Divorce." *Century*, 23 (1882), 411–420.

———. "Is Marriage Holy?" *Atlantic Monthly*, 25 (March 1870), 360–368.

James, William. *Letters of William James*. Ed. Henry James. Boston: The Atlantic Monthly Press, 1920.

———. *Pragmatism and Other Essays*. Intro. Joseph L. Blau. 1896; rpt. New York: Washington Square Press, 1963.

———. *Varieties of Religious Experiences*. 1902; rpt. New York: Random House, 1929.

Jobes, Gertrude. *Dictionary of Mythology Folklore and Symbols*. New York: The Scarecrow Press, Inc., 1961.

Johnson, Wendell Stacy. *Sex and Marriage in Victorian Poetry*. Ithaca: Cornell University Press, 1975.

Jones, Howard Mumford. "The Genteel Tradition." In *The Age of Energy: Varieties of American Experience 1865–1915*. New York: Viking Press, 1970, pp. 216–252.

Jung, C. G. "Jung on Freud." Ed. Aniela Jaffe. *Atlantic Monthly*, 210 (November 1962), 47–58.

———. *The Portable Jung*. Ed. and intro. Joseph Campbell. Trans. R. F. C. Hull. New York: Penguin Books, 1971.

———. *Psyche and Symbol: A Selection from the Writings of C. G. Jung*. Ed. Violet S. de Laszlo. Garden City, N.Y.: Doubleday & Company, Inc., 1958.

———. *Symbols of Transformation: An Analysis of the Prelude to a Case of Schizophrenia*. Trans. R. F. C. Hull. Princeton: Princeton University Press, 1956.

Kaplan, Harold. *Democratic Humanism and American Literature*. Chicago: University of Chicago Press, 1972.

Kerr, Howard. *Mediums, and Spirit-Rappers, and Roaring Radicals: Spiritualism in American Literature, 1850–1900*. Urbana: University of Illinois Press, 1972.

Kolb, Harold H., Jr. *The Illusion of Life: American Realism as a Literary Form*. Charlottesville: The University Press of Virginia, 1969.

Kris, Ernst. *Psychoanalytic Explorations in Art.* New York: International Universities Press, Inc., 1952.

Kubie, Lawrence, S., M.D. *Neurotic Distortion of the Creative Process.* New York: Farrar, Straus and Giroux, 1958.

Lawrence, D. H. *Sex, Literature and Censorship.* Ed. Harry T. Moore. 1928; rpt. New York: The Viking Press, 1953.

Laemmel, Klaus. "Sex and the Arts." In *The Sexual Experience.* Ed. Benjamin J. Sadock, M.D.; Harold I. Kaplan, M.D.; and Alfred Freedman, M.D. Baltimore: Williams and Wilkins, 1976, pp. 527–565.

Lesser, Simon O. *Fiction and the Unconscious.* Intro. Ernest Jones. Chicago: The University of Chicago Press, 1957.

Lewis, R. W. B. *The American Adam: Innocence, Tragedy and Tradition in the Nineteenth Century.* Chicago: The University of Chicago Press, 1955.

Lipton, Robert Jay. "The Appeal of the Death Trap." *The New York Times Magazine,* January 7, 1979, pp. 26–31.

Mann, Thomas. "Freud and the Future." In *Criticism: The Major Texts.* Ed. Walter Jackson Bate. New York: Harcourt Brace Jovanovich, Inc., 1952, pp. 666–674.

Marcus, Steven. *The Other Victorians: A Study of Sexuality and Pornography in Mid-Nineteenth-Century England.* New York: Basic Books, Inc., Publishers, 1964.

Marcuse, Herbert. *Eros and Civilization: A Philosophic Inquiry into Freud.* Vintage Books. New York: Random House, 1962.

Martin, Jay. *Harvests of Change: American Literature 1865–1914.* Englewood Cliffs, N.J.: Prentice-Hall, Inc., 1967.

Matlaw, Ralph E., ed. *Tolstoy: A Collection of Critical Essays.* Englewood Cliffs, N.J.: Prentice-Hall, Inc., 1967.

May, Rollo. *Love and Will.* New York: Dell Publishing Co., Inc., 1969.

————. *The Meaning of Anxiety.* New York: Ronald Press Co., 1950.

Miller, J. Hillis. "Bleak House and the Moral Life." In *Dickens' Bleak House: A Casebook.* Ed. A. E. Dyson. Nashville, Tenn.: Aurora Publishers Incorporated, 1969, pp. 157–191.

Mitchell, S. Weir, M.D. *Doctor and Patient.* Philadelphia: J. B Lippincott Company, 1901.

Moore, Harry T. Intro. in *American Dreams, American Nightmares.* Ed. David Madden. Carbondale: Southern Illinois University Press, 1970.

Mordell, Albert. *The Erotic Motive in Literature.* New York: Boni and Liveright, 1919.

Mullahy, Patrick. *Oedipus: Myth and Complex: A Review of Psychoanalytic Theory.* New York: Grove Press, Inc., 1955.

Nuttin, Joseph. *Psychoanalysis and Personality: A Dynamic Theory of Normal Personality.* Trans. George Lamb. New York: Mentor Books, 1953.

Ober, William B. "Lady Chatterley's What?" In *Boswell's Clap and Other Essays: Medical Analyses of Literary Men's Afflictions.* Carbondale: Southern Illinois University Press, 1979, pp. 89–117.

Ortega y Gasset, José. *On Love: Aspects of a Single Theme.* Trans. Roby Talbot. New York: The New American Library, Inc., 1957.

Pachter, Marc, ed. *Telling Lives: The Biographer's Art.* Washington, D.C.: New Republic Books, 1979.

Partridge, Eric. *A Dictionary of Slang and Unconventional English.* New York: The Macmillan Company, 1961.

————. *Shakespeare's Bawdy: A Literary and Psychological Essay and Comprehensive Glossary.* London: Routledge & Kegan Paul, 1968.

Pearsall, Ronald. *The Worm in the Bud: The World of Victorian Sexuality.* New York: Macmillan, 1972.

Perkins, Michael. *The Secret Record: Modern Erotic Literature.* New York: William Morrow & Co., Inc., 1976.

Perry, Thomas Sergeant. "Zola's Last Novel." *Atlantic Monthly*, 45 (May 1880), 693–699.

Phillips, William, ed. and intro. *Art and Psychoanalysis.* New York: Criterion Books, 1957.

Poulet, Georges. *The Metamorphoses of the Circle.* Trans. Carley Dawson and Elliott Coleman. Baltimore: The Johns Hopkins Press, 1966.

Price, Reynolds. "What Did Emma Bovary Do in Bed?" *Esquire*, 80 (August 1973), 80–146.

Pritchett, V. S. "The Passions of Emile Zola." *The New York Review of Books*, November 10, 1977, pp. 10–11.

Rougemont, Denis de. *Love in the Western World.* Trans. Montgomery Belgion. New York: Harper & Row Publishers, 1956.

Rudofsky, Bernard. *The Unfashionable Human Body.* Garden City, N.Y.: Doubleday & Company, Inc., 1971.

Rugoff, Milton. *Prudery and Passion.* New York: G. P. Putnam's Sons, 1971.

Russell, Bertrand. *Marriage and Morals.* New York: Bantam Books, 1929.

Santayana, George. *The Genteel Tradition at Bay.* New York: Charles Scribner's Sons, 1931.

Schopenhauer, Arthur. "The Metaphysics of the Love of the Sexes." In *The Works of Schopenhauer.* Ed. Will Durant. New York: Simon & Schuster, pp. 330–363.

Shakespeare, William. *As You Like It.* Ed. Ralph M. Sargent. Baltimore: Penguin Books, 1959.

———. *Hamlet Prince of Denmark.* Ed. Willard Farnham. New York: Penguin Books, 1957.

———. *Othello.* Ed. Mark Eccles. New York: Appleton-Century-Crofts, Inc., 1946.

Smith, Goldwin. "Pessimism." *Atlantic Monthly*, 45 (February 1880), 195–214.

Sontag, Susan. "On Pornography." *Partisan Review*, 34 (Spring 1967), 181–212.

Steiner, George. "Night Words: Human Privacy and High Pornography." In *The New Eroticism: Theories, Vogues and Canons.* Ed. Philip Nobile. New York: Random House, 1970, pp. 120–132.

———. *Tolstoy or Dostoevsky: An Essay in the Old Criticism.* New York: E. P. Dutton & Company, Inc., 1971.

Stendhal. *Love.* Trans. Gilbert and Suzanne Sale. Intro. Jean Stewart and B. C. J. G. Knight. Harmondsworth, England: Penguin Books, 1957.

Stern, E. Mark. "Narcissism and the Defiance of Time." In *The Narcissistic Condition: A Fact of Our Lives and Times.* Ed. Marie Coleman Nelson. New York: Human Sciences Press, 1977.

Swedenborg, Emanuel. *The Delights of Wisdom pertaining to Conjugial Love: After which Follow the Pleasures of Insanity pertaining to Scortatory Love.* Trans. Samuel M. Warren. 1768; rpt. Boston: Houghton Mifflin Company, 1907.

Taneyhill, Richard H. *The Leatherwood God.* Ed. George Kummer. 1869–1870; rpt. Gainesville, Fla.: Scholars' Facsimiles & Reprints, 1966.

Taylor, G. Rattray. *Sex in History.* New York: Harper & Row, Publishers, 1970.

Thielicke, Helmut. *The Ethics of Sex.* Trans. John W. Doberstein. New York: Harper & Row, Publishers, 1964.

Tocqueville, Alexis de. *Democracy in America.* Trans. Henry Reeve. Ed. Philipps Bradley, Vol. II. New York: Vintage Books, 1945.

Toksvig, Signe. *Emanuel Swedenborg: Scientist and Mystic.* New Haven: Yale University Press, 1948.

Tolstoy, Leo. *Anna Karenina*. Trans. Constance Garnett. New York: Airmont Publishing Company, Inc., 1966.
———. *Childhood, Boyhood, Youth*. Trans. and Intro. Rosemary Edmonds. Baltimore: Penguin Books, 1964.
———. *My Confession*. Trans. Leo Wiener. Boston: Colonial Press Co., 1904.
Tragedy: Modern Essays in Criticism. Ed. Lawrence Michel and Richard B. Sewall. Englewood Cliffs, N.J.: Prentice-Hall, Inc., 1963.
Turgenev, Ivan S. *Liza*. Trans. W. R. Shelden Ralston. New York: E. P. Dutton & Co., Inc., 1914.
———. *Smoke*. Trans. Constance Garnett. New York: The Macmillan Company, 1920.
Updike, John. *The Centaur*. Greenwich, Conn.: Fawcett Publications, Inc., 1963.
von Franz, M. L. "The Process of Individuation." In *Man and His Symbols*. Ed. Carl G. Jung. New York: Dell Publishing Co., Inc., 1964, pp. 159–254.
Walcutt, Charles Child. *American Literary Naturalism, A Divided Stream*. Minneapolis: University of Minnesota Press, 1956.
Walker, Benjamin. *Sex and the Supernatural: Sexuality in Religion and Magic*. New York: Harper & Row, Publishers, 1970.
Walker, Philip D. *Emile Zola*. London: Routledge & Kegan Paul, 1968.
Walters, Ronald E., ed. *Primers for Prudery: Sexual Advice to Victorian America*. Englewood Cliffs, N.J.: Prentice-Hall, Inc., 1974.
Wasserstrom, William. *Heiress of All the Ages: Sex and Sentiment in the Genteel Tradition*. Minneapolis: University of Minnesota Press, 1959.
Watts, Isaac. *Hymns and Spiritual Songs*. London, 1779.
Wilson, Angus. *Emile Zola: An Introductory Study*. New York: William Morrow & Company, 1952.
Wilson, Colin. *Origins of the Sexual Impulse*. New York: G. P. Putnam's Sons, 1963.
Worcester, Joseph Emerson. *A Comprehensive Dictionary of the English Language*. Boston: Swan, Brewer, and Tilleston, 1860.
Zola, Emile. *L'Assommoir*. Trans. and Intro. Leonard Tancock. Baltimore: Penguin Books, 1970.
———. *La Bete Humaine*. Trans. and Intro. Leonard Tancock. New York: Penguin Books, 1977.
———. *Nana*. Trans. and Intro. George Holden. Baltimore: Penguin Books, 1972.
———. *La Terre*. Trans. and Intro. Douglas Parmee. New York: Penguin Books, 1980.

Index

Elizabeth Stevens Prioleau took her Ph.D. in English at Duke University. She has published articles on Victorian literature in *Twentieth Century Literature* and *Victorian Poetry* and has contributed essays on medicine and literature to *The American Journal of Dermatopathology*, for which she is a literary consultant.